Lecture Notes in Computer Science 14053

Founding Editors

Gerhard Goos
Juris Hartmanis

Editorial Board Members

The series Lecture Notes in Computer Science (LNCS), including its subseries Lecture Notes in Artificial Intelligence (LNAI) and Lecture Notes in Bioinformatics (LNBI), has established itself as a medium for the publication of new developments in computer science and information technology research, teaching, and education.

LNCS enjoys close cooperation with the computer science R & D community, the series counts many renowned academics among its volume editors and paper authors, and collaborates with prestigious societies. Its mission is to serve this international community by providing an invaluable service, mainly focused on the publication of conference and workshop proceedings and postproceedings. LNCS commenced publication in 1973.

Ioannis Chatzigiannakis · Ioannis Karydis
Editors

Algorithmic Aspects of Cloud Computing

8th International Symposium, ALGOCLOUD 2023
Amsterdam, The Netherlands, September 5, 2023
Revised Selected Papers

Editors
Ioannis Chatzigiannakis (ID)
Sapienza University of Rome
Rome, Italy

Ioannis Karydis (ID)
Ionian University
Corfu, Greece

ISSN 0302-9743 ISSN 1611-3349 (electronic)
Lecture Notes in Computer Science
ISBN 978-3-031-49360-7 ISBN 978-3-031-49361-4 (eBook)
https://doi.org/10.1007/978-3-031-49361-4

This Springer imprint is published by the registered company Springer Nature Switzerland AG
The registered company address is: Gewerbestrasse 11, 6330 Cham, Switzerland

Paper in this product is recyclable.

Preface

The International Symposium on Algorithmic Aspects of Cloud Computing (ALGO-CLOUD) is an annual event aiming to tackle the diverse new topics in the emerging area of algorithmic aspects of computing and data management in modern cloud-based systems interpreted broadly so as to include edge- and fog-based systems, cloudlets, cloud micro-services, virtualization environments, decentralized systems, as well as dynamic networks.

The symposium aims to bring together researchers, students, and practitioners to present research activities and results on topics related to the algorithmic, design, and development aspects of modern cloud-based systems. ALGOCLOUD is particularly interested in novel algorithms in the context of cloud computing, cloud architectures, as well as experimental work that evaluates contemporary cloud approaches and pertinent applications. ALGOCLOUD also welcomes demonstration manuscripts which discuss successful system developments, as well as experience/use-case articles and high-quality survey papers.

Topics of interest include, but are not limited to:

- Algorithms for Decentralized Systems
- Algorithms for Dynamic Networks
- Cloud-Edge Continuum
- IoT and Cloud Computing
- Fog and Edge Computing
- Mobile Edge Computing
- Stream Processing for Cloud-Edge Continuum
- In-Network Stream Processing
- Machine Learning for Cloud-Edge
- Federated Learning in Cloud-Edge Architectures
- Resource Management and Scheduling
- Resource Management in Mobile Edge Computing
- Data Center and Infrastructure Management
- Distributed Caching and Load Balancing
- Distributed Storage Management
- Privacy, Security and Anonymization
- Game-Theoretic Approaches for Cloud-Edge Computing
- Economic Models and Pricing
- Cloud-Edge Deployment Tools and Their Analysis
- Novel Code Deployment Models
- Energy and Power Management
- Analysis of Algorithms and Data Structures
- Search and Retrieval Algorithms for Cloud Infrastructures
- Caching and Load-Balancing
- Storage Structures and Indexing for Cloud Databases

ALGOCLOUD 2023 took place on September 5th, 2023, in Amsterdam, the Netherlands. It was part of ALGO 2023 (September 4–8, 2023), the major annual congress that combines the premier algorithmic conference European Symposium on Algorithms (ESA) along with a number of specialized symposia and workshops, all related to algorithms and their applications, making ALGO the major European event for researchers, students, and practitioners in algorithms and their application.

In response to the call for papers, a total of 24 submissions were received from researchers and practitioners from the field of science and engineering working towards the vision of Cloud Computing. The diverse nature of papers submitted demonstrates the vitality of the algorithmic aspects of cloud computing. All submissions went through a rigorous peer-review process and were reviewed by at least three Program Committee (PC) members. They were evaluated on their quality, originality, and relevance to the symposium. Following the reviewers' recommendations, the PC accepted twelve original research papers covering a variety of topics that were presented at the symposium. We would like to thank all PC members for their significant contribution to the review process.

Apart from the contributed talks, ALGOCLOUD 2023 included an invited keynote presentation by Chris Schwiegelshohn titled "Fitting Data on a Grain of Rice".

We wish to thank all authors who submitted their research to this conference, contributing to the high-quality program, the Program Committees for their scholarly effort, and all referees who assisted the Program Committees in the evaluation process. We also thank the Steering Committee of ALGOCLOUD 2023 for its continuous support.

We thank Springer for sponsoring the best paper and best student paper awards taking into account the reviews and selection process followed by the Program Committee. The best paper award was given to Marianna Tzortzi, Charalampos Kleitsikas, Agis Politis, Sotirios Niarchos, Katerina Doka, and Nectarios Koziris for their work titled "Planning workflow executions over the Edge-to-Cloud Continuum". The best student paper award was given to Themistoklis Sarantakos, Daniel Mauricio Jimenez Gutierrez, and Dimitrios Amaxilatis for their work titled "Olive Leaf Infection Detection using the Cloud-Edge Continuum".

We hope that these proceedings will help researchers, students, and practitioners understand and be aware of state-of-the-art algorithmic aspects of cloud computing, and that they will stimulate further research in the domain of algorithmic approaches in cloud computing in general.

October 2023

Ioannis Chatzigiannakis
Ioannis Karydis

Organization

Steering Committee

Spyros Sioutas	University of Patras, Greece
Peter Triantafillou	University of Warwick, UK
Christos D. Zaroliagis	University of Patras, Greece

Symposium Chairs

Ioannis Chatzigiannakis	Sapienza University of Rome, Italy
Ioannis Karydis	Ionian University, Greece

Program Committee

Dimitrios Amaxilatis	University of Patras, Greece
Roberto Beraldi	Sapienza University of Rome, Italy
Ioannis Chatzigiannakis	Sapienza University of Rome, Italy
Charalampos Chelmis	University at Albany - State University of New York, USA
Marc Frincu	Nottingham Trent University, UK
Jonathan Fürst	NEC Labs Europe, Germany
Domenico Garlisi	University of Palermo, Italy
Anastasios Gounaris	Aristotle University of Thessaloniki, Greece
Ioannis Karydis	Ionian University, Greece
Dimitrios Katsaros	University of Thessaly, Greece
Panagiotis Kokkinos	National Technical University of Athens, Greece
Weifa Liang	City University of Hong Kong, China
Haris Mouratidis	University of Essex, UK
Christoforos Ntantogian	Ionian University, Greece
George Pallis	University of Cyprus, Cyprus
Apostolos Papadopoulos	Aristotle University of Thessaloniki, Greece
Antonio Skarmeta Gomez	Universidad de Murcia, Spain
Eirini Tsiropoulou	University of New Mexico, USA
Vassilios Verykios	Hellenic Open University, Greece

Contents

Fitting Data on a Grain of Rice

Chris Schwiegelshohn[(✉)] [iD]

Aarhus University, Aarhus, Denmark
cschwiegelshohn@gmail.com

Abstract. Coresets are among the most successful compression
paradigms. For clustering, a coreset B of a point set A preserves the
clustering cost for any candidate solution C. In general, we are interested in finding a B that is as small as possible. In this overview, we will
survey techniques for constructing coresets for clustering problems, their
applications, and potential future directions.

Keywords: Clustering · Compression · Learning

1 Introduction

An efficient algorithm is an algorithm that runs in polynomial time, according
to conventional wisdom. Unfortunately, in the age of big data, this is not an
accurate assessment of an algorithm's performance. The large the data set is, the
less viable quadratic or even cubic running times become. Algorithms designed
with scalability issues in mind try to tackle this problem from two fronts. First,
they are typically limit to running in linear or even sublinear time. Second,
they aim to compress the data set such that the key features of the problem are
retained, while consisting of significantly fewer input points. This solves the issue
of large datas by both directly addressing the volume of the data, but also by
making slower algorithms viable if they are only executed on the compression.

There are many successful, and often related, concepts and computational
models with scalability issues in mind. Examples are sublinear algorithms, that
ask what can be inferred by making few randomized queries to a data set, streaming algorithms, who take a single passes over the data while retaining the most
important properties in a space constrained data structure, and distributed and
parallel computing, that aim to study how modern architectures can help with
scalability.

In the intersecting all of these lie coresets, a compression paradigm that
has seen substantial success over the past years, in particular for clustering
problems. In this overview, we will detail coresets, with an emphasis on center
based clustering objectives such as k-means clustering.

2 Coresets

The coreset notion has been applied to many problems, but it is perhaps best
understood via a specific example to clustering. Consider a (potentially weighted)

I. Chatzigiannakis and I. Karydis (Eds.): ALGOCLOUD 2023, LNCS 14053, pp. 1–8, 2024.
https://doi.org/10.1007/978-3-031-49361-4_13

point set A in d dimensional Euclidean space. For a given set of k-centers C, the k-means cost is defined

$$\text{cost}_w(A, C) := \sum_{p \in A} \min_{c \in C} \|p - c\|^2 \cdot w_p,$$

where w_p denotes the (nonnegative) weight and $\|x\| := \sqrt{\sum_{i=1}^d x_i^2}$. We say that a (potentially weighted) point set B is an k-means coreset of A if for all candidate solutions C

$$|\text{cost}_w(A, C) - \text{cost}_w(B, C)| \cdot \varepsilon \cdot \text{cost}_w(A, C).$$

Composability. The important property that a compression must satisfy to typically be called a coreset is composability. Composability means that given disjoint point sets A_1 and A_2 and corresponding coresets B_1 and B_2, we have that $B_1 \cup C_2$ is a coreset of $A_1 \cup A_2$. This property holds for any point-wise loss function satisfying the above guarantee, that is, it in particular holds for k-means. Composability means that coresets immediately imply distributed and parallel algorithms. A data set can be partitioned arbitrarily, sent to available computing units which compress the data and send the computed coreset back. Composability also enables easy streaming algorithms via the merge and reduce technique in a black box way, though better streaming algorithms for k-means are known to exist.

Related Notions. Many compression notions such as sketching or sparsification are similar to coresets in spirit as well as on a technical level. Sketching algorithms are typically understood to be compressions obtained by mapping a high-dimensional vector to a low-dimensional one via a randomized sketching matrix, see Woodruff for an overview [44]. For problems in numerical linear algebra, both coresets as well as sketching algorithms have seen much success [6,43]. In the context of dimension reduction, sketching is frequently used and indeed coreset constructions for clustering typically rely on the existence of efficient dimension reduction techniques.

Though typically not expressed through the lense of coresets, graph sparsifiers [4] are closely related. In particular, spectral sparsifiers and cut sparsifiers approximate the value of any cut. The sampling distributions used to compute such sparsifiers are closely related to sensitivity sampling described further below.

Coresets also have a lot in common with kernels studied in the context of fixed parameter tractable approximation algorithms. Indeed, a coreset is a lossy kernel in that, having computed a computed a coreset of size $\text{poly}(k, \varepsilon^{-1})$, typically in time $O(ndk)$[1], one may solve the problem on the coreset exactly in time $\exp(\text{poly}(k, \varepsilon^{-1}))$, yielding a $(1 + \varepsilon)$ approximate solution.

---

[1] Faster algorithms are possible, but not discussed here.

3 Algorithms

In this section, we detail some of the algorithmic techniques used to compute coresets, in particular coresets for the Euclidean k-means problem, which arguably has driven most coreset-based research for center-based clustering. This section also serves as a survey over related work.

Geometric Decompositions. The earliest coreset algorithms for clustering relied heavily on the following observation. If we compute an m-clustering B, such that for sufficiently high value of m the cost of B is substantially smaller than the cost of any k-clustering, then surely we must have a coreset? This observation can be made formal, specifically, if $\text{cost}(A, B) \leq \varepsilon^2 \cdot \min_{C, |C|=k} \text{cost}(A, C)$, then the point set B where each point is weighted by the number of points in A assigned to it, is an $O(\varepsilon)$ coreset. Unfortunately, there exist data sets where $m \in \Omega(n)$ for this to be the case, the high dimensional simplex being such an example. Nevertheless, geometric decompositions yielded the first coreset results in low dimensional Euclidean space, typically with an exponential dependency on the dimension [20, 21].

Sampling. Sampling based algorithms were not used to construct coresets until the seminal work by Chen [9]. Though it seems natural to study uniform sampling as a compression tool, and indeed it is popular for sublinear algorithms [24], it is also easy to construct instances where uniform sampling fails to produce any bounded approximation factor. To see this, merely consider that a single outlier can dominate the entire cost of the data. Uniform sampling cannot find such a point. Chen countered this by partitioning the data into multiple sets for which there are no outliers.

The power of sampling was subsequently fully realized with the introduction of sensitivity sampling [18, 34]. The sensitivity of a point p is defined as

$$\sigma_p = \sup_C \frac{\text{cost}(p, C)}{\text{cost}(A, C)}, \tag{1}$$

and the total sensitivity $\mathfrak{S} := \sum_{p \in P} \sigma_p$. The sensitivity is the maximum impact a point can have in any given solution. Thus, the higher σ_p, the more important it is to sample it.

Computing the sensitivities exactly is infeasible, but the following algorithm computes approximate scores that are sufficient for the analysis.

Variants of this algorithms are now the main focus of coreset research. The state of the art coreset bounds summarized via the following theorem are obtained by this algorithm.

Theorem 1. *There exists an algorithm that computes an ε coreset for Euclidean k-means of size $\tilde{O}(k\varepsilon^{-2} \min(\sqrt{k}, \varepsilon^{-2}))^2$.*

Typically, they proceed via the following two steps.

---

[2] $\tilde{O}(x)$ hides terms polylog(x).

Algorithm 1. Sensitivity Sampling(P, k, m)

1: **Input:** data A, number of clusters k
2: Find approx. solution $\tilde{C} = \{\tilde{c}_1, ..., \tilde{c}_k\}$ on A
3: Let $C_i = \tilde{\sigma}^{-1}(c_i)$. Compute the 1-mean c_i of each C_i.
4: For each point $p \in C_i$, define $\sigma'(p) = \frac{\|p - c_i\|^2}{\text{cost}(C_i, c_i)} + \frac{1}{|C_i|}$ and $\mathfrak{S}' = \sum_{p \in A} \sigma'(p)$.
5: Sample a set B of m points independently with replacement from P proportionate to σ'.
6: **Output:** the coreset B, with weights $w(p) = \frac{\mathfrak{S}'}{\sigma'(p) \cdot m}$

- Bounding the error for a single solution: We analyze the variance of the sample coreset. It turns out that the variance is determined by the total sensitivity $\mathfrak{S}$. It is possible to show that $\mathfrak{S} \in O(k)$, while a point set consisting of k distinct points also immediately shows that $\mathfrak{S} \geq k$. Thus, roughly $\mathfrak{S} \cdot \varepsilon^{-2}$ many points are sufficient to have a small error for any arbitrary solution.
- Bounding the error for all solutions: This is the most complicated step in the analysis. One typically has to characterize similar solutions such as a bound on one solution implies a bound on all similar solutions. Feldman and Langberg [18] showed to use VC-dimension basesd characterizations. Cohen-Addad et al. [15] later provided an alternative condition which also yielded coresets for metric spaces where the VC-dimension is unbounded. Subsequently, Cohen-Addad et al. [11,12,14] introduced the chaining technique to coresets, which, combined with dimension reduction techniques described further below, yielded the optimal coreset bounds of $\tilde{O}(k\varepsilon^{-2}\min(\sqrt{k}, \varepsilon^{-2}))$. Chaining is a deep technique and describing it is out of scope in this overview.

The aforementioned bounds were recently shown to be optimal [26]. We note that while these methods were used for high-dimensional point sets, they also readily lend themselves to low-dimensional cases, see [7,22].

Dimension Reduction. Even with sampling based techniques, coreset sizes still depended on the dimension. In a seminal work, Feldman, Schmidt and Sohler [19] showed that using the singular value decomposition, one could replace the dependency on d with one on k/ε^2. For related clustering objectives like k-median, similar results were achieved by Sohler and Woodruff [42]. This was important milestone, but the results quickly fell out of fashion in favor of terminal embeddings. Given a point set $A \in \mathbb{R}^d$ a terminal embedding $f : \mathbb{R}^d \to \mathbb{R}^\ell$ satisfies for all points $p \in A$ and $q \in \mathbb{R}^d$

$$(1 - \varepsilon) \cdot \|p - q\|^2 \leq \|f(p) - f(q)\|^2 \leq (1 + \varepsilon) \cdot \|p - q\|^2.$$

This is related to the Johnson-Lindenstrauss lemma, but stronger in that not only are pairwise distances preserved, but distances of A to all points of $\mathbb{R}^d$. Terminal embeddings [35,39] are now known to have the same dependency on the dimension as the Johnson-Lindenstrauss lemma, meaning that $\ell \in O(\varepsilon^{-2} \log |A|)$ is sufficient. In a series of works [5,8,27], these methods were used to improve coreset sizes for k-means and other k-clustering objectives such k-median.

We note that Johnson-Lindenstrauss based dimension reduction methods proposed by [10, 36] are related in spirit, but do not seem to combine well with coresets.

4   Other Coreset Variants

While Euclidean spaces no doubt received most of the attention, numerous works have also investigated other important metric spaces, such as finite metrics [9, 18], doubling metrics [16, 23], graph metrics [2, 8]. The overall approach remains largely the same as the sampling based program used for Euclidean spaces, but the characterization of similar solutions typically requires metric-dependent insights.

Another important notion that has recently received attention are coresets for clustering problems with capacity constraints. This includes upper bounded capacities, lower bounded capacities, and group-fairness based notions. Despite substantial attention [3, 7, 13, 25, 41], there are many problems left open here which we will describe later.

Finally, coresets may be defined for many problems beyond k-clustering. Examples include decision trees [32], kernel methods [31, 33, 40], determinant maximization [29], diversity maximization [30], and logistic regression [28, 38]. A more comprehensive treatments can be found in surveys [1, 17, 37].

5   Open Problems

With coresets for unconstrained k-means in Euclidean spaces being resolved, the biggest open problem is whether for capacitated and cardinality constrained inputs a similar result can be achieved. Specifically, do there exist coresets of size $\tilde{O}(k)$ for this problem?

Another interesting direction is to obtain results that bypass the $\Omega(k\varepsilon^{-2}, \min(\sqrt{k}, \varepsilon^{-2}))$ lower bound. This requires either a different compression guarantee, or a different estimator. Does there exist such a notion that still retains important properties such as composability?

Acknowledgements. The author acknowledges the support of the Independent Research Fund Denmark (DFF) under a Sapere Aude Research Leader grant No. 1051-00106B.

References

1. Agarwal, P.K., Har-Peled, S., Varadarajan, K.R.: Geometric approximation via coresets. Comb. Computat. Geom. **52**, 1–30 (2005)
2. Baker, D., Braverman, V., Huang, L., Jiang, S.H.C., Krauthgamer, R., Wu, X.: Coresets for clustering in graphs of bounded treewidth (2020)
3. Bandyapadhyay, S., Fomin, F.V., Simonov, K.: On coresets for fair clustering in metric and Euclidean spaces and their applications. In: Bansal, N., Merelli, E., Worrell, J. (eds.) 48th International Colloquium on Automata, Languages, and Programming, ICALP 2021, 12–16 July 2021, Glasgow, Scotland (Virtual Conference). LIPIcs, vol. 198, pp. 23:1–23:15. Schloss Dagstuhl - Leibniz-Zentrum für Informatik (2021). https://doi.org/10.4230/LIPIcs.ICALP.2021.23

4. Batson, J.D., Spielman, D.A., Srivastava, N., Teng, S.: Spectral sparsification of graphs: theory and algorithms. Commun. ACM **56**(8), 87–94 (2013). https://doi.org/10.1145/2492007.2492029

5. Becchetti, L., Bury, M., Cohen-Addad, V., Grandoni, F., Schwiegelshohn, C.: Oblivious dimension reduction for k-means: beyond subspaces and the Johnson-Lindenstrauss lemma. In: Proceedings of the 51st Annual ACM SIGACT Symposium on Theory of Computing, STOC 2019, Phoenix, AZ, USA, 23–26 June 2019, pp. 1039–1050 (2019). https://doi.org/10.1145/3313276.3316318

6. Boutsidis, C., Drineas, P., Magdon-Ismail, M.: Near-optimal coresets for least-squares regression. IEEE Trans. Inf. Theor. **59**(10), 6880–6892 (2013). https://doi.org/10.1109/TIT.2013.2272457

7. Braverman, V., et al.: The power of uniform sampling for coresets. In: 63rd IEEE Annual Symposium on Foundations of Computer Science, FOCS 2022, Denver, CO, USA, 31 October–3 November 2022, pp. 462–473. IEEE (2022). https://doi.org/10.1109/FOCS54457.2022.00051

8. Braverman, V., Jiang, S.H., Krauthgamer, R., Wu, X.: Coresets for clustering in excluded-minor graphs and beyond. In: Marx, D. (ed.) Proceedings of the 2021 ACM-SIAM Symposium on Discrete Algorithms, SODA 2021, Virtual Conference, 10–13 January 2021, pp. 2679–2696. SIAM (2021). https://doi.org/10.1137/1.9781611976465.159

9. Chen, K.: On coresets for k-median and k-means clustering in metric and Euclidean spaces and their applications. SIAM J. Comput. **39**(3), 923–947 (2009)

10. Cohen, M.B., Elder, S., Musco, C., Musco, C., Persu, M.: Dimensionality reduction for k-means clustering and low rank approximation. In: Proceedings of the Forty-Seventh Annual ACM on Symposium on Theory of Computing, STOC 2015, Portland, OR, USA, 14–17 June 2015, pp. 163–172 (2015)

11. Cohen-Addad, V., Larsen, K.G., Saulpic, D., Schwiegelshohn, C.: Towards optimal lower bounds for k-median and k-means coresets. In: Leonardi, S., Gupta, A. (eds.) 54th Annual ACM SIGACT Symposium on Theory of Computing, STOC 2022, Rome, Italy, 20–24 June 2022, pp. 1038–1051. ACM (2022). https://doi.org/10.1145/3519935.3519946

12. Cohen-Addad, V., Larsen, K.G., Saulpic, D., Schwiegelshohn, C., Sheikh-Omar, O.A.: Improved coresets for Euclidean k-means. In: NeurIPS (2022). http://papers.nips.cc/paper_files/paper/2022/hash/120c9ab5c58ba0fa9dd3a22ace1de245-Abstract-Conference.html

13. Cohen-Addad, V., Li, J.: On the fixed-parameter tractability of capacitated clustering. In: 46th International Colloquium on Automata, Languages, and Programming, ICALP 2019, 9–12 July 2019, Patras, Greece, pp. 41:1–41:14 (2019). https://doi.org/10.4230/LIPIcs.ICALP.2019.41

14. Cohen-Addad, V., Saulpic, D., Schwiegelshohn, C.: Improved coresets and sublinear algorithms for power means in Euclidean spaces. In: NeurIPS (2021)

15. Cohen-Addad, V., Saulpic, D., Schwiegelshohn, C.: A new coreset framework for clustering. In: Khuller, S., Williams, V.V. (eds.) 53rd Annual ACM SIGACT Symposium on Theory of Computing, STOC 2021, Virtual Event, Italy, 21–25 June 2021, pp. 169–182. ACM (2021). https://doi.org/10.1145/3406325.3451022

16. Cohen-Addad, V., Saulpic, D., Schwiegelshohn, C.: A new coreset framework for clustering. In: Khuller, S., Williams, V.V. (eds.) 53rd Annual ACM SIGACT Symposium on Theory of Computing, STOC 2021, Virtual Event, Italy, 21–25 June 2021. ACM (2021). https://doi.org/10.1145/3406325.3451022

17. Feldman, D.: Core-sets: an updated survey. WIREs Data Mining Knowl. Discov. **10**(1) (2020). https://doi.org/10.1002/widm.1335

18. Feldman, D., Langberg, M.: A unified framework for approximating and clustering data. In: Proceedings of the 43rd ACM Symposium on Theory of Computing, STOC 2011, San Jose, CA, USA, 6–8 June 2011, pp. 569–578 (2011)
19. Feldman, D., Schmidt, M., Sohler, C.: Turning big data into tiny data: constant-size coresets for k-means, PCA, and projective clustering. SIAM J. Comput. **49**(3), 601–657 (2020). https://doi.org/10.1137/18M1209854
20. Har-Peled, S., Kushal, A.: Smaller coresets for k-median and k-means clustering. Discrete Computat. Geom. **37**(1), 3–19 (2007)
21. Har-Peled, S., Mazumdar, S.: On coresets for k-means and k-median clustering. In: Proceedings of the 36th Annual ACM Symposium on Theory of Computing, Chicago, IL, USA, 13–16 June 2004, pp. 291–300 (2004)
22. Huang, L., Huang, R., Huang, Z., Wu, X.: On coresets for clustering in small dimensional Euclidean spaces. In: Krause, A., Brunskill, E., Cho, K., Engelhardt, B., Sabato, S., Scarlett, J. (eds.) Proceedings of the International Conference on Machine Learning Research, ICML 2023, 23–29 July 2023, Honolulu, Hawaii, USA, vol. 202, pp. 13891–13915. PMLR (2023). https://proceedings.mlr.press/v202/huang23h.html
23. Huang, L., Jiang, S.H., Li, J., Wu, X.: Epsilon-coresets for clustering (with outliers) in doubling metrics. In: 59th IEEE Annual Symposium on Foundations of Computer Science, FOCS 2018, Paris, France, 7–9 October 2018, pp. 814–825 (2018). https://doi.org/10.1109/FOCS.2018.00082
24. Huang, L., Jiang, S.H., Lou, J.: The power of uniform sampling for k-median. CoRR abs/2302.11339. arXiv arXiv:2302.11339 (2023)
25. Huang, L., Jiang, S.H., Vishnoi, N.K.: Coresets for clustering with fairness constraints. In: NeurIPS, pp. 7587–7598 (2019)
26. Huang, L., Li, J., Wu, X.: Towards optimal coreset construction for (k, z)-clustering: breaking the quadratic dependency on k. CoRR abs/2211.11923. arXiv arXiv:2211.11923 (2022). https://doi.org/10.48550/arXiv.2211.11923
27. Huang, L., Vishnoi, N.K.: Coresets for clustering in Euclidean spaces: importance sampling is nearly optimal. In: Makarychev, K., Makarychev, Y., Tulsiani, M., Kamath, G., Chuzhoy, J. (eds.) Proceedings of the 52nd Annual ACM SIGACT Symposium on Theory of Computing, STOC 2020, Chicago, IL, USA, 22–26 June 2020, pp. 1416–1429. ACM (2020). https://doi.org/10.1145/3357713.3384296
28. Huggins, J., Campbell, T., Broderick, T.: Coresets for scalable Bayesian logistic regression. In: Advances in Neural Information Processing Systems, pp. 4080–4088 (2016)
29. Indyk, P., Mahabadi, S., Gharan, S.O., Rezaei, A.: Composable core-sets for determinant maximization problems via spectral spanners. In: Chawla, S. (ed.) Proceedings of the 2020 ACM-SIAM Symposium on Discrete Algorithms, SODA 2020, Salt Lake City, UT, USA, 5–8 January 2020, pp. 1675–1694. SIAM (2020). https://doi.org/10.1137/1.9781611975994.103
30. Indyk, P., Mahabadi, S., Mahdian, M., Mirrokni, V.S.: Composable core-sets for diversity and coverage maximization. In: Hull, R., Grohe, M. (eds.) Proceedings of the 33rd ACM SIGMOD-SIGACT-SIGART Symposium on Principles of Database Systems, PODS 2014, Snowbird, UT, USA, 22–27 June 2014, pp. 100–108. ACM (2014). https://doi.org/10.1145/2594538.2594560
31. Jiang, S.H., Krauthgamer, R., Lou, J., Zhang, Y.: Coresets for kernel clustering. CoRR abs/2110.02898 (2021). https://arxiv.org/abs/2110.02898
32. Jubran, I., Shayda, E.E.S., Newman, I., Feldman, D.: Coresets for decision trees of signals. CoRR abs/2110.03195 (2021)

33. Karnin, Z.S., Liberty, E.: Discrepancy, coresets, and sketches in machine learning. In: Beygelzimer, A., Hsu, D. (eds.) Conference on Learning Theory, COLT 2019, 25–28 June 2019, Phoenix, AZ, USA, vol. 99, pp. 1975–1993. Proceedings of Machine Learning Research (PMLR) (2019). http://proceedings.mlr.press/v99/karnin19a.html

34. Langberg, M., Schulman, L.J.: Universal ε-approximators for integrals. In: Proceedings of the Twenty-First Annual ACM-SIAM Symposium on Discrete Algorithms, SODA 2010, Austin, Texas, USA, 17–19 January 2010, pp. 598–607 (2010)

35. Mahabadi, S., Makarychev, K., Makarychev, Y., Razenshteyn, I.P.: Nonlinear dimension reduction via outer Bi-Lipschitz extensions. In: Proceedings of the 50th Annual ACM SIGACT Symposium on Theory of Computing, STOC 2018, Los Angeles, CA, USA, 25–29 June 2018, pp. 1088–1101 (2018). https://doi.org/10.1145/3188745.3188828. http://doi.acm.org/10.1145/3188745.3188828

36. Makarychev, K., Makarychev, Y., Razenshteyn, I.P.: Performance of Johnson-Lindenstrauss transform for k-means and k-medians clustering. In: Proceedings of the 51st Annual ACM SIGACT Symposium on Theory of Computing, STOC 2019, Phoenix, AZ, USA, 23–26 June 2019, pp. 1027–1038 (2019). https://doi.org/10.1145/3313276.3316350. https://doi.org/10.1145/3313276.3316350

37. Munteanu, A., Schwiegelshohn, C.: Coresets-methods and history: a theoreticians design pattern for approximation and streaming algorithms. Künstliche Intell. **32**(1), 37–53 (2018). https://doi.org/10.1007/s13218-017-0519-3. https://doi.org/10.1007/s13218-017-0519-3

38. Munteanu, A., Schwiegelshohn, C., Sohler, C., Woodruff, D.P.: On coresets for logistic regression. In: Bengio, S., Wallach, H.M., Larochelle, H., Grauman, K., Cesa-Bianchi, N., Garnett, R. (eds.) Advances in Neural Information Processing Systems 31: Annual Conference on Neural Information Processing Systems 2018, NeurIPS 2018, 3–8 December 2018, Montréal, Canada, pp. 6562–6571 (2018)

39. Narayanan, S., Nelson, J.: Optimal terminal dimensionality reduction in Euclidean space. In: Charikar, M., Cohen, E. (eds.) Proceedings of the 51st Annual ACM SIGACT Symposium on Theory of Computing, STOC 2019, Phoenix, AZ, USA, 23–26 June 2019, pp. 1064–1069. ACM (2019). https://doi.org/10.1145/3313276.3316307

40. Phillips, J.M., Tai, W.M.: Near-optimal coresets of kernel density estimates. Discret. Comput. Geom. **63**(4), 867–887 (2020). https://doi.org/10.1007/s00454-019-00134-6

41. Schmidt, M., Schwiegelshohn, C., Sohler, C.: Fair coresets and streaming algorithms for fair k-means. In: 17th International Workshop on Approximation and Online Algorithms, WAOA 2019, Revised Selected Papers, Munich, Germany, 12–13 September 2019, pp. 232–251 (2019). https://doi.org/10.1007/978-3-030-39479-0_16

42. Sohler, C., Woodruff, D.P.: Strong coresets for k-median and subspace approximation: goodbye dimension. CoRR abs/1809.02961 (2018). http://arxiv.org/abs/1809.02961

43. Tukan, M., Maalouf, A., Feldman, D.: Coresets for near-convex functions. In: Larochelle, H., Ranzato, M., Hadsell, R., Balcan, M., Lin, H. (eds.) Advances in Neural Information Processing Systems 33: Annual Conference on Neural Information Processing Systems 2020, NeurIPS 2020, Virtual, 6–12 December 2020 (2020)

44. Woodruff, D.P.: Sketching as a tool for numerical linear algebra. Found. Trends Theoret. Comput. Sci. **10**(1–2), 1–157 (2014). https://doi.org/10.1561/0400000060

Planning Workflow Executions over the Edge-to-Cloud Continuum

Marianna Tzortzi, Charalampos Kleitsikas, Agis Politis, Sotirios Niarchos,
Katerina Doka$^{(\boxtimes)}$, and Nectarios Koziris

Computing Systems Laboratory, National Technical University of Athens,
Athens, Greece
{mtzortzi,ckleitsikas,apolitis,sniarchos,katerina,
nkoziris}@cslab.ece.ntua.gr

Abstract. In the ever growing field of Data Science, Cloud Computing
is a well established computational paradigm, while Edge Computing
is an emerging and promising alternative when it comes to the novel
challenges introduced in the Internet of Things (IoT) landscape. The
combination of the two as a unified paradigm forms the Edge-to-Cloud
continuum, which allows the execution of applications and services to
span both edge and cloud resources in a transparent way. In such heterogeneous and volatile environments, the scheduling of data intensive
workloads is a difficult task, usually performed manually and requiring
careful and educated decisions on the type of devices used to optimally
exploit the underlying hardware and achieve any user-defined higher level
policy. In this paper we present the *EC-Planner*, a planning component
for Edge-Cloud environments, which can make intelligent, automated
decisions both on how and where to map arbitrary data analytics tasks
to the underlying heterogeneous infrastructure, which may consist of a
mix of devices and processing units, including CPUs and hardware accel-
erators both in the Cloud and at the Edge.

1 Introduction

Cloud Computing is a decade-old technology developed to provide users and
organizations with scalable, secure, uninterrupted and consistent computational
and storage services [5]. Soon it became clear that the processing power and
the storage capacity of the Cloud could be leveraged by mobile and/or lower
capability devices, what we nowadays refer to as the Edge, by outsourcing all
or part of their services to the Cloud [11]. However, the bandwidth of the networks that carry data between the devices and the Cloud has failed to keep up
with the rapid increase in processing power of modern Cloud infrastructures
and data centers, introducing a bottleneck in cloud-based applications that,
given the ever-increasing rate of data produced at the Edge, becomes harder
and harder to ignore. Moreover, modern edge devices like smartphones, tablets,
smart devices etc., have significant processing and/or storage capabilities that
remain untapped. Last but not least, a significant portion of the data that is

© The Author(s), under exclusive license to Springer Nature Switzerland AG 2024
I. Chatzigiannakis and I. Karydis (Eds.): ALGOCLOUD 2023, LNCS 14053, pp. 9–24, 2024.
https://doi.org/10.1007/978-3-031-49361-4_1

produced at the Edge is sensitive (e.g., medical data as recorded by a smart watch), thus its transfer anywhere outside the device where it was initially produced/stored would raise major privacy concerns [16].

The Edge Computing paradigm, where the data generated at the Edge stay and get processed at the Edge, emerged as a natural way to overcome the aforementioned limitations, by utilizing the computational power of edge devices. In this new computing paradigm, the execution of services and functions originally run in the Cloud is moved closer to the user, leading to lower latency and alleviating the network's high traffic congestion.

However, because of the IoT devices' limited onboard resources, supporting resource-intensive applications, such as AI algorithms and big-data analytics is an extremely challenging task. Therefore, the Edge Computing paradigm should not be considered as a substitute for Cloud Computing, but as a complementary means of enhancing the capacity of both. Wouldn't it be nice to combine the best of both worlds, namely the processing power of the Cloud and the security and flexibility of the Edge? This idea gave birth to the notion of the Edge-Cloud Continuum, which aims to bridge the gap between the Cloud and Edge Computing ecosystems by providing ways to seamlessly integrate distributed computing resources at the Edge and the Cloud.

Designing and implementing systems that serve the Edge-Cloud Continuum though is by no means an easy task. On the one hand, resources in Edge-Cloud environments are heterogeneous, having diverse capacity and capabilities (e.g., different hardware, storage space, processing power, reliability of network connection etc.). On the other hand, the business workflows that operate over the datasets produced in such environments are becoming ever more complex, containing operators ranging from simple relational ones (e.g., filters) to sophisticated machine learning tasks. Thus, decisions as to where each task - or part of it - should be executed over an Edge-Cloud environment is a strenuous task even for the most experienced developer. Extra constraints concerning application Service Level Agreements (SLAs) and data privacy render the problem of producing an optimal execution plan even harder. Moreover, the volatility of edge topologies calls for dynamic solutions that can quickly adapt to frequent changes.

Existing platforms and schedulers that assume heterogeneous environments either focus on servers within an HPC or Cloud datacenter or consider the case of offloading tasks to edge devices in an Edge-Cloud environment without leveraging any knowledge of the anticipated task [8,9]. More sophisticated solutions [10] that rely on ML models to estimate the task performance over the available devices and select the optimal device mapping do not consider the additional challenges that an Edge-Cloud environment introduces.

As a remedy, we design and implement the *EC-Planner*, a planning/scheduling component for the Edge-Cloud Continuum that relies on machine learning to make automated decisions on both how and where to map arbitrary data analytics tasks to an underlying infrastructure that consists of Cloud servers as well as edge devices, in order to optimize for any user-defined policy. More precisely, *EC-Planner* takes into account:(a) the available resources, be it Cloud or edge, and their topology; (b) the characteristics of the application to be executed (derived from raw code); (c) the size of the data to be processed and (d) additional constraints, such as privacy-related ones and form an optimization problem for any user-defined policy (e.g., maximize performance, minimize energy consumption), which is solved using a well known heuristic. The decision making relies on performance and cost estimations of the various tasks when executed over the different resources available. Such estimations result from sophisticated machine learning models produced for this purpose, which form the intelligence of the proposed planner. We envision the *EC-Planner* to complement existing orchestrators such as Kubernetes, which is usually the platform of choice in Edge-Cloud scenarios, with intelligent execution planning capabilities.

2   Related Work

The field of scheduling in Edge-Cloud environments has attracted the interest of many researchers, who have taken various approaches to determine the most beneficial ways of allocating applications to the available resources, edge devices or Cloud servers, according to performance indices like total execution time, energy consumption and resource utilization. Most of the relevant works concentrate on the aspects of computation offloading, resource allocation and resource provisioning, considering computing, communication and storage resources.

Hong et al. [8] studied the multi-hop computation offloading for industrial IoT devices and proposed a game-theoretic approach where each task chooses to be executed on the device that minimizes its computation time and energy consumption. More specifically, they developed two distributed algorithms to address their game- theoretic problem and prove that they lead to a Nash equilibrium state. In [15] Wang et al. studied the problem of computation offloading in heterogeneous multi-layer mobile networks and developed a latency minimization algorithm that schedules efficiently the execution of tasks between edge devices, mobile edge servers and cloud servers in order to optimize the total computing and transmission time on all layers. Their main objective was to move the execution of tasks that could not be processed on time in edge devices to the cloud layer. Finally, COM [17], is a computation offloading method that uses the NSGA-III algorithm to address the multi-objective of execution time and energy consumption minimization of tasks in an edge-cloud environment.

In [18], the authors enhanced the edge-cloud model by inserting cloudlet[1] infrastructures into the network. They studied the problem of optimally placing cloudlets into the network and allocating tasks between the cloudlets and cloud servers, proposing a Benders decomposition-based algorithm that achieved near-optimal performance in terms of execution time and energy consumption.

In [4], Fan et al. presented a deadline-oriented task allocation mechanism for a tiered IoT infrastructure. They represented the problem as a NP-hard multi-dimensional 0–1 knapsack problem and adopted an algorithm based on ant

---

[1] https://searchcloudcomputing.techtarget.com/definition/cloudlet.

colony optimization to increase the resources' provider profit while meeting the deadline and resource constraints of the task. Finally, Mahmud et al. [9] proposed an allocation mechanism based on and Integer Linear Programming model that places user's applications to the available resources, aiming to maximize the provider's profit while ensuring the user's QoS.

However, none of these works rely on the characteristics of the application to be scheduled in order to make a device mapping decision. Contrarily, the *EC-Planner* bases its decisions on knowledge derived from the task at hand through the use of Machine Learning.

Closely related to our work is also the field of ML-assisted scheduling and device mapping. Relevant works mainly focus on the automatic selection of CPU vs. GPU for the execution of a code segment based on ML models. Most works in the field consider static code features that affect performance (e.g., loop range of a parallel loop, number of instructions per iteration, number of array accesses, etc.) to create ML classifiers using traditional methods like Support Vector Machines or Neural Networks [6,7]. DeepTune [3] contrarily relies on machine learning over source code, bypassing the code feature selection stage. More precisely, sequences of raw code tokens are translated into sequences of embedding vectors that capture the semantic relationship between tokens. A Long Short-Term Memory (LSTM) neural network is then used to extract a single, fixed size vector that characterizes the entire code. The learned representations of the source code are finally fed to a fully connected, two-layer neural network to make the optimization prediction. PROGRAML [2], by the same authors, goes a step further, maintaining the graph representation of programs, which can then be processed natively by Graph Neural Networks (GNNs). Such solutions, however, work at the task level and do not consider applications that are essentially translated to a graph of inter-dependent tasks. The *EC-Planner* addresses the device mapping of a graph of tasks, heavily relying on the fundamental concepts of PROGRAML to build its intelligence.

3   Motivation and Overview

In this section, we motivate our work by providing a real-life scenario that could benefit from a component like the *EC-Planner* and discuss the importance of Edge-Cloud systems for data processing. The described application is driven by actual business needs and has been specified in the context of the EU-funded ELEGANT project[2].

Let us consider a stream processing engine that is used for the real-time detection of arrhythmia in a stream of electrocardiography (ECG) data. In this scenario, ECG data are produced in real-time by sensors attached to patients through wearable devices. The data are processed to extract features from the ECG traces (e.g., count of peaks, average amplitude etc.), which are then fed to a Machine Learning model to infer if a patient suffers from arrhythmia. As the

---

[2] https://www.elegant-h2020.eu/.

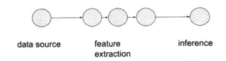

Fig. 1. Arrhythmia detection application graph.

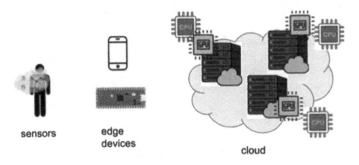

Fig. 2. Topology of motivating scenario

output of a task is needed as input for another one, different tasks interact with each other through well-defined data-dependencies. This way, we can imagine the application as a graph of tasks where data flow among its vertices. Figure 1 presents the application graph for our motivating scenario.

Figure 2 depicts the available resources of the Edge-Cloud environment, which include heterogeneous devices, both Cloud (servers) and Edge (mobile phones, raspberry pi), with different capacities and various hardware (both CPUs and GPUs).

Decisions concerning where each task should execute depend on a plethora of factors, such as the capabilities of each device, the nature of each task, the size of the data involved and the quality of the network connections among the available resources, since data transfer is required. Moreover, the application-related optimization objectives and possible constraints also affect execution plan decisions. It is clear that the application described is highly sensitive to latency. After experimentation it was found that as data grows bigger, the Cloud-only execution performs better. However, this entails the transfer of data from the Edge to the Cloud, which may be prohibitively slow in the case of a low bandwidth connection. Moreover, since medical data are involved, privacy constraints may exist, which do not allow data to leave the edge device. In this case, all execution should take place at the Edge. But even so, in the presence of multiple heterogeneous devices at the Edge, which device is the most beneficial (e.g., the CPU or the GPU of a raspberry pi)?

The answers to these questions are automatically provided by the *EC-Planner*, a component that, given the code of an application and a set of available resources, can identify the optimal mapping between tasks and devices without any manual intervention, addressing any user-defined policy.

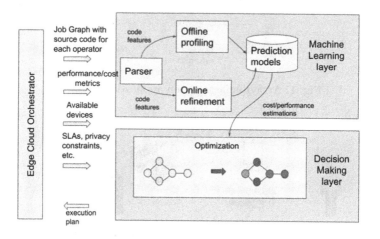

Fig. 3. EC-Planner architecture.

4   Architecture

The goal of the *EC-Planner* is to produce the optimal execution plan of complex data analytics applications containing both compute and data intensive operators in an Edge-Cloud environment. In a nutshell, the procedure is as follows: The application code is written using any framework of choice and translated to a Directed Acyclic Graph (DAG) of tasks. Using performance and cost estimations for each one of them, the planner allocates them to the underlying heterogeneous infrastructure, be it in the Cloud or at the Edge, taking additionally into account constraints such as privacy. This is done essentially by solving an optimization problem, using heuristics. The optimization policy is user-defined and can be single (e.g., minimize execution time) or multi- objective (e.g., minimize execution time and power consumption). Once the optimal execution plan is available, it is handed to the execution framework that enforces it. During its execution, the workflow is being monitored for failures and/or performance degradation. Such events trigger the creation of a new execution plan for the remaining tasks, to ensure the dynamic adaptation of the planner to the volatility of Edge-Cloud environments.

Figure 3 depicts the architecture of the *EC-Planner*, including its internal components and their interaction with other internal component or external systems. The *EC-Planner* consists of two layers: (1) the Machine Learning layer, depicted on top, which is a Machine Learning modeling framework that derives knowledge from both offline profiling and dynamic runs; and (2) the Decision Making layer, at the bottom, that communicates with the Machine Learning layer and performs the decision making of where to allocate code for execution on the available Cloud and edge devices.

In a nutshell, the modules of the *EC-Planner* cooperate towards the optimization of workflow executions over Edge-Cloud infrastructures with respect to the policy provided by the user. The *Optimization* module determines in real-time where each task is to be run and whether data need to be moved to/from their current locations and between devices and/or processing units. Such a decision must rely on the characteristics of the involved tasks, derived as code features by the *Parser*, and the underlying hardware they are executed upon. The code features, which act like a signature, take into account the type and sequence of operations involved, the input data, the control flow of the code etc., and are to be used as input for the model training process.

The training process is initially performed by the *Offline Profiling* module that profiles benchmark code over the available edge and Cloud resources. Profiling parameters are both data- (e.g., the type of data used and its size) and resource-related (e.g., type of hardware, type of device, etc.). Each profiling run logs performance and cost, such as end-to-end execution time, throughput, power consumption, etc., under each combination of the input parameter values. Code features along with profiling results are used as training data for ML models, which are then stored within the *Prediction Models library*.

Initial models are refined in an online manner by the *Online Refinement* module, which feeds monitoring information of the actual run back to the existing models. This mechanism allows for the dynamic adaptation of the models to the current infrastructure conditions, which are prone to change due to the volatility of Edge-Cloud environments. Thus, the *EC-Planner* is able to base its decisions on the most up-to-date knowledge.

In the next sections, we will delve into the implementation details of each layer.

5   The ML Layer

The Machine Learning Layer of the Planner serves as its intelligence, helping the Decision-Making layer to optimally decide on the most suitable device for executing different implementations of typical data-intensive calculations. During an offline phase, the Machine Learning model captures the performance characteristics of arbitrary code executing on a specific hardware device. Specifically, each program is represented by a graph, containing representative features extracted from its LLVM Intermediate Representation (IR), while appropriate labels for each program execution over the various devices are also provided.

Since we are interested in the device mapping problem, we have opted for OpenCL code, which is portable and can be compiled and executed on any device, be it CPU or GPU, that supports it. In the OpenCL terminology, a code function that can be executed over various devices is called kernel. We use this term throughout the paper.

For creating the graphs we use PROGRAML [2], a novel graph-based representation of programs, using a low-level, language-agnostic, and portable format. This representation is a directed attributed multi-graph, where statements, identifiers, and immediate values are vertices, and relations between vertices are edges. Edges are typed to differentiate control-, data-, and call- flow.

After creating the graphs out of the kernels and gathering all the runtime metrics, we convert the PROGRAML graphs into Pytorch Geometric graphs by using the Pytorch Geometric library. These graphs are used as the input to a Graph Transformer model, so as to learn to predict the execution time of kernels seen for the first time. The core component of Graph Transformers is the attention mechanism [1]. Attention-based models are state-of-the-art in a large range of applications. One important aspect of the attention mechanism is that it allows inputs of variable length. All the stages are described in more detail in the following.

5.1 Data Collection and Preparation

Training data highly impact the quality of an ML model, thus we need a large corpus of OpenCL kernels. We rely on the dataset of [3], which is publicly available. In particular, for our experiments, we use 93 unique OpenCL kernels. Each of these kernels has been executed with increasing input buffer sizes, on 4 machines, containing CPU and GPU devices. Table 1 summarizes all the machines used in our experiments along with their devices. For each execution, we log the execution time as well as the power consumption. In total, we have collected data from 7071 runs.

Table 1. Machines for our experiments.

Machines	Device Type	Platform Type
epyc7	NVIDIA A100-PCIE-40GB	NVIDIA CUDA
	pthread-AMD EPYC 7402 24-Core Processor	PoCL
silver1	Tesla V100-SXM2-32GB	NVIDIA CUDA
	pthread-Intel(R) Xeon(R) Silver 4114 CPU @ 2.20 GHz	PoCL
gold2	GeForce GTX 1060 6GB	NVIDIA CUDA
	Intel(R) Xeon(R) Gold 5120 CPU @ 2.20 GHz	Intel(R) OpenCL
dungani	Quadro M4000	NVIDIA CUDA
	Tesla K40	NVIDIA CUDA
	pthread-Intel(R) Core(TM) i7-4820K CPU @ 3.70 GHz	PoCL

The next step in our process is to convert the OpenCL kernels into LLVM IR. For this, we used the Clang compiler, an LLVM compiler front end for C-based languages[3]. For each pair of LLVM-IR and its corresponding measurements, we generate a single PROGRAML graph representation. PROGRAML graphs are directed attributed multi-graphs where nodes represent statements, identifiers, and values while edges represent control-, data-, and call-flow relationships between vertices. Thus, node features include the node type (instruction, variable, or constant), the number of input bytes as well as the device of execution,

---
[3] https://clang.llvm.org/.

and the block to which each node belongs, while edge features include information about the edge type (control, data, and call).

Continuing the pre-processing of our dataset, we group our data creating two sets for each device type, i.e., two for CPUs and two for GPUs, based on the year of manufacture of each device. Thus, we have groups A and B containing runs on the high-end GPU and CPU devices of our testbed respectively and groups C and D containing runs on the lower-end GPUs and CPUs respectively. The last column of Table 1 summarizes this information.

5.2 Model Setup

To have a more robust and organized approach for the evaluation of our machine learning model, we make use of cross-validation with dynamic directory creation. Cross-validation helps in gaining a less biased estimate of the model skill than other methods, such as a simple train/test split.

In particular, we split each team into a 5-fold dataset (training) and test dataset, based on unique kernels, so as to avoid any possibility of data leakage. For training, we keep 90% of our dataset and the rest 10% is for the test set.

An attention-based graph neural network has been used. Specifically, we use the Graph Transformer operator from [12]. This architecture adopts from [14] its vanilla multi-head attention into graph learning and takes into account the case of edge features. First of all, we prepare the node features and the edge attributes converting them into node embeddings and edge embeddings. Due to the nature of our dataset (for example, we have 1 kernel corresponding to many different runs/graphs, depending on the different input buffer sizes), we follow two approaches for creating them: (a) per batch of graphs and (b) for the entire dataset. In the first approach, we process the node features independently for each batch, and the embeddings are learned specifically for that batch. In the second approach, we combine all the graphs from the training dataset into a single large graph and compute the embeddings on this combined graph. Then for the per batch training, we index the single large graph to get the embeddings for each batch graph. This way the model captures global patterns across the entire dataset.

In addition to the embeddings, we normalize each target value separately by using Min-Max scaler. This way all features are transformed into the range [0,1]. All neural networks are regularized with Dropout for generalization and Batch Normalization in order to be uniformly applicable to vastly different scales of auxiliary input features. We also use the Adam optimizer with lr=0.001 to train our model, and we set weight decay to 0.0005 for our model to prevent overfitting.

For the implementation of the Graph Transformer, we make use of the graph transformer operator, which is available in the Pytorch Geometric library. Our experiments have consistently showed that by using the second approach of computing the embeddings for the entire dataset, we achieve better results. This is logical, because our dataset is small, and the interactions between the graphs of different kernels are essential to learn meaningful embeddings. We choose different epochs and batch sizes for the CPU datasets, in comparison with the GPU datasets, because of their difference in length.

For groups B and D (high and low-end CPUs), we have trained the models for 50 epochs with 32 batch size, and selected the model with the lowest mean L1 loss value, between the kfolds in the cross-validation experiment. The Mean Absolute Error (MAE) is calculated out of the normalized target and normalized predictions, so for group B is 0.0078, and for group D is 0.0054.

For the GPU datasets, we have trained the models for 70 epochs, with 64 batch size, and selected the lowest mean L1 loss value, as in the CPU dataset. For group A we have a MAE of 0.074 and for group C a MAE of 0.0126.

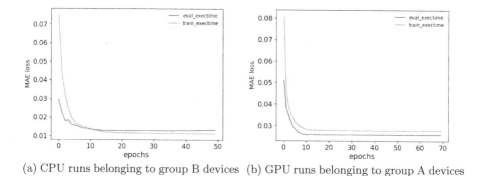

(a) CPU runs belonging to group B devices   (b) GPU runs belonging to group A devices

Fig. 4. Mean train and eval MAE loss for execution time

Figure 4 plots the training and evaluation MAE for execution time based on runs belonging to groups A and B. These groups correspond to the most recent machines based on the year of manufacture. Based on the size and the nature of our dataset, there is a good convergence. In Fig. 4 we can see that the evaluation loss is below the training loss, and that is because the validation data, even with the cross-validation procedure, is scarce but in the same time widely represented by the training dataset. So the model performs extremely well on these few examples. Finding bigger and more diverse dataset will be valuable for our future directions.

Using pre-trained language models to better exploit the text of a node, e.g., the contents of a statement, or the name of an identifier, as well as incorporating more sophisticated graph-specific inductive bias would improve the performance of the model and is subject to future work.

6   The Decision-Making Layer

The main goal of the Decision Making layer is to produce a (near) optimal scheduling plan based on one or multiple given objectives, for instance, the minimization of the end-to-end execution time, the minimization of power consumption, or both. It receives the user's application, represented as a DAG of tasks, and the available nodes in the network topology - along with the specific hardware devices of each node and their network transfer rates - from the execution framework used. Moreover, it needs the estimations of execution time and power consumption for each task in the DAG derived from the ML layer. After that, it produces a (near) optimal execution plan and returns it to the execution framework.

Our approach for tackling the DAG scheduling problem is based on the *HEFT* (Heterogeneous Earliest Finish Time) [13] algorithm, which is a list-scheduling algorithm designed to minimize the execution time of a given task graph in a heterogeneous hardware environment. The reason we chose *HEFT* is that it has been proven to produce highly efficient scheduling plans, over a wider range of graph structures in very low running time, making it a viable and highly competitive algorithm for real-time application scheduling.

Briefly, *HEFT* consists of two major phases: (i) a task prioritizing phase in which all tasks are sorted based on precedence constraints, and (ii) a processor selection phase in which the chosen task is assigned to the processor that minimizes the task's finish time. One limitation of *HEFT* is that it considers only the minimization of execution time when making its scheduling decisions. Since we consider multi-objective optimization in our case, we enhance the original algorithm to optimize for a function of metrics (e.g., 0.5×`execution time` +0.5× `power consumption`). The overhead introduced by possible data transfers is also taken into account by the algorithm. Moreover, we further modify the original version of the algorithm to support specific, user-defined task-to-device assignments, i.e., pinned tasks, and to consider network topologies that are not fully connected, which is typical for edge-to-cloud environments.

The following is dedicated to the experimental evaluation of the Decision Making layer, which is written in Python 3.7. We aim to assess (a) the overhead of the planning procedure, i.e., the time needed for *EC-Planner* to come up with the final execution plan, especially as workflow sizes increase, (b) the performance gain when executing the *EC-Planner* selected device placement vs. baseline placement strategies and (c) the closeness of the *EC-Planner* resulting plans to the optimal ones.

To this end, we use synthetically generated workflow graphs using our own workflow generator. Our generator can produce DAGs of arbitrary sizes and edge densities in order to be able to test the scalability and performance of our system in a wide range of task graph sizes and structures. It also generates the computation, communication, and power costs of the tasks across all the available devices. We set the computation cost on CPU devices to be a uniform variable in the interval (0–10] sec and the corresponding cost on GPUs to be 2 to 4 times less. As for the power consumption on CPUs, it is uniform in the interval [50–100] Watt, while on GPUs it is 3 to 4 times more. Finally, the computation costs are set in a way that the CCR (Communication to Computation Ratio) values of the generated graphs are in the range (0–1).

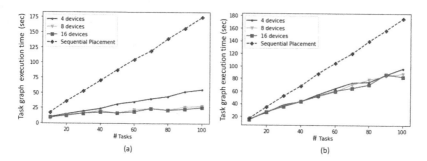

Fig. 5. Execution time of the resulting plan vs. the size of (a) sparse or (b) dense task graphs, when optimizing for performance.

All the experiments have been executed for workflows of sizes ranging from 10 to 100 tasks with step size 10 and for 4, 8, and 16 devices (half of which are CPUs and the other half GPUs at each time). In each scenario, we generate 10 different graphs to reduce the variance and provide more accurate results. We also considered two types of graphs regarding their number of edges, one that has the same number of edges as nodes (tree-like structure) and one that has approximately edges that are three times the number of nodes. We refer to the first type as sparse and the second as dense.

Two baselines are provided (one for end-to-end execution time and one for power consumption) to illustrate the performance of our method in a clearer way: 1) the makespan end-to-end execution time of the scheduling where all tasks are assigned sequentially to the fastest executor (called *sequential placement*) and 2) the power consumption when each task is assigned for execution to the device that minimizes its power consumption. The former is a common baseline used in scheduling algorithms and essentially provides an upper bound that we don't want to surpass, and the latter is the lower bound of the power consumption that we want to approach.

Efficiency of Produced Plans
In this experiment, we study the efficiency of the plans produced by *EC-Planner* when considering single multiple optimization objectives, namely the minimization of the tasks graph's end-to-end execution time and the minimization of power consumption respectively.

Figure 5 plots the execution time of the resulting plan vs. the size of sparse (a) or dense (b) task graphs, for various number of available devices and a single optimization objective, i.e., the minimization of execution time. Our planner produces highly efficient scheduling plans that significantly improve the sequential placement strategy, with the difference in performance increasing as the number of tasks grows, reaching a 7× improvement at 100 tasks, in Fig. 5(a). The same applies to the case of dense graphs, Fig. 5(b). Despite the more complex dependencies in the task graph, the *EC-Planner* manages again to generate low-cost scheduling plans, improving performance by over 50% in the case of 100 tasks.

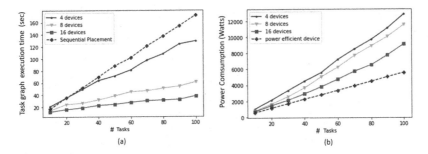

Fig. 6. (a) Execution time and (b) power consumption of the resulting plan vs. the size of the task graph, when optimizing for both objectives.

Another observation worth noticing is that where in the case of sparse graphs increasing the number of devices leads to better results, while the same does not apply to the case of denser graphs. This is because in the former case, the tasks have very few dependencies among them and can take advantage of the larger number of devices to execute in parallel, while in the latter the excess devices cannot be exploited for parallel execution.

Figure 6 depicts the results of the placement strategies that aim to minimize both the execution time and the power consumption of task graphs. Equal weights were assigned to both objectives. We present results for sparse graphs, as dense graphs results are qualitatively similar. As can be seen from Fig. 5(a), the number of available devices plays an important role in the execution time of the produced schedules - the more the devices the better the performance. Our planner still manages to achieve lower execution times than the baseline, while at the same time significantly improving the consumed power, as seen in Fig. 6(b). The most noticeable example is one of 16 devices where our planner achieves a 50% improvement in power consumption with an almost zero increase in execution time.

Scalability of the EC-Planner
This section aims to demonstrate the scalability of our planner for different graph sizes and edge densities. Figures 7(a) and 7(b) plot the overhead (in terms of time) of the planning process when the number of tasks increases, for sparse and more dense graphs respectively. The EC-Planner planning overhead scales almost linearly with the number of tasks, remaining, however, in the sub-second scale (slightly above 0.01 s) even in the extreme case of 16 devices and 100 tasks of a dense graph, thus being a viable solution even for large-scale scientific or industrial applications. As expected, the number of devices is of critical importance for the planning overhead. As for the graph density, it slightly increases the running time of the *EC-Planner* by about 15%.

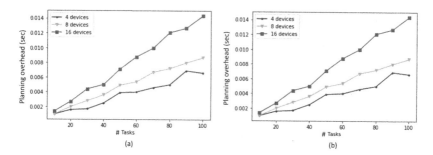

Fig. 7. Overhead in sec of planning vs. the size of the workflow graph, for (a) sparse and (b) dense graphs.

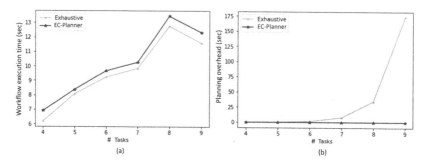

Fig. 8. Comparison of EC-Planner with exhaustive search of optimal plan in terms of (a) end-to-end execution time of resulting plan and (b) overhead of planning.

Comparison with Optimal

Finally, we implemented an exhaustive algorithm that calculates and evaluates all possible scheduling plans for the given task graph. Its complexity is exponential to the number of tasks and highly affected by the number of available hardware devices. For these experiments, we used smaller synthetic graphs of up to 9 nodes and 4 hardware devices. This is the largest graph size on which the exhaustive algorithm successfully runs in our machine. We present plots for the single objective of minimizing the end-to-end execution time of the task graph. The goal is to assess how close the placements produced by *EC-Planner* are to the optimal solution in terms of execution time minimization.

As seen in Fig. 8(a), our planner manages to generate placements that are close to the optimal, less than 15% off for all cases. This ensures that, especially for task graphs of small sizes, the generated schedules are of high quality. Figure 8(b) plots the time needed to generate the execution plan for both algorithms. As expected the overhead of the exhaustive scheduler grows exponentially to the number of tasks making it a non-feasible solution even for relatively small graphs.

7 Conclusions

In this paper we presented the *EC-Planner*, a planning component designed and implemented for heterogeneous and volatile Edge-Cloud environments. The *EC-Planner* makes intelligent, automated decisions on the mapping of tasks to devices, both in the Cloud and at the Edge, for data intensive applications. Experimental results show that the *EC-Planner* produces near-optimal plans for any user-defined policy, incurring only minimal overhead.

Acknowledgment. This work has been supported by the European Commission in terms of the H2020 ELEGANT Project (Grant Agreement 957286).

References

1. Bahdanau, D., Cho, K., Bengio, Y.: Neural machine translation by jointly learning to align and translate. arXiv preprint arXiv:1409.0473 (2014)
2. Cummins, C., Fisches, Z.V., Ben-Nun, T., Hoefler, T., O'Boyle, M.F., Leather, H.: Programl: a graph-based program representation for data flow analysis and compiler optimizations. In: International Conference on Machine Learning, pp. 2244–2253. PMLR (2021)
3. Cummins, C., Petoumenos, P., Wang, Z., Leather, H.: End-to-end deep learning of optimization heuristics. In: 2017 26th International Conference on Parallel Architectures and Compilation Techniques (PACT), pp. 219–232. IEEE (2017)
4. Fan, J., Wei, X., Wang, T., Lan, T., Subramaniam, S.: Deadline-aware task scheduling in a tiered IoT infrastructure. In: GLOBECOM 2017–2017 IEEE Global Communications Conference, pp. 1–7. IEEE (2017)
5. Francis, T.: A comparison of cloud execution mechanisms fog, edge, and clone cloud computing. Int. J. Electr. Comput. Eng. 8(6), 2088–8708 (2018)
6. Grewe, D., O'Boyle, M.F.P.: A static task partitioning approach for heterogeneous systems using OpenCL. In: Knoop, J. (ed.) CC 2011. LNCS, vol. 6601, pp. 286–305. Springer, Heidelberg (2011). https://doi.org/10.1007/978-3-642-19861-8_16
7. Hayashi, A., Ishizaki, K., Koblents, G., Sarkar, V.: Machine-learning-based performance heuristics for runtime cpu/gpu selection. In: Proceedings of the principles and practices of programming on the Java platform, pp. 27–36 (2015)
8. Hong, Z., Chen, W., Huang, H., Guo, S., Zheng, Z.: Multi-hop cooperative computation offloading for industrial IoT-edge-cloud computing environments. IEEE Trans. Parallel Distrib. Syst. 30(12), 2759–2774 (2019)
9. Mahmud, R., Srirama, S.N., Ramamohanarao, K., Buyya, R.: Profit-aware application placement for integrated fog-cloud computing environments. J. Parall. Distrib. Comput. **135**, 177–190 (2020)
10. Mytilinis, I., Bitsakos, C., Doka, K., Konstantinou, I., Koziris, N.: The vision of a heterogenerous scheduler. In: 2018 IEEE International Conference on Cloud Computing Technology and Science (CloudCom), pp. 302–307. IEEE (2018)
11. Shi, W., Dustdar, S.: The promise of edge computing. Computer 49(5), 78–81 (2016)
12. Shi, Y., Huang, Z., Feng, S., Zhong, H., Wang, W., Sun, Y.: Masked label prediction: Unified message passing model for semi-supervised classification. arXiv preprint arXiv:2009.03509 (2020)

13. Topcuoglu, H., Hariri, S., Wu, M.Y.: Performance-effective and low-complexity task scheduling for heterogeneous computing. IEEE Trans. Parallel Distrib. Syst. **13**(3), 260–274 (2002)

14. Vaswani, A., et al.: Attention is all you need. In: Advances in neural information processing systems 30 (2017)

15. Wang, P., Zheng, Z., Di, B., Song, L.: Hetmec: latency-optimal task assignment and resource allocation for heterogeneous multi-layer mobile edge computing. IEEE Trans. Wireless Commun. **18**(10), 4942–4956 (2019)

16. Wang, T., Zhang, G., Liu, A., Bhuiyan, M.Z.A., Jin, Q.: A secure IoT service architecture with an efficient balance dynamics based on cloud and edge computing. IEEE Internet Things J. **6**(3), 4831–4843 (2018)

17. Xu, X., et al.: A computation offloading method over big data for Iot-enabled cloud-edge computing. Futur. Gener. Comput. Syst. **95**, 522–533 (2019)

18. Yang, S., Li, F., Shen, M., Chen, X., Fu, X., Wang, Y.: Cloudlet placement and task allocation in mobile edge computing. IEEE Internet Things J. **6**(3), 5853–5863 (2019)

Olive Leaf Infection Detection Using the Cloud-Edge Continuum

Themistoklis Sarantakos[1] , Daniel Mauricio Jimenez Gutierrez[2] ,
and Dimitrios Amaxilatis[1]([envelope])

[1] SparkWorks Ltd., Galway, Ireland
{tsaradakos,d.amaxilatis}@sparkworks.net
[2] Sapienza University of Rome, Rome, Italy
jimenezgutierrez@diag.uniroma1.it

Abstract. The use of computer vision, deep learning, and drones has revolutionized agriculture by enabling efficient crop monitoring and disease detection. Still, many challenges need to be overcome due to the vast diversity of plant species and their unique regional characteristics. Olive trees, which have been cultivated for thousands of years, present a particularly complex case for leaf-based disease diagnosis as disease symptoms can vary widely, both between different plant variations and even within individual leaves on the same plant. This complexity, coupled with the susceptibility of olive groves to various pathogens, including bacterial blight, olive knot, aculus olearius, and olive peacock spot, has hindered the development of effective disease detection algorithms. To address this challenge, we have devised a novel approach that combines deep learning techniques, leveraging convolutional neural networks, vision transformers, and cloud computing-based models. Aiming to detect and classify olive tree diseases the experimental results of our study have been highly promising, demonstrating the effectiveness of the combined transformer and cloud-based machine learning models, achieving an impressive accuracy of approximately 99.6% for multiclass classification cases including healthy, aculus olearius, and peacock spot infected leaves. These results highlight the potential of deep learning models in tackling the complexities of olive leaf disease detection and the need for further research in the field.

Keywords: Computer Vision · Olive Leaf Infection · Machine Learning · Image Analysis

1 Introduction

The use of advanced technologies in agriculture has revolutionized traditional farming practices, enabling more efficient and precise methods for crop monitoring and disease detection. Among these transformative technologies, computer vision and drones have emerged as powerful tools for the detection of leaf infections in olive trees, offering new possibilities for early disease diagnosis and

I. Chatzigiannakis and I. Karydis (Eds.): ALGOCLOUD 2023, LNCS 14053, pp. 25–37, 2024.
https://doi.org/10.1007/978-3-031-49361-4_2

effective disease management. By leveraging the capabilities of computer vision algorithms and aerial surveillance provided by drones, farmers and researchers can now detect and respond to leaf infections in olive trees more accurately and promptly than ever before.

Olive trees are an integral part of the agricultural landscape, providing valuable yields of olives and olive oil. However, they are susceptible to various diseases, including leaf infections caused by fungal pathogens, bacteria, and viruses. Identifying and addressing these infections in their early stages is crucial for preventing severe crop damage and yield losses. Traditional methods of disease detection often involve manual inspection of individual trees, which can be time-consuming, labor-intensive, and prone to human error. Fortunately, computer vision technologies and drones have emerged as promising solutions to overcome these limitations.

Computer vision refers to the field of artificial intelligence that enables machines to analyze and interpret visual data, such as images or videos. By employing sophisticated algorithms, computer vision systems can extract meaningful information from visual inputs, enabling them to identify patterns, detect anomalies, and classify objects accurately. In the context of olive tree leaf infection detection, computer vision algorithms can be trained to recognize specific disease symptoms, such as discoloration, spots, lesions, or other visible signs of infection. By analyzing high-resolution images captured by drones, these algorithms can quickly scan vast olive tree groves and identify potentially infected trees with remarkable speed and precision.

Drones, or unmanned aerial vehicles (UAVs), have rapidly gained popularity in agriculture due to their versatility and ability to provide an aerial perspective of crops and farmland. Equipped with high-resolution cameras and advanced sensors, drones can capture detailed images of olive trees from various angles and altitudes. These images offer a comprehensive view of the entire grove, allowing farmers and researchers to monitor the health and condition of individual trees remotely. Combined with computer vision algorithms, drones can autonomously survey large areas and generate real-time insights on the presence and severity of leaf infections. This enables farmers to make data-driven decisions and implement targeted interventions for disease control.

The integration of computer vision technologies and drones for olive tree leaf infection detection offers several advantages over traditional methods. Firstly, it significantly reduces the time and effort required for disease surveillance, allowing farmers to cover large areas quickly and accurately. Secondly, by enabling early detection, this technology facilitates timely intervention, thereby minimizing the spread of infections and potential crop losses. Additionally, the use of drones eliminates the need for manual tree inspection, reducing the risk of human error and improving overall efficiency in disease management.

The rest of the paper is structured as follows: Section 2 presents the literature state of the art on the fields of computer vision, machine learning, and edge computing technologies. Section 3 describes our methodology and the proposed architecture for identifying the condition of olive leaves. The evaluation of this methodology and its comparison with other systems is showcased in Sect. 4. Finally, in Sect. 5 we present our conclusions and future directions.

2 Related Work

Image processing and analysis have been utilized by many proposed solutions in past years in literature to efficiently detect plant and crop diseases. In [3] disorders in tomato plants are detected in leaf images using contour tracing, feature extraction, and Convolutional Neural Network (CNN) or K-Nearest Neighbor (KNN) machine learning approaches. [6] showcases a similar system that was developed in the Kingdom of Saudi Arabia that uses Deep Learning techniques like *ResNet-50* and MobileNet models to classify olive leaf images collected through remote-controlled UAVs with high accuracy reaching up to 97%. X-FIDO [2] is a vision-based program to detect symptoms of Olive Quick Decline Syndrome. It showcases how transfer learning can be leveraged when collecting thousands of new leaf images is impossible, using only a few hundred images of healthy and infected leaves reaching over 98% accuracy. Olive tree disease analysis and classification is also to target of [8]. In more details, the infected area is isolated using the histogram thresholding and k-means segmentation methodologies with the latter being evaluated as more accurate. Finally, [10] solves a problem close to the one we face, by providing an automated methodology for detecting and counting olive trees using a multi-step classification system using colored satellite images. In [1] the authors explore the utilization of transformers for multiclass classification to predict olive leaf disease. They present their findings, highlighting the effectiveness of this approach in accurately identifying and categorizing various diseases affecting olive leaves.

2.1 Computer Vision Approaches

Convolutional Neural Networks (CNNs) are a powerful class of deep learning models specifically designed for computer vision applications. CNNs excel at automatically learning and extracting meaningful features from visual data, such as images or videos. They employ a series of convolutional layers that apply learnable filters to capture local patterns and features. These filters scan the input data, enabling the network to detect edges, textures, shapes, and other visual attributes. By stacking multiple convolutional layers, CNNs can progressively learn more complex and abstract representations of the input. Additionally, pooling layers are used to downsample the learned features and retain important information while reducing spatial dimensions. The final layers of a CNN typically consist of fully connected layers that map the learned features to specific outputs, such as object classes or semantic labels. CNNs have demonstrated remarkable performance in various computer vision tasks, including image classification, object detection, image segmentation, and image generation. Their ability to automatically learn and extract relevant features from visual data has made them a fundamental and widely-used tool in the field of computer vision.

Transfer learning is a machine learning technique where knowledge gained from training one model on a specific task is applied to a related task. A pre-trained model is used as a starting point and adapted to the new task by fine-tuning or retraining specific parts leveraging the pre-trained model's learned features and representations, leading to improved performance, especially when data is limited. *ResNet-50* is a highly regarded transfer learning model in the field of computer vision. Originally trained on the extensive ImageNet dataset, it has acquired intricate image representations. As a transfer learning technique, *ResNet-50*'s pre-trained layers can serve as feature extractors for novel tasks. This capability allows researchers to achieve remarkable performance, even when faced with limited annotated data. Due to its adaptability, *ResNet-50* finds extensive utility across diverse computer vision applications, including image classification, object detection, and image segmentation. The versatility and effectiveness of *ResNet-50* make it a widely favored choice in the field of computer vision. *VGG-19*, like *ResNet-50*, is a renowned convolutional neural network architecture that stands out as a potent transfer learning model. Like its counterpart, *VGG-19* was initially trained on the ImageNet dataset, which has played a crucial role in shaping its effectiveness across diverse computer vision tasks. By harnessing the pre-trained weights and learned features of *VGG-19*, researchers can tap into its vast knowledge and extend its applicability to new domains or tasks, particularly in scenarios where labeled data is scarce. The extensive capabilities of *VGG-19* make it a valuable asset for leveraging transfer learning in the realm of computer vision.

You Only Look Once (YOLO) stands as a groundbreaking object detection framework, ushering in a new era in computer vision. It diverges from traditional methods by adopting a singular-stage approach, resulting in exceptional speed and efficiency. YOLO revolutionizes object detection by dividing the input image into a grid and directly predicting bounding boxes, object probabilities, and class labels from each grid cell. Through the ingenious employment of a solitary neural network, YOLO concurrently identifies multiple objects in a single pass, achieving remarkable real-time performance that proves invaluable in time-sensitive applications. With its precise and swift object detection capabilities, YOLO has become an indispensable tool across diverse domains, including autonomous driving, surveillance systems, and image analysis.

Amazon Rekognition stands at the forefront of cutting-edge computer vision technology, offering a comprehensive and powerful solution for image and video analysis. Developed by Amazon Web Services (AWS), this state-of-the-art service provides an array of advanced features, including object recognition, facial analysis, emotion detection, text recognition, and more. With its deep learning algorithms and extensive training on vast datasets, Amazon Rekognition exhibits remarkable accuracy and robust performance, allowing users to extract valuable insights from visual content. *Roboflow* Roboflow is a powerful platform and suite of tools designed to streamline the process of building computer vision models and managing image datasets. It offers a comprehensive set of functionalities that simplify and accelerate various stages of the computer vision workflow. With Roboflow, users can annotate and label images, enabling the creation of high-quality datasets for training models. The platform also provides pre-processing capabilities, allowing users to resize, augment, and transform their image data to enhance model performance. Furthermore, Roboflow offers integration with popular machine learning frameworks and APIs, making it easy to train and deploy models in different environments.

2.2   Edge Computing

Edge computing is a distributed computing approach that brings processing and storage closer to the devices and sensors at the edge of the network. It reduces latency by processing data locally and enables real-time decision-making. Edge computing offers benefits such as improved efficiency, enhanced privacy and security, offline capabilities, and scalability. It is applied in various industries and use cases to optimize data processing, reduce network bandwidth usage, and enable faster insights and better user experiences. Using edge computing in agriculture enables farmers to make timely decisions based on on-site data processing, reduces reliance on cloud connectivity, and ensures continuous farm operations even in remote areas. Edge computing empowers farmers with actionable insights, improves resource allocation, and promotes sustainable farming practices [5,7,9].

2.3   Learning at the Cloud-Edge Continuum

Federated Learning is a decentralized machine learning approach that prioritizes data privacy by keeping training data on local or edge devices instead of a central server or cloud. In this method, the model is distributed to edge devices for local training, with only model updates transmitted back and aggregated to improve the global model. The key objective is to protect data privacy and security by minimizing data sharing risks. Federated learning facilitates distributed model training while respecting privacy constraints and reducing the need for large-scale data transfers. Its benefits include personalized model training on individual devices, preserving data privacy, collaborative learning from diverse sources, and applicability in various scenarios such as mobile and IoT devices as well as edge computing environments.

2.4   Leaf Datasets

Most of the systems presented above utilize a set of existing open datasets that contain curated images of plant leaves and fruits. These images contain mostly clean views of plant leaves, in neutral backgrounds, so their classification will be most accurate. One such dataset is the PlantVillage [4] dataset. It is a widely used and publicly available dataset for plant disease detection and classification research created by the PlantVillage project, that aims to assist in the development and evaluation of computer vision algorithms for plant disease diagnosis. It consists of 54303 healthy and unhealthy leaf images divided into 38 categories by species and diseases. The Olive Leaf Dataset[1] was created for olive tree disease detection and classification using convolutional neural networks (CNNs). It is intended to aid researchers and developers working on olive leaf disease analysis and machine learning algorithms for olive tree health monitoring and consists of high-resolution images, of three distinct classes: 2068 images of leaves infected by aculus orealus, 3717 images of leaves infected by peacock spot and 2155 healthy leaves.

---

[1] https://github.com/sinanuguz/CNN_olive_dataset

3   Proposed Methodology

Our proposed solution focuses on the analysis of the collected olive tree images collected using on-field hardware like drones or autonomous vehicles that can traverse the olive grove with limited or no human intervention. These images contain as expected a portion of the olive tree, with multiple leaves, photographed from a close or medium distance. The pipeline followed for the analysis of the images collected is depicted in Fig. 1. As depicted there, all collected images are bundled into a dataset, that are to be analyzed. This analysis consists of two parts:

– The segmentation of the leaves from each one of the tree images collected.
– The characterization of each detected leaf as healthy or unhealthy and the decision on the parasite it is infected with.

These two processes can be either performed in two steps, using two discrete ML models, or as a single step using a single ML model trained to detect all 3 possible conditions. The first approach allows us to optimize the two ML models performing each operation, and increase their expected accuracy, resulting in better results, but on the other hand, requires more computational power for the analysis of each image. Using the second approach, we are able to perform both operations with a single prediction, that can both extract the olive leaves in each image and categorize them in one of the 3 available categories.

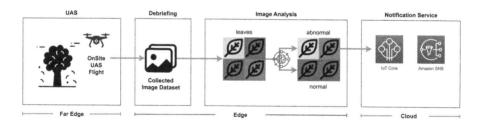

Fig. 1. Leaf image collection pipeline across the Cloud-Edge continuum.

After careful and extensive evaluation of all available software solutions, we were able to identify the best configuration for the two approaches we will evaluate in the rest of this paper. To implement the first approach and in scenarios where accuracy and flexibility are key, we determined that a combination of a self-trained YOLO ML model for image segmentation, complemented by a *ResNet-50* ML model using transfer learning techniques, is expected to provide the best outcome. This hybrid approach allows us to leverage the strengths of YOLO's real-time object detection capabilities while benefiting from the high accuracy of *ResNet-50*. However, in situations where efficiency takes precedence over flexibility, we identified that leveraging the advanced capabilities of a single YOLO multi-class segmentation ML model would be a viable alternative. That is why we based on it the second approach described above.

Moving parts of the leaf infection detection to the edge of the network offers a multitude of significant benefits. Firstly, it helps reduce the burden of data transfer to cloud services. By processing data locally at the edge of the network, the need to transmit the total volume of images or video footage to centralized cloud services is minimized, resulting in more efficient data management, lower network congestion and lower communication costs. Additionally, edge computing accelerates the delivery of results. With data processing occurring on-site or close to the data source, the latency associated with sending data to a distant data center is substantially reduced, leading to faster and more real-time outcomes. Finally, moving computing to the edge helps keep sensitive data under our own control, enhancing data security and privacy, and reducing the exposure of critical information to external networks.

3.1 Leaf Extraction

The process of detecting the exact position of olive leaves inside a photo taken by an autonomous vehicle can be quite a complex task. Most applications that we investigated from the previous work (presented in Sect. 2) dealt with images of single leaves. These leaves were mostly placed in neutral backgrounds without any other information that could affect the process. Our goal was to be able to detect much more than single leaves and identify and extract each leaf from high-resolution images that contain portions or even whole olive trees. To achieve such a result we had to move of course from the single leaf images to branches of olive trees and finally high-resolution images as the ones available in Fig. 2.

In the pursuit of robust solution for object segmentation, our research led us to YOLOv8, an advanced framework renowned for its exceptional performance. In parallel, we delved into the available tools for the preparation of the datasets for YOLO ML model training, exploring two state-of-the-art applications: trainYOLO[2] and roboflow[3]. With these applications, we could easily label

Fig. 2. Single leaf, branch of leaves and tree image used to evolve the leaf extraction ML model.

---

[2] https://trainyolo.com/.
[3] https://roboflow.com/.

and annotate the specific regions of interest in our experiments, the olive leaves. To ensure the model's efficiency, we divided the dataset into training and validation subsets. Following an extensive training process, we evaluated our model against a diverse set of tree images that contained either single leaves, branches with multiple leaves in neutral backgrounds, or multiple leaves in images of trees in natural surroundings. Once the leaves were detected, we are able to use the YOLO bounding boxes detected to precisely crop and extract each individual leaf as a separate image, ready for their subsequent analysis (in the first approach) or their exact categorization (in the second approach).

3.2   Leaf Classification

In the image classification part, our exploration led us to four distinct approaches. Firstly, we experimented with custom-built CNN trained from scratch, leveraging our domain expertise to develop a tailored architecture. The image classification model we employed is a sequential model with a series of convolutional and pooling layers followed by fully connected layers. The model begins with an initial convolutional layer with 8 filters and a 3×3 kernel, utilizing the ReLU activation function. Subsequently, a max pooling layer with a pool size of 2×2 and stride of 2 downsamples the feature maps. This is followed by two more convolutional layers, each with increasing filter size, and their corresponding max pooling layers. After the final pooling layer, the features are flattened into a 1D vector. Two fully connected layers are then applied, with the first layer consisting of 64 units and ReLU activation, and the final layer producing class probabilities using the softmax activation function. This model architecture enables extracting and learning hierarchical features from the input images, facilitating accurate image classification. The CNN model structure was carefully chosen through a comprehensive grid search process, which involved evaluating its performance on our specific dataset.

Secondly, we evaluated models that harness the power of transfer learning, utilizing pre-trained *VGG-19* and *ResNet-50* models, originally trained on the ImageNet dataset, and further fine-tuned them with our own dataset. This approach allowed us to benefit from the models' learned features and representations, enabling enhanced classification performance. These two models was selected based on thorough research and analysis of literature papers. We observed that *VGG-19* and *ResNet-50* demonstrated superior performance on our dataset compared to other models or variations.

Finally, we experimented with cloud computing tools, more specifically AWS Rekognition, to train a ML model using our own dataset. This cloud-based approach would provide us with easy-to-scale infrastructures for efficient training and inference operations.

Throughout the implementation and evaluation of these diverse methodologies, we aimed to understand the best configurations for our system and find the optimal strategies for achieving accurate and reliable image classification results.

4   Evaluation

4.1   Metrics

To evaluate the performance of classification ML models we use the most commonly used metrics of the field, accuracy, precision, recall, and f1 score. Each metric provides a different perspective on the model's effectiveness. In more detail, *accuracy* (1) measures the proportion of correct predictions to the total number of predictions made; *precision* (2) calculates the ratio of true positive predictions to the total number of positive predictions, indicating how well the model correctly identifies positive instances; *recall* (3) calculates the ratio of true positive predictions to the total number of actual positive instances, indicating how well the model captures all positive instances; *f1 score* (4) is the harmonic mean of precision and recall providing a single metric that combines both precision and recall, giving a balanced measure of the model's performance.

$$Accuracy = \frac{TP + TN}{Predictions} \quad (1)$$

$$Precision = \frac{TP}{TP + FP} \quad (2)$$

$$Recall = \frac{TP}{TP + FN} \quad (3)$$

$$F1 = 2 \times \frac{Precision \times Recall}{Precision + Recall} \quad (4)$$

TP: True Positive, TN: True Negative, FP: False Positive, FN: False Negative

4.2   Leaf Segmentation

Figure 3 showcases the result of using the YOLO-based ML model we developed for the leaf segmentation operations of our system. This model is trained on a dataset consisting of more than 200 annotated images with more than 1000 objects belonging to one each of the three classes we use (healthy, aculus orealus, and peacock spot).

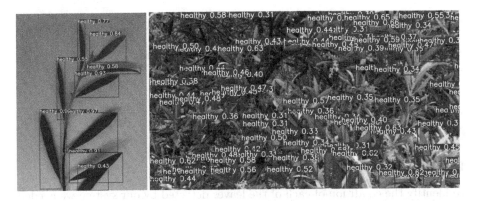

Fig. 3. Leaf detection on a branch and tree image using a YOLOv8 image segmentation ML model.

In Fig. 4 we showcase the evolution of all the available metrics during the training of our model for the whole 50 epochs of the training procedure. By minimizing the training losses (box loss, segmentation loss, classification loss, and localization loss) over time, the model improves its ability to accurately classify objects and predict their bounding box coordinates. This indicates that the model is learning to make more precise and accurate predictions. Simultaneously, the metrics such as precision, recall, mAP@0.5, and mAP@0.5:0.95 are all increasing. This suggests that the model's performance in object detection is improving. Higher precision indicates a lower rate of false positive detections, while higher recall indicates a lower rate of false negative detections.

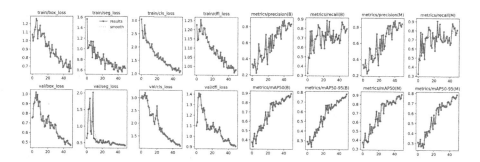

Fig. 4. Metrics for the training of the YOLO-based segmentation model.

Additionally, in Table 1 we present the results achieved by our YOLO-based segmentation ML model, for the two-step and approach. In the two-step approach, we can see the amount of leaves the system can detect out of the total number of leaves available in the dataset. This total number of leaves available is not the actual leaves presented in the image but the leaves that are usable, in focus, and in correct distance from the camera.

Table 1. Statistics for the olive leaves detected in the YOLO-based approach.

Class	Expected	Detected	Rate
Single Leaf	212	197	93%
Branch	135	130	96%
Tree	1761	1509	85%

4.3   Leaf Classification

To identify the condition of each of the leaves detected by our system we needed to develop a ML model that is capable of classifying each cropped image to one of the 3 available categories. In our attempts to find the best possible ML model,

Table 2. Accuracy scores achieved in the evaluation of multiple ML models for the classification of single olive leaves.

ML Model	Accuracy	Precision	Recall	F1 Score
CNN	91.2	82.1	84.96	83.4
ResNet-50	99.3	90.2	96.5	93.3
VGG-19	98.2	89	93.3	91.1
AWS Rekognition	99.6	99.5	99.7	99.6

we evaluated multiple configurations and design: a CNN-based ML model, a ResNet-50 ML model, a VGG-19 ML model and AWS Rekognition.

The accuracy of each model is noted in Table 2. We can there identify that our custom CNN model has achieved the lower accuracy across all our attempts with 91.2%. The VGG-19 model showed a huge improvement, that reached 98.2% as it is designed for similar tasks. ResNet-50 and AWS Rekognition were capable of reaching an accuracy score of more than 99% using our combined dataset.

4.4   Comparison with Other Solutions

In [6] a custom ML solution called *MobilResNet* was presented to facilitate the task of olive leaf classification. As this task is similar to our goal, based on transfer learning techniques in this section we will try to replicate these experiments and evaluate our own ML models in the same dataset to evaluate their performance. The same is with [1], where the authors use transformers for multi-class classification. Taking their exceptional achievements as the state of the art, characterized by high accuracy and remarkable precision, recall, and F1 score values, we aimed to surpass their performance. To achieve this, we leveraged the powerful Amazon Rekognition API, which proved to be crucial in our experiments and produced the best results.

Table 3. Comparison of our cloud-based model with models described in [1, 6]

Model	Accuracy	Precision	Recall	F1 Score
MobiResnet	97.08	97.61	97.4	96.86
Transformers	95	94	98	96
AWS Rekognition	99.6	99.5	99.7	99.6

The results of our experiments are presented in Table 3. Based on the outcome, it is evident that we achieved remarkable results, surpassing the initial objectives in our research on olive leaf classification. Our findings represent a significant advancement in this field, opening up new possibilities for further exploration and development.

5 Conclusions

The combination of computer vision technologies and drones presents a promising approach to revolutionize the detection of leaf infections in olive trees. By harnessing the power of computer vision algorithms and aerial surveillance capabilities, farmers and researchers can gain valuable insights into the health of olive tree groves, detect infections at an early stage, and implement targeted interventions for effective disease control. As these technologies continue to advance, the future holds great potential for optimizing olive tree health and ensuring sustainable olive production.

Our end-to-end system provides a robust solution for olive grove inspections, implemented with real-world photos, captured by UAVs within Mediterranean olive groves. The system is capable of detecting infections on images containing hundreds of leaves at a time, instead of individual leaves with remarkable accuracy even when compared to solutions existing in the literature.

Acknowledgements. This work has been supported by the European Union's Horizon 2020 research and innovation programme under Secure and Seamless Edge-to-Cloud Analytics (GA 957286), EU H2020, ICT-50-2020 - Software Technologies and Next Generation IoT as part of Next Generation Internet project (GA 957246), EU H2020, ICT-56-2020 - Next Generation Internet of Things.

References

1. Alshammari, H., Karim, G., Ben Ltaifa, I., Krichen, M., Ben Ammar, L., Mahmood, M.: Olive disease classification based on vision transformer and cnn models. Computational Intelligence and Neuroscience 2022, 1–10 (07 2022). https://doi.org/10.1155/2022/3998193
2. Cruz, A.C., Luvisi, A., De Bellis, L., Ampatzidis, Y.: X-fido: an effective application for detecting olive quick decline syndrome with deep learning and data fusion. Front. Plant Sci. **8** (2017). https://doi.org/10.3389/fpls.2017.01741, https://www.frontiersin.org/articles/10.3389/fpls.2017.01741
3. Harakannanavar, S.S., Rudagi, J.M., Puranikmath, V.I., Siddiqua, A., Pramodhini, R.: Plant leaf disease detection using computer vision and machine learning algorithms. Global Trans. Proc. **3**(1), 305–310 (2022)
4. Hughes, D., Salathé, M., et al.: An open access repository of images on plant health to enable the development of mobile disease diagnostics. arXiv preprint arXiv:1511.08060 (2015)
5. Kalyani, Y., Collier, R.: A systematic survey on the role of cloud, fog, and edge computing combination in smart agriculture. Sensors **21**(17) (2021). https://doi.org/10.3390/s21175922, https://www.mdpi.com/1424-8220/21/17/5922
6. Ksibi, A., Ayadi, M., Soufiene, B.O., Jamjoom, M.M., Ullah, Z.: Mobires-net: a hybrid deep learning model for detecting and classifying olive leaf diseases. Applied Sciences 12(20) (2022). https://doi.org/10.3390/app122010278, https://www.mdpi.com/2076-3417/12/20/10278
7. O'Grady, M., Langton, D., O'Hare, G.: Edge computing: a tractable model for smart agriculture? Artif. Intell. Agricultu. **3**, 42–51 (2019)

8. Sinha, A., Shekhawat, R.S.: Olive spot disease detection and classification using analysis of leaf image textures. Proc. Comput. Sci. **167**, 2328–2336 (2020).   https://doi.org/10.1016/j.procs.2020.03.285https://www.sciencedirect. com/science/article/pii/S1877050920307511, international Conference on Computational Intelligence and Data Science

9. Uddin, M.A., Ayaz, M., Mansour, A., Aggoune, e.H.M., Sharif, Z., Razzak, I.: Cloud-connected flying edge computing for smart agriculture. Peer-to-Peer Network. Appl. **14**(6), 3405–3415 (2021)

10. Waleed, M., Um, T.W., Khan, A., Khan, U.: Automatic detection system of olive trees using improved k-means algorithm. Remote Sensing **12**(5), 760 (2020)

Application of Federated Learning Techniques for Arrhythmia Classification Using 12-Lead ECG Signals

Daniel Mauricio Jimenez Gutierrez[(✉)][iD], Hafiz Muuhammad Hassan,
Lorella Landi, Andrea Vitaletti[iD], and Ioannis Chatzigiannakis[iD]

Sapienza University, Rome, Italy
{jimenezgutierrez,vitaletti,ichatz}@diag.uniroma1.it

Abstract. Artificial Intelligence-based (AI) analysis of large, curated medical datasets is promising for providing early detection, faster diagnosis, and more effective treatment using low-power Electrocardiography (ECG) monitoring devices information. However, accessing sensitive medical data from diverse sources is highly restricted since improper use, unsafe storage, or data leakage could violate a person's privacy. This work uses a Federated Learning (FL) privacy-preserving methodology to train AI models over heterogeneous sets of high-definition ECG from 12-lead sensor arrays collected from six heterogeneous sources. We evaluated the capacity of the resulting models to achieve equivalent performance compared to state-of-the-art models trained in a Centralized Learning (CL) fashion. Moreover, we assessed the performance of our solution over Independent and Identical distributed (IID) and Non-IID federated data. Our methodology involves machine learning techniques based on Deep Neural Networks and Long-Short-Term Memory models. It has a robust data preprocessing pipeline with feature engineering, selection, and data balancing techniques. Our AI models demonstrated comparable performance to models trained using CL, IID, and Non-IID approaches. They showcased advantages in reduced complexity and faster training time, making them well-suited for cloud-edge architectures.

Keywords: Federated Machine Learning · Deep Learning · Low-power devices · Arrhythmia and Multilead ECG classification · 12-channel ECG · Medical Data Privacy

1 Introduction

Significant advancements in Artificial Intelligence (AI) have revolutionized the field of medical data analysis, leveraging technologies like big data, machine learning (ML), and deep learning (DL) [21,42]. These innovations have the potential to significantly enhance the efficiency and effectiveness of preventive measures, diagnoses, and treatments in healthcare [7]. Modern AI models

© The Author(s), under exclusive license to Springer Nature Switzerland AG 2024
I. Chatzigiannakis and I. Karydis (Eds.): ALGOCLOUD 2023, LNCS 14053, pp. 38–65, 2024.
https://doi.org/10.1007/978-3-031-49361-4_3

rely on vast datasets and millions of parameters to achieve clinical-grade accuracy while ensuring safety, fairness, equity, and robust generalization to new data [59]. Recent studies highlight the collaboration of low-power devices across borders to harness large volumes of data for AI systems, which can either outperform or significantly aid medical specialists. However, despite the promise of AI in healthcare, practical implementation faces challenges, including a lag in adoption compared to technological development [36,46]. Integrating AI into healthcare operations necessitates incorporating medical data from diverse edge devices [24], a task made complex by data sensitivity and privacy concerns [58]. Even anonymizing data often falls short of ensuring privacy, highlighting the need for robust privacy protection measures in the evolving landscape of AI-driven healthcare [50].

Recently, Federated learning (FL) has been introduced as a decentralized training paradigm of an AI model that enables collaborative learning without exchanging the data itself [62]. FL utilizes distributed consensus algorithms that allow organizations to gain insights collaboratively so that patient data are not transferred outside the organization's firewalls. Consider, for example, multiple hospitals (equipped with low-powered medical devices) collaboratively learning from a shared medical predictive model while keeping data sources in their original location in each hospital, decoupling the ability to do ML from the need to store the data in a single place. Some recent studies examine the performance levels achieved by AI models trained using FL techniques on isolated single-organizational data. They compare them with models trained on centrally hosted data, indicating comparable results [56]. Therefore, FL offers a promising path with a potentially significant impact on large-scale precision medicine, resulting in models that make impartial judgments, best reflect an individual's physiology, and are sensitive to uncommon illnesses while respecting privacy issues.

In this work, we apply the FL paradigm to train AI models that can assist doctors in closely and efficiently monitoring arrhythmias, a common Cardiovascular disease (CVD) recognized as one of the leading causes of death globally.[1] Arrhythmia is a disorder of the heart rate (pulse) or heart rhythm, being too slow, fast or irregular. Today, the most effective tool to identify variations in heart rhythm along with other patterns of the heart's electrical impulses is based on low-power Electrocardiography (ECG) monitoring devices [43]. Such devices use multiple sensors, and the ECG leads to capture the heart's electrical activity from different angles and positions. Automatic analysis of the ECG signal has become one of the essential tools in diagnosing heart disease. It has been used as the basis for the design of algorithms for many years [53].

We introduce a multi-step privacy-preserving methodology for training AI models for arrhythmia detection and classification using 12-lead ECG recordings. The process can be applied to various ML techniques, ranging from deep neural networks to recurrent neural networks with long short-term memory. Moreover, the methodology is generic enough for several classification problems. A detailed

---

[1] https://www.who.int/en/news-room/fact-sheets/detail/cardiovascular-diseases-(cvds).

feature extraction stage is included that examines the morphology of all the channels of the ECG signals both in the time domain and the frequency domain and the cardiac rhythm of consecutive heartbeats, resulting in about 650 features. The methodology introduces a novel feature selection stage where a subset of the features is selected so that the overall training time of the model and performance achieved is optimized.

We employ the FL approach on the PhysioNet in Cardiology Challenge 2020 dataset [47], comprising 12-lead ECG recordings from 43,059 patients across six diverse geographical centers. This dataset stands out due to its comprehensive collection of cardiac abnormalities, making it valuable for training AI models to detect various cardiac arrhythmias. Additionally, the heterogeneity of recordings from different centers, with varying patient numbers and arrhythmia distributions, adds complexity. We assess the AI models' performance in three scenarios: (a) *centralized* training with data collected in a single location, (b) simplified federated learning with independent and identically distributed data on *multiple homogeneous devices*, and (c) the most realistic scenario of federated learning with non-independent and non-identically distributed data on *multiple heterogeneous devices*, reflecting variations in arrhythmia types across hospitals.

2   Previous Related Work

2.1   Arrythmia Detection

The development of AI models for ECG signal analysis and arrhythmia detection has been based on free-access datasets, such as the MIT-BIH Arrhythmia database [40]. This database is popular because it includes recordings of all five arrhythmia classes suggested by the AAMI standards [38]. Two cardiologists annotate it, making it suitable for supervised and unsupervised learning techniques. However, the MIT-BIH dataset has limitations, including only two ECG leads and a small dataset size, which restrict the generality of the trained AI models. Recent ML and DL advances have led to the development of models that can rapidly detect cardiac abnormalities in 12-lead ECGs [2,6] and achieve comparable performance to clinical cardiologists on many ECG analysis tasks and arrhythmia/disease detection [10,22]. However, these models are often trained on small datasets, which limits their ability to detect a wide range of arrhythmias. Additionally, many deep-learning models focus on heartbeat classification [33,54], while others designed for rhythmic arrhythmia classification only deal with a few arrhythmias [48,51].

To encourage more multidisciplinary research, PhysioNet in Cardiology Challenge 2020 (Challenge 2020) [47] provided high-quality 12-lead ECG data obtained from multiple centers with a large set of cardiac abnormalities. The aim of Challenge 2020 was to identify clinical diagnoses from 12-lead ECG recordings, providing an opportunity to employ various advanced methods to address clinically important questions that are either unsolved or not well-solved [4].

Forty-one teams were selected during this challenge, and others were discarded due to failing to achieve high scores or appear at the conference. One can observe that most teams use common techniques by looking at the 41 teams' papers published in PhysioNet [47]. Among these techniques, signal processing, DNNs, convolutional neural networks (CNNs), and end-to-end and multi-binary classifications are used by all of the top 10 teams. In addition, there are several important points 1) deep-learning methods were more popular than traditional methods in Challenge 2020; 2) all the teams that employed deep-learning methods used CNNs; and 3) none of the top 10 teams used hand-labeled features (except demographic features); they all adopted end-to-end models instead.

One can also notice that the three highest-ranking teams used the model ensemble [44,65,67], but only 14 out of 41 teams employed this strategy. It is also important to note that model ensemble only helps if used for a single model rather than structurally different models. Most of the team also used only age and sex as features rather than using demographic features or 12-lead ECG-based features. The training data in Challenge 2020 suffer from heavy class imbalance, so most teams used threshold optimization [14,17,65] and weighted loss [12,39] to handle the imbalance class issue. In addition, over-sampling [68], down-sampling [27], and other methods have been employed in Challenge 2020.

2.2 Federated Learning

FL applied to health has gained interest in the last few years. Specifically, employing FL to classify ECG arrhythmias shows relevant advances and results [57]. For example, [49] implemented explainable artificial intelligence (XAI) and convolutional neural networks (CNN) for ECG-based healthcare. They employed the baseline Massachusetts Institute of Technology - Boston's Beth Israel Hospital (MIT-BIH) Arrhythmia database. The trained classifier obtained an accuracy of up to 94.5% and 98.9%.

Utilizing the same MIT-BIH, [29] proposed an algorithm to identify the best number of epochs per training round in FL. They showed that using its algorithm's suggested number of epochs decreases the training time and resource consumption while keeping the accuracy level. In detail, their approach obtained an accuracy close to 97.5%.

Using ECG collected from different medical institutions, the authors of [64] obtained a dataset where the arrhythmia's distribution is diverse from one hospital to another. The latter may lead to the non-convergence of the FL-based algorithm. To address that challenge, they optimized the FL-based algorithm using a sharing strategy for partial ECG data of each medical institution combined with the elastic weight consolidation (EWC) algorithm. As a result, their model's performance measured through the F1-Score got 0.7.

FL can be classified into different types depending on how the data is divided among the devices (data partitioning) [62]. One of those classifications is the so-called **Horizontal data partitioning**, in which the data of various local nodes share the same properties (i.e., features). However, there is a limited sample space intersection (i.e., the patients differ from device to device). Moreover, the most common FL architecture is horizontal partitioning [41].

FL has relevant advantages over centralized (traditional) systems [11]. The most remarkable is that the data remains locally (in each hospital) and does not require transmitting personal information along the network. It only sends the weights of the models. A second advantage is that models continuously enhance by utilizing local nodes' input, eliminating the requirement to aggregate data for continual learning. In third place, FL generates technological efficiency. This technique employs less complex hardware since FL models do not require a single central server to train data.

FL, on the other hand, faces several difficulties. Firstly, models could be poisoned by providing model updates resulting from mislabeled data, even though only models, not raw data, are sent to the central server. FL is vulnerable to adversarial assaults in the form of backdoors during training, as seen in [60]. A backdoor aims to tamper with the trained model's performance on specified sub-tasks. Secondly, device-specific characteristics may prevent models from generalizing from some local nodes, decreasing the global model's performance [11]. The mentioned difficulties and how to tackle them are out of the scope of this work.

3   Methodology

In this study, we assume *a group of healthcare organizations (equipped with low-powered medical devices)* that wish to collectively train an arrhythmia classification AI-based module without sharing their medical records. For each organization, we envision a *single, local module* that coordinates all the activities related to collecting, storing, and analyzing medical records. Moreover, we assume that each organization can access high-definition electrocardiogram monitoring devices to record the patient's heart activity. Each monitoring session produces a short 12-channel ECG recording, i.e., about 16 s, that is transferred from the device to the local, private database of the organization.[2] One or more healthcare experts examine the ECG recordings and provide a diagnosis stored in the local database.

We assume that the healthcare organizations have agreed upon a *single, global, trusted cloud server*. The role of the global server is to coordinate all the activities of the local modules. The global server does not maintain any database with medical records. The only information stored is related to the standard AI model and the system's operating parameters. We also assume that

---

[2] Remark that several different interconnection architectures are used in ECG technologies available in the market and studied in the relevant literature, such as wireless technologies like WI-FI or BLE, or wire technologies such as USB, or non-volatile memory formats. Such interconnections aspects are beyond the scope of this paper.

all organizations have agreed on a standard length for the ECG recordings, e.g., 16 seconds, and a common sampling frequency, e.g., $257KHz$.[3,4]

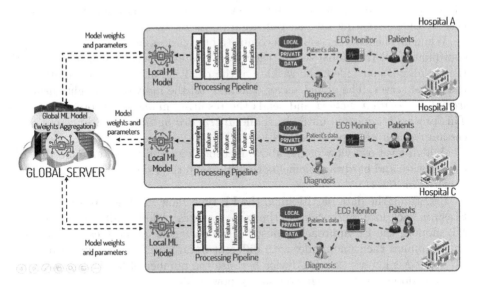

Fig. 1. High-level overview of the proposed federated learning methodology and software and hardware components.

Periodically, the global server starts *a global training session* by notifying all the local servers (a.k.a, clients or local nodes) of the organizations that participate in the federation. Upon receiving this notification, each organization's device independently goes through *a local training session*. During a local training session, all the records available in the local, private database are analyzed using local computing resources based on a *a processing pipeline* made up of four steps. First, each recording passes through a *Feature Extraction* phase, where they are analyzed independently, and critical information connected to the heartbeats that will help the training of the AI model is extracted. Second, a *feature normalization* step follows, where statistics are used to scale the features to improve the robustness of the data. In coordination with the global server, the local servers compute the necessary robust measures over the federated dataset without revealing sensitive information. Third, all the original records, along with the normalized features, are examined. To this end, a *feature selection* is carried out to remove redundant features that may hinder the performance of the

---

[3] Note that in case the recording has a different sampling frequency, various algorithms exist in the relevant literature to change the sampling frequency to a lower or a higher one without affecting the accuracy [66].

[4] Note that ECG recordings that are longer than the agreed length can be split into multiple ones without loss of generality.

trained model and reduce the computational cost since they use a smaller number of features to train the local model. The fourth and final *data balancing* step examines the diagnosis attached to all the records in the local database to identify and remove any imbalances found between the representation of arrhythmia classes, thus increasing the generalization power of the model.

When all the local servers have completed the processing pipelines, under the coordination of the global server, they start training their local models. When the training is concluded, the weights of the resulting model are transmitted to the global server. The global server examines all the individual weights using a *weight aggregation method* and sends the resulting model to all organizations. This process is repeated until either the *distributed optimization converges* or a certain number of steps is reached.

A high-level overview of the above methodology and the interconnection of the software and hardware elements that make up the federated architecture are depicted in Fig. 1.

Regarding the data partitioning, the FL type shown in Fig. 1 is a Horizontal FL since each local node collects the same features. Additionally, regarding the ML models, the FL approach exposed is homogeneous because each hospital's device applies the same model with different data. Finally, regarding scale, the FL defined is known as cross-device because the number of local nodes is high, but they do not have enough computing power [63].

3.1   Problem Formulation

We assume that an ECG recording s_i has $c \in [1, 12]$ channels with fixed samplings rate, producing d samples per channel, $s_i = \left\{ x_1^1 \ldots x_d^1, x_1^2 \ldots x_d^2, \ldots, x_1^{12} \ldots x_d^{12} \right\}$ where x_j^c, is the jth sample of channel c, where $j \in [1, d]$. The ECG multiclass arrhythmia classification task considered here takes as input a local data set of n 12-channel ECG recordings ($\mathcal{S} = \{s_1, \ldots, s_n\}$). It outputs a sequence of labels, one for each signal $\mathcal{L} = [l_1, \ldots, l_n]$, where each $l_i \in \mathcal{A}$, and $\mathcal{A}$ represents the different rhythm classes considered. We focus on $|\mathcal{A}| = 27$ diagnoses of arrhythmia classes as defined by the AAMI standard [38] that are of clinical interest and more likely to be recognizable from ECG recordings [3]. Table 1 summarizes the complete list of diagnoses considered.

3.2   Feature Extraction

First, each 12-channel ECG recording is analyzed by examining the morphology of all the heart cycles included. The QRS complex represents a heart cycle, illustrated in Fig. 2, which corresponds to the depolarization of the right and left ventricles of the human heart. Detecting the QRS complex is essential for time-domain signal analysis, that is, the heart rate variability. For each found QRS complex, a series of representative *morphological features*[5] is extracted in

---

[5] Code for morphological features: https://github.com/physionetchallenges/python-classifier-2020/blob/master/get_12ECG_features.py.

Table 1. Diagnoses and abbreviations for the selected diagnoses

Diagnosis	Abbreviation
1st degree AV block	IAVB
Abnormal QRS	abQRS
Atrial fibrillation	AF
Left atrial enlargement	LAE
Left axis deviation	LAD
Left bundle branch block	LBBB
Left ventricular hypertrophy	LVH
Low QRS voltages	LQRSV
Myocardial infarction	MI
Myocardial ischemia	MIs
Nonspecific st t abnormality	NSSTTA
Old myocardial infarction	OldMI
Pacing rhythm	PR
Premature atrial contraction	PAC
Prolonged QT interval	LQT
Q wave abnormal	QAb
Right bundle branch block	RBBB
Sinus arrhythmia	SA
Sinus bradycardia	SB
Sinus rhythm	NSR
Sinus tachycardia	STach
ST depression	STD
ST elevation	STE
ST interval abnormal	STIAb
T wave abnormal	TAb
T wave inversion	TInv
Ventricular ectopics	VEB

terms of slope, amplitude, and width, such as the *R peak*, the highest amplitude of the complex; *PR interval*, the period between the P peak and the R peak; *QRS interval*, the period between the Q and the S segments; *ST interval*, the period between the S and T segments; *QT interval*, the period between the Q and T segments; the *RR interval*, the period between two consecutive R peaks.

An alternative type of feature based on *Spectral analysis* was employed in this work. The latter is a frequency-based signal analysis that uses a Discrete

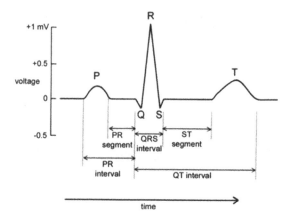

Fig. 2. Typical ECG waveform from the Lead II position for one cardiac cycle.

Wavelet Transform (DWT) followed by spectral analysis.[6] For each of the coefficients of the DWT, as well as the original complete signal, the percentiles (5, 25, 50, 75, 95), mean, standard deviation, variance, skewness, and kurtosis, are calculated along with Shannons Entropy (information of the distribution). The DWT coefficients were obtained using the *wavedec* function of the *pywt* Python package. The age and sex of patients are also included as features, resulting in a total of 650 features (14 morphological and demographical and 636 spectral). Note that this step is done only once for each record, and the extracted features are stored on the local database for future training sessions.

3.3 Feature Normalization

Towards enhancing the performance of the AI models, the values of each feature are centered and scaled independently according to the median value and the interquartile range (IQR) between the first and third quartiles, i.e., the 25th and 75th percentiles, using the *RobustScaler* Python function. The specific formula is as follows:

$$\text{norm}\left(_f x_i^c\right) = \frac{_f x_i^c - _f \bar{x}^c}{_f x_{q_{75}}^c - _f x_{q_{25}}^c} \tag{1}$$

where f is one of the 636 spectral features, $_f \bar{x}^c$ is the median, $_f x_{q_{35}}^c$ and $_f x_{q_{75}}^c$ are the 25th and 75th percentiles computed over all the values in the entire federated data set for the given feature f in channel c.

3.4 Feature Selection

Since the extraction of the majority of the features is conducted over each of the 12 channels and due to the nature of multi-channel ECG recording, in many

---

[6] Code for spectral features: https://github.com/onlyzdd/ecg-diagnosis/blob/dfa9033d5ae7be135db63ff567e66fdb2b86d76d/expert_features.py.

cases, there is redundancy between pairs of features. Moreover, environmental noise from nearby appliances or noise originating from muscular activity frequently produces abnormalities in a recording identified and removed by the ECG monitor at the hardware level [55]. The latter leads to temporal loss of some values of one or more of the 12 channels [35]. Since redundant or missing features can potentially lower the performance of the classification model, it is crucial to identify and remove them. Besides improving our model's predictive performance, it will also reduce the overall computational requirements of AI model training [16].

Several methods have been proposed for feature selection in the relevant bibliography [20]. Here we offer a simple and automated way to rank features based on their importance. We calculate the embedded feature importance scores based on tree ensemble models. The central concept here is that given the feature sub-sampling and bootstrapping in an ensemble of trees, the importance scores of two or more redundant features are expected to be spread evenly among the trees. Then the resulting scores of the candidate features are re-examined following a sequential boosting process based on the XG-Boost model [15]. The boosting process allows re-examining some of the features that received a low rank due to specific limitations of the tree-based feature importance calculation in large datasets, datasets with missing values, and datasets with both numerical and categorical features [5].

3.5 Dataset Balancing

Various nationwide register-based cohort studies conducted over a very long period, such as in Denmark [61] and Canada [52], indicate an inequality of arrhythmia incidence rate between highest and lowest income groups and the existence of significant geographical variation even in countries with free access to healthcare and even when accounting for socioeconomic differences at an individual level. Therefore when the organizations do not share their medical records, the observed distribution of the local diagnoses of the arrhythmia classes will differ across each healthcare organization. As each organization is training its local model based only on the data locally available, it is expected that the resulting model will have certain biases towards the most populated classes, learning too much about their characteristics and failing to recognize the differentiating factors of the others, resulting in poor performance for the minority classes [23].

Various techniques have been proposed to overcome this problem in the relevant literature, such as the Random Over Sampling (ROS) [34], Random Under Sampling (RUS) [23], and Synthetic Minority Oversampling Technique (SMOTE-SMT) [13]. The approaches implemented were ROS + RUS and SMT + RUS. The latter aimed to overcome the well-known problem of ROS resulting from the generation of exact copies of the minority class samples.

In more detail, for a local dataset made up of n recordings and diagnoses represented as $\mathcal{D} = \{(s_1, l_1), \ldots, (s_n, l_n)\}$. Then b_u is the number of signals belonging to the under-balanced classes, and b_o is the number of over-balanced classes. In this case, $b_u \leq b_o$. Clearly $b_u + b_o = n$. Our balancing method will make a total of $\tau = (m_l - m_s) \cdot \beta$ random duplications (or interpolations) and eliminations, where $\beta \in [0,1]$, and m_l and m_s represent the numbers of recordings in the largest class and the smallest class, respectively. Here β is user-defined. For example, if $\beta = 1$, the resulting dataset is completely balanced.

The proposed algorithm uses an appropriate mix of random duplication (or interpolation) of the minority, under-balanced class samples, and random elimination of the majority, over-sampled classes. Thus, after identifying the changes that need to be made, the algorithm randomly chooses a sample x_i. If it belongs to an under-balanced class, it will duplicate it, while if it belongs to an over-balanced class, it will eliminate it. The resulting approach is simple to implement and has shallow requirements in terms of computational resources.

3.6   Multiclass Arrhythmia Classification

Model 1 - (DNN) Deep Neural Networks. In this context, deep neural networks (DNN) refer to organic or artificial systems of neurons. DNN can adapt to changing input and produce the best possible result without modifying the output criteria because they can adjust to variable inputs [18]. DNN, an artificial intelligence-based concept, has gained popularity for developing health classification systems.

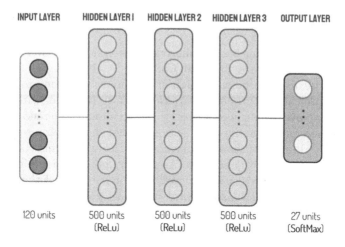

Fig. 3. DNN architecture

As depicted in Fig. 3, the DNN defined, inspired by [43], has one input layer, three hidden layers, and one output layer. For the input layer, 120 units were considered since they represent the number of features used in the training set. The three hidden layers contain 500 hidden units each. Furthermore, the last layer was formed by 27 neurons, related to the number of diagnoses to predict. Moreover, the hidden layers employed the ReLu activation and the SoftMax

Table 2. Fine-tuning grid for DNN

Hyperparameter	Possible values	Best approach
Number of hidden layers	2, 3, 5, 10	3
Number of hidden neurons	50, 100, 500, 1000	500
Activation function (Hidden layers)	ReLu, Tanh, SeLu	ReLu
Activation function (Output layer)	Sigmoid, SoftMax	SoftMax

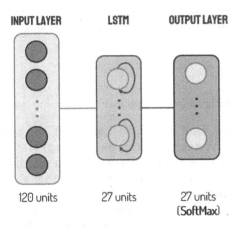

Fig. 4. LSTM architecture

for the output layer. The hidden layers, neurons, and activation functions arose after the hyperparameter fine-tuning method, using the possibilities in Table 2. In detail, one model was trained for every combination of parameters. Then, Accuracy, Precision, Recall, and F1-Score were calculated over the test set and the fitted model. Finally, the best approach ended up as the model obtaining the highest F1-Score among all the combinations.

Model 2 - (LSTM) Long-Short Term Memory. Long-short-term memory (LSTM) networks are a type of DNN. It is a Recurrent Neural Networks (RNNs) class that can learn long-term dependencies and functionals to solve sequence prediction issues. Besides, for single data points like pictures, LSTM has feedback connections, which means it can process a complete data sequence [25].

Figure 4 depicts the architecture used for the LSTM methodology, motivated by [43]. Then, 120 neurons were employed in the input layer because those variables were used to predict. Moreover, both the LSTM cell and the output layer were composed of 27 neurons, as many as the number of classes predicted. Regarding the hyperparameters mentioned, their values were selected after the fine-tuning process, providing the best performance. Table 3 depicts the possibilities tested during the hyperparameter fine-tuning procedure. Notice that the number of LSTM cell neurons has an upper limit of 27, corresponding to the number of classes (arrhythmias) considered in this work.

Table 3. Fine-tuning grid for LSTM

Hyperparameter	Possible values	Best approach
Number of LSTM cell neurons	1, 5, 10, 20, 27	27
Activation function (LSTM layer)	None, ReLu, Tanh	None
Activation function (Output layer)	Sigmoid, SoftMax	SoftMax

3.7 Distributed Weight Aggregation

When the weights from each local model arrive at the global node, they are aggregated. Federated Average Aggregation (FedAvg) is typically used for that task [32]. The latter enables local nodes to perform multiple batch updates on local data, exchanging averaged updated weights rather than raw data [37].

In an FL environment exists a concept so-called **communication round** (comm round) [8]. The latter begins when a model is trained inside each local node, and later the models' weights are passed to the global node to be aggregated there. Finally, the communication round finishes when each local model gets updated with the new weights. Then, as a result, in each comm round, the model's performance increases. Moreover, it should get stable after some trials [9].

The training process in the proposed architecture works as follows. First, each local node trains the model using the correspondent local data. In the second place, every client sends the weights of the obtained model to the global server. The weights are aggregated and sent back to each client in the latter. Finally, each local node updates its parameters. The previous process is repeated until the performance of the global model converges.

4   Experimental Settings and Fine-Tuning

4.1   Data

We utilized the 2020 PhysioNet Challenge dataset [3] to classify cardiac arrhythmias from ECG records, consisting of 12-lead ECG recordings from 43,059 patients. Furthermore, it adds data from different hospitals, making it suitable for an FL approach to address privacy concerns. It offers heterogeneous data and a wide range of 82 cardiac arrhythmias, representing a realistic scenario. The data are from five sources summarized in Table 4.

Table 4. Relevant information for each data set

Dataset	Number of Recordings	Mean Duration (seconds)	Mean Age (years)	Sex (male/female)	Sample Frequency (Hz)
CPSC (all data)	13256	16.2	61.1	53%/47%	500
CPSC Training	6877	15.9	60.2	54%/46%	500
CPSC-Extra Train	3453	15.9	63.7	53%/46%	500
Hidden CPSC	2926	17.4	60.4	52%/48%	500
INCART	72	1800.0	56.0	54%/46%	257
PTB	516	110.8	56.3	73%/27%	1000
PTB-XL	21837	10.0	59.8	52%/48%	500
G12EC (all data)	20678	10.0	60.5	54%/46%	500
G12EC Training	10344	10.0	60.5	54%/46%	500
Hidden G12EC	10344	10.0	60.5	54%/46%	500
Undisclosed	10000	10.0	63.0	53%/47%	300

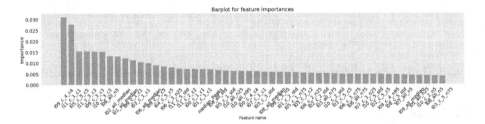

Fig. 5. Feature importance from XG-Boost algorithm (only the 50 best)

Processing Pipeline Fine-Tuning. The bar plot in Fig. 5 shows the most important features for predicting classes using the XG-Boost method. After obtaining importance scores for all 650 features, trial-and-error was conducted to remove unimportant features, ending with 120 features keeping the Accuracy and F1-Score. The best features included entropy for leads 9, 11, and 10, the lead six's 5th percentile, and the median for leads 1 and 2.

$$feature_s = l(lead_i)\_c\_(coefficient_j)\_(operation_k) \tag{2}$$

Each 636 spectral feature is based on *lead* denoted as l, their *coefficient* as c, and *operation* applied on it. Also, $lead_i$ represents ECG lead number from 00–11, $coefficient_j$ represents a coefficient number from DWT (there are five coefficients in total 1–5), and $operation_k$ represents the operation name like average, standard deviation as std, variance as var, percentiles represents as n5(percentile 5), n25(percentile 25), n50(percentile 50), n75(percentile 75), n95(percentile 95) and entropy applied on coefficient got represented as $c1 - c5$. In Fig. 5, names of features are represented by the 2 mnemotechnic structure.

The ROS and SMT approaches were applied to the dataset with a down-sampling to have as many recordings as the filtered dataset, with 43,200 recordings for each method. Thus, as depicted in Fig. 6, the distribution of the labels is much more similar among the arrhythmia categories.

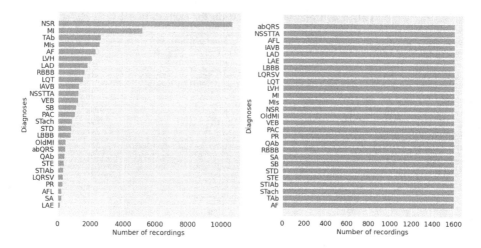

Fig. 6. (Left) Selected diagnoses distribution. (Right) Diagnoses distribution for ROS and SMOTE datasets.

4.2 Scenarios

We present an FL approach for classifying 12-channel ECG arrhythmias. Two FL scenarios, IID and Non-IID, were developed and tested (see Fig. 7). The IID combined six databases into one dataset, resulting in 41,894 (a.k.a. filtered dataset) recordings after selecting the most representative diagnoses. The dataset was randomly split into train (90%), validation (5%), and test (5%) sets. Stratified random splitting was used for the label distributions to be the same for each partition. Different partition sizes, such as 2, 4, 6, 8, and 10, are possible depending on the 12-leads ECG data, which will be explored in Sect. 5.4.

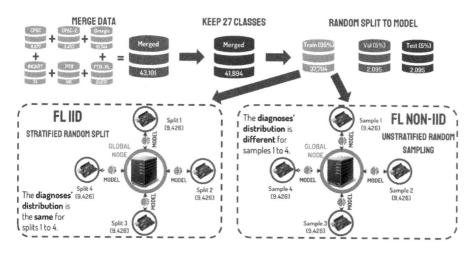

Fig. 7. IDD and Non-IID architecture

The Non-IID approach has the same two steps of the IID (data appending and splitting of Fig. 7). The main difference is the generation of the local nodes. Thus, to get those clients, an Unstratified random sampling (with replacement) method [28] was employed. As a result, each local node has a varied distribution of diagnoses. Furthermore, some recordings may be missing entirely from the synthesized dataset.

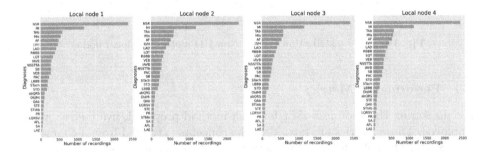

Fig. 8. Label distribution for the filtered dataset by each local node

As depicted in Fig. 8, the distribution among the four local nodes seems IID. The latter means that the diagnoses along the devices are equally distributed, containing 9,426 recordings per local node. The same occurs for the ROS and SMOTE datasets, as is shown in Fig. 9.

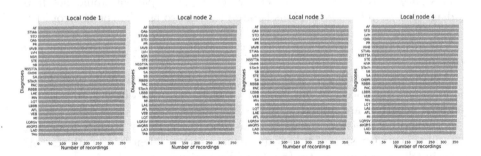

Fig. 9. Label distribution for the ROS and SMOTE datasets by each local node

For the Non-IID approach, the method drew four random samples with repetition from the 41,894 recordings (local nodes) dataset. The given data in each local node (or client) is Non-IID approaches due to the unstratified random sampling, as shown in Fig. 10. This scenario is far more plausible since most 12-channel ECGs shared across several devices are Non-IID.

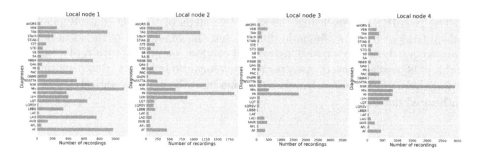

Fig. 10. Label distribution for the Non-IID method by local node

4.3 Performance Metrics

For measuring the goodness-of-fit for each method proposed, five metrics were employed. Those metrics are related to the concepts extracted from a confusion matrix [26]. The following are explanations about each term, using as an example a fictitious diagnosis A:

- *True negatives (TN):* The model predicted a patient wouldn't have diagnosis A, and he did not have it.
- *True positives (TP):* These were examples when the model predicted yes (the recording has the diagnosis A), and the patient does have it.
- *False positives (FP):* The model predicted that a patient would have the diagnosis A, but he does not. (also referred to as a "Type I error.")
- *False negatives (FN):* The model predicted that a patient would not have diagnosed A, yet he does. (This is often referred to as a "Type II error.")

Then, the metrics to measure the classification power of the algorithms proposed are:

Accuracy: $Accuracy = \frac{TP+TN}{TP+FP+FN+TN}$: A metric measuring correct predictions out of all observations. Useful for balanced data where false positives and false negatives are similar.

Precision: $Precision = \frac{TP}{TP+FP}$: The ratio of accurately predicted positives to total expected positives. It reflects the accuracy of identifying patients with a specific diagnosis and relates to a low false-positive rate.

Recall: $Recall = \frac{TP}{TP+FN}$: The ratio of successfully predicted positives to all actual class observations. It measures the identification of patients with arrhythmia A.

F1-Score: $F1-Score = \frac{2*(Recall*Precision)}{(Recall+Precision)}$: A weighted average of Precision and Recall, considering false positives and false negatives. It is more valuable than accuracy, particularly when dealing with unequal class distribution or significant differences in the cost of false positives and negatives.

It is relevant to highlight that the current work deals with a multi-class problem (more than two classes as labels). Due to it, for Precision, Recall, and

F1-Score, the final metrics values were calculated as the weighted average of the metric measured in each pairwise class [19].

In FL is relevant to measure the **Execution time** that a model takes to be trained [29]. The latter helps compare the FL architecture to the centralized one, expecting the FL approach to be faster in each local node. This time accounts for the time elapsed since the model started to train until it finished and returned the results. During the experimentation of this work, the execution times were measured in **minutes**. The hardware specification used to train and evaluate the models is shown in Table 5.

Table 5. Hardware specification used to train models

Component	Specification
Disk size	108 GB
Processors' model	Intel(R) Xeon(R) CPU @ 2.20 GHz
Number of processors	2
Memory	13.2 GB
Operating System	(Linux) Ubuntu 18.04.5 LTS
GPU	GeForce RTX 3070 8 GB
Python version	3.7.13

5   Results

5.1   Performance of Centralized

A Centralized (traditional) Learning approach was employed to evaluate the dataset's performance without dividing it among hospitals and devices. Feature engineering, data balancing, and classification methods (DNN, LSTM) were applied to the complete dataset. The model of the second-best team (TEAM2) [66] in the Physionet competition was replicated for fair comparisons[7]. Imbalanced datasets for each arrhythmia type were addressed using ROS and SMT techniques. ROS was also applied to the TEAM2 strategy but did not yield better results. The SMT strategy was not tested within the TEAM2 approach. Table 6 depicts the tested and best approaches we got regarding the classification metrics.

Within the results in Fig. 11, the best model was TEAM2's approach, which got an F1-Score close to 0.63. Nevertheless, the DNN over the ROS data had similar behavior, with the mentioned metric at 0.61. Finally, LSTM does not perform well compared to the other models, with metrics between 0.39 and 0.47 for all the scenarios.

---

[7] TEAM2's code: https://github.com/ZhaoZhibin/Physionet2020model.

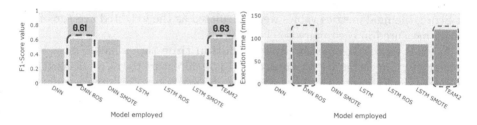

Fig. 11. (Left) F1-Score for methods employed in CL on the test set. (Right) Execution times for the methods used in CL.

Table 6. Scenarios tested for centralized learning

Characteristic	Scenarios	Best approach
Data Split	%Train-%Validation-%Test: Option 1: 60%-20%-20% Option 2: 70%-10%-10% Option 3: 80%-10%-10% Option 4: 90%-5%-5%	Option 4: 90%-5%-5%
Features normalization	Option 1: MinMaxScaler Option 2: StandardScaler Option 3: RobustScaler	Option 3: RobustScaler
Sampling rate	Option 1: 257 Hz Option 2: 500 Hz	Option 1: 257 Hz
Features employed	Option 1: Baseline features (morphological and demographic) Option 2: Baseline features (morphological and demographic) and Spectral features	Option 2: Baseline features and Spectral features

Finally, as shown in Fig. 11, TEAM2's approach took almost 122 min to run. On the other hand, DNN and LSTM took lower execution times (close to 89 min on average). Thus, TEAM2 is the slowest method, although it generates the best results. On the contrary, DNN is a fast method, and the performance is NOT quite different from TEAM2.

5.2   Performance of IID Federated

Then, the modeling part was executed in the IID FL paradigm using four clients. Therefore, DNN and LSTM methodologies classified the 12-leads ECG's arrhythmias. Hence, the aggregation technique employed to get the weights of the global model was FedAvg [31].

As depicted in Fig. 12, the best results arise using the TEAM2 method with an F1-Score of 0.58. On the other hand, DNN got an F1-Score of 0.54, placing it as the second-best option. In addition, the best performance for LSTM was obtained with the original data, although it is worst than the TEAM2 and DNN ROS models. Then, applying oversampling for LSTM does not improve the result of the models. However, using ROS, the performance of the FL model increases.

Considering Fig. 12 results, the TEAM2 generates the slowest procedure with a time of 78 min. In addition, the second less time-consuming approach was the DNN ROS with 32 min, where using oversampling techniques makes the

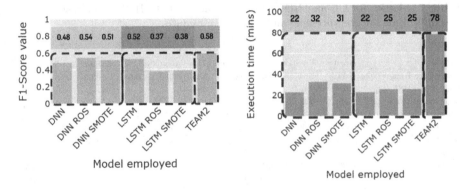

Fig. 12. (Left) F1-Score for methods employed in FL on the test set (IID). (Right) Execution times for the methods used in FL (IID).

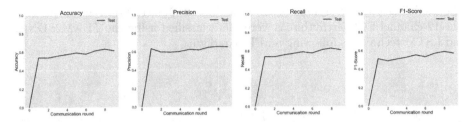

Fig. 13. Metrics along communication rounds for TEAM2 (the best model) on the test set

execution time increase [30]. Compared to the CL approach, the TEAM2 FL method has a faster execution with similar performance. Similarly, DNN ROS and SMOTE ran fast, performing comparably to their CL versions.

Figure 13 establishes the behavior of each metric for each communication round. As depicted, the performance stabilizes after the eighth comm round. Notice that all the metrics start low in the first comm round, but the measurements get steady after some updates. DNN and LSTM methods performed similarly, but for the sake of the extension, it is not included in this work.

Table 7 depicts the metrics obtained over the test dataset and the execution time of the training phase and all the state-of-the-art competitors. The CL TEAM2 model outperforms all the proposals by at least two percentage points, but it is the slowest method. Concerning the FL architecture, the TEAM2 FL is close enough to the centralized TEAM2 model, showing that the FL applied over an IID set behaves well, although the execution time is better for DNN ROS.

Table 7. Metrics for CL and IID Federated Learning (FL -IID) in the test data set. Execution time for preprocessing and training in minutes.

Method	CL					FL IID				
	Accuracy	Precision	Recall	F1-Score	Time	Accuracy	Precision	Recall	F1-Score	Time
Competence Team #2 [66]	**0.64**	0.64	**0.64**	**0.63**	122	**0.63**	**0.64**	**0.63**	**0.58**	78
Inspirational DNN [43]	0.50	0.46	0.50	0.47	**88**	–	–	–	–	–
Inspirational LSTM [43]	0.50	0.45	0.50	0.46	89	–	–	–	–	–
DNN	0.50	0.47	0.50	0.47	89	0.46	0.53	0.45	0.49	**22**
DNN ROS	0.61	**0.66**	0.61	0.61	90	0.55	0.59	0.54	0.54	32
DNN SMOTE	0.60	0.64	0.60	0.60	91	0.52	0.58	0.52	0.51	31
LSTM	0.51	0.47	0.51	0.39	91	0.48	0.58	0.48	0.52	**22**
LSTM ROS	0.38	0.51	0.38	0.39	91	0.39	0.48	0.38	0.38	25
LSTM SMOTE	0.39	0.49	0.39	0.39	89	0.39	0.47	0.39	0.38	25

5.3 Performance of Non-IID Federated

The modeling phase was done again with the four Non-IID datasets extracted. The 12-channel ECG arrhythmias were then classified using the TEAM2, DNN, and LSTM techniques following an FL paradigm.

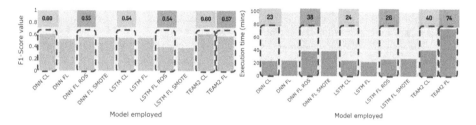

Fig. 14. (Left) F1-Score for methods employed in FL Non-IID on the test set. (Right) Execution times for the methods used in FL Non-IID.

We employed a CL strategy to compare the Non-IID FL and CL implementations. In terms of classification performance, the best results were for TEAM2 with the original datasets, as shown in Fig. 14, while the DNN ROS and DNN LSTM techniques also performed well, with an F1-Score of around 0.58 on the test set. On the other hand, the highest performance for LSTM was with the original data, yet it was worse than the DNN ROS model.

As shown in Fig. 14, the TEAM2 method was the slowest, clocking in at 74 min. Compared to the CL method, the TEAM2 methodology with FL is faster and produces equivalent results. The same behavior applies to DNN ROS and SMOTE; however, while LSTM performs worse than TEAM2 and DNN, it is significantly quicker in producing the results.

5.4 Performance Changing Local Nodes

We implemented a model's performance evaluation by changing the number of local nodes diverse to 4 (i.e., 2, 4, 6, 8, 10). Per each client, we trained a CL to determine how well the FL training fits regarding that CL for IID and Non-IID scenarios. Still, for the sake of the extension of this document, only the Non-IID result is reported because the performances of both methods were quite similar.

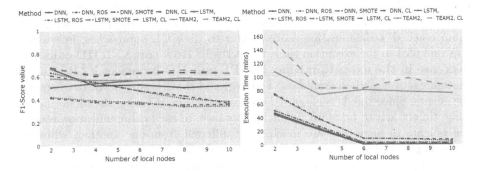

Fig. 15. (Left) F1-Score changing number of local nodes with FedAvg in test set. (Right) Running time changing number of local nodes with FedAvg.

Figure 15 represents the F1-Score for all the methods while changing the number of local nodes. TEAM2 CL, DNN CL, and LSTM CL are reference models trained with all the data appended to a single dataset, where the best solution when considering two local nodes is DNN ROS. On the other hand, with four or more clients, the best solution is TEAM2, keeping steady behavior when increasing the number of clients. Nevertheless, when considering six or more nodes, LSTM on the original data is a good option, similar to the TEAM2 metric.

Typically, the higher the local nodes' quantity, the faster the algorithms run, as depicted in Fig. 15. Moreover, all the techniques drastically decreased the running time when increasing the number of clients, but the performance also decreased.

6 Discussion

Analyzing the CL setting experiments results, the highest classification performance was reached by TEAM2, which combined Convolutional Recurrent Neural Networks (CRNN) and cross-validation. Nevertheless, our proposed DNN on the augmented ROS dataset had a competitive classification performance. In addition, the execution time for DNN was more than twice as fast as TEAM2. **Why can a DNN model perform similarly to a CRNN while reducing the execution time?** This is possible since we employed a solid pre-processing pipeline selecting powerful spectral and morphological features. Moreover, the architecture of DNN was considerably less complex (fewer hidden layers, fewer hidden neurons, not using cross-validation) than TEAM2's approach.

Concerning the FL IID experiments results, TEAM2 and DNN using the ROS balanced data have similar F1-Score to their CL versions while having a decrease of around 36% and 64% in the execution time, respectively. **Why does employing FL cause such execution time reduction?** That is an expected behavior supporting scientific evidence [1] since running models in an FL fashion can be done parallelly in each client, removing the burden of transmitting large amounts of data, and causing the execution time to drop substantially.

Regarding the FL non-IID experiment results, TEAM2 and DNN using ROS again reached a classification score similar to their CL approaches, increasing 85% and 65% in the execution time, respectively. **How come FL IID causes a decrease in the execution time, but FL non-IID increases it?** It involves the aggregation method employed (FedAvg) and the diversity of the data among the clients. Since the data is non-IID by construction, it causes the model's converge time taken to be more significant because, in each communication round, the weights to aggregate are much more different from one another, which is something that does not occur in the IID (and not quite real) setting.

The most accurate models for the FL Non-IID using less than four clients were DNN and TEAM2. Even so, when considering six or more clients, LSTM performed comparably while drastically decreasing the execution time. **Why does the number of clients involved in the FL experiment cause LSTM to outperform DNN and become more similar to TEAM2's approach?** The FL approach under DNN may overfit when training with fewer data in each client since the model becomes too specialized for a smaller dataset. Besides, the LSTM algorithm has been studied as a more robust solution to overfitting (mitigating the vanishing gradient problem) [45]. In this case, the model is not as complex as the DNN, having a better performance while increasing the number of clients (decreasing the number of samples per client). CRNN may also overfit the given data, but that effect is mitigated by using cross-validation in TEAM2's solution, causing a comparable performance between TEAM2 and LSTM.

7   Conclusions and Future Work

Our team implemented a 12-lead arrhythmia classification leveraged on an FL paradigm over multiple ML and AI algorithms to evaluate their performance compared to a centralized (traditional) approach. Although the solution from TEAM2 provided good results, our proposal, using DNN over augmented datasets (ROS), produced a comparable performance with the benefit of a drastic reduction in the execution time. In addition, considering a Non-IID scenario over a few clients, TEAM2 and DNN ROS attained equivalent behaviors to their respective CL and FL approaches. At the same time, our DNN ROS solution acutely reduced the execution time. Alternatively, using our proposed LSTM for larger clients demonstrated steady and analogous behavior to the obtained in a CL with a drastic reduction of the execution time compared to the state-of-the-art.

In future work, the FL architecture could use a different data partition. For example, each original database can be used as a client with a Non-IID distribution of arrhythmias. Moreover, alternative aggregation methods may deal with the Non-IID property, such as Fedprox, SCAFFOLD, or FedNova [31]. Another venue for future research is using Catboost and XG-Boost in an FL architecture to check their performance for the 12-leads ECG arrhythmia classification.

Acknowledgements. This work was partially supported by project SERICS (PE00000014) under the MUR National Recovery and Resilience Plan funded by the European Union - NextGenerationEU and PNRR351 TECHNOPOLE - NEXT GEN EU Roma Technopole - Digital Transition, FP2 - Energy transition and digital transition in urban regeneration and construction.

References

1. AbdulRahman, S., Tout, H., Ould-Slimane, H., Mourad, A., Talhi, C., Guizani, M.: A survey on federated learning: the journey from centralized to distributed on-site learning and beyond. IEEE Internet Things J. **8**(7), 5476–5497 (2020)
2. Al-Zaiti, S., Besomi, L.B.Z.: Machine learning-based prediction of acute coronary syndrome using only the pre-hospital 12-lead electrocardiogram. National Library of Medicine (2020). https://doi.org/10.1038/s41467-020-17804-2
3. Alday, E.A.P., et al.: Classification of 12-lead ecgs: the physionet/computing in cardiology challenge 2020. Physiol. Meas. **41**(12), 124003 (2020)
4. Alday, E.A.P., et al.: Classification of 12-lead ECGs: the PhysioNet/computing in cardiology challenge 2020. Physiol. Meas. **41**(12), 124003 (2020). https://doi.org/10.1088/1361-6579/abc960
5. Alsahaf, A., Petkov, N., Shenoy, V., Azzopardi, G.: A framework for feature selection through boosting. Expert Syst. Appl. **187**, 115895 (2022)
6. Ana Minchole, Julia Camps, A.L.: Machine learning in the electrocardiogram. In: National Library of Medicine, pp. S61–S64 (2019). https://doi.org/10.1016/j.jelectrocard.2019.08.008
7. Arnold, D., Wilson, T.: What doctor? why AI and robotics will define new health. In: PwC (2017)
8. Asad, M., Moustafa, A., Ito, T.: Fedopt: towards communication efficiency and privacy preservation in federated learning. Appl. Sci. **10**, 1–17 (2020). https://doi.org/10.3390/app10082864
9. Asad, M., Moustafa, A., Ito, T., Aslam, M.: Evaluating the communication efficiency in federated learning algorithms (2020). https://doi.org/10.48550/ARXIV.2004.02738. https://arxiv.org/abs/2004.02738
10. Attia, Z.I., et al.: An artificial intelligence-enabled ECG algorithm for the identification of patients with atrial fibrillation during sinus rhythm: a retrospective analysis of outcome prediction. Lancet **394**(10201), 861–867 (2019)
11. Bogdanova, A., Attoh-Okine, N., Sakurai, T.: Risk and advantages of federated learning for health care data collaboration. ASCE-ASME J. Risk Uncertainty Eng. Syst. Part A: Civil Eng. **6**, 04020031 (2020). https://doi.org/10.1061/AJRUA6.0001078
12. Bos, M.N., et al.: Automated comprehensive interpretation of 12-lead electrocardiograms using pre-trained exponentially dilated causal convolutional neural networks. In: 2020 Computing in Cardiology, pp. 1–4 (2020). https://doi.org/10.22489/CinC.2020.253
13. Chawla, N.V., Bowyer, K.W., Hall, L.O., Kegelmeyer, W.P.: Smote: synthetic minority over-sampling technique. J. Artif. Intell. Res. **16**, 321–357 (2002)

14. Chen, J., et al.: SE-ECGNET: multi-scale se-net for multi-lead ECG data. In: 2020 Computing in Cardiology, pp. 1–4 (2020). https://doi.org/10.22489/CinC.2020.085

15. Chen, T., Guestrin, C.: Xgboost: a scalable tree boosting system. In: Proceedings of the 22nd ACM SIGKDD International Conference on Knowledge Discovery and Data Mining, KDD 2016, pp. 785–794. Association for Computing Machinery, New York (2016). https://doi.org/10.1145/2939672.2939785

16. Dhal, P., Azad, C.: A comprehensive survey on feature selection in the various fields of machine learning. Appl. Intell. 1–39 (2022)

17. Fayyazifar, N., Ahderom, S., Suter, D., Maiorana, A., Dwivedi, G.: Impact of neural architecture design on cardiac abnormality classification using 12-lead ECG signals. In: 2020 Computing in Cardiology, pp. 1–4 (2020). https://doi.org/10.22489/CinC. 2020.161

18. Gallo, C.: Artificial Neural Networks: tutorial, chap, p. 10 (2015)

19. Grandini, M., Bagli, E., Visani, G.: Metrics for multi-class classification: an overview (2020). https://doi.org/10.48550/ARXIV.2008.05756. https://arxiv.org/abs/2008.05756

20. Guyon, I., Elisseeff, A.: An introduction to variable and feature selection. J. Mach. Learn. Res. 3(Mar), 1157–1182 (2003)

21. Hamet, P., Tremblay, J.: Artificial intelligence in medicine. Metabolism 69, S36–S40 (2017)

22. Hannun, A.Y., Rajpurkar, P.H.M.: Cardiologist-level arrhythmia detection and classification in ambulatory electrocardiograms using a deep neural network. Nat. Med. 25, 65–69 (2019). https://doi.org/10.1038/s41591-018-0268-3

23. He, H., Garcia, E.A.: Learning from imbalanced data. IEEE Trans. Knowl. Data Eng. 21(9), 1263–1284 (2009)

24. He, J., Baxter, S.L., Xu, J., Xu, J., Zhou, X., Zhang, K.: The practical implementation of artificial intelligence technologies in medicine. Nat. Med. 25(1), 30–36 (2019)

25. Hochreiter, S., Schmidhuber, J.: Long short-term memory. Neural Comput. 9, 1735–1780 (1997). https://doi.org/10.1162/neco.1997.9.8.1735

26. Hossin, M., Sulaiman, M.N.: A review on evaluation metrics for data classification evaluations. Int. J. Data Mining Knowl. Manag. Process 5, 01–11 (2015). https://doi.org/10.5121/ijdkp.2015.5201

27. Hsu, P.Y., Hsu, P.H., Lee, T.H., Liu, H.L.: Multi-label arrhythmia classification from 12-lead electrocardiograms. In: 2020 Computing in Cardiology, pp. 1–4 (2020). https://doi.org/10.22489/CinC.2020.134

28. Hsu, T.M.H., Qi, H., Brown, M.: Measuring the effects of non-identical data distribution for federated visual classification (2019). https://doi.org/10.48550/ARXIV. 1909.06335. arxiv.org/abs/1909.06335

29. Ibraimi, L., Selimi, M., Freitag, F.: Bepoch: improving federated learning performance in resource-constrained computing devices. In: 2021 IEEE Global Communications Conference (GLOBECOM), pp. 1–6 (2021). https://doi.org/10.1109/GLOBECOM46510.2021.9685095

30. Jamali-Rad, H., Abdizadeh, M., Singh, A.: Federated learning with taskonomy for non-iid data. IEEE Trans. Neural Netw. Learn. Syst. 34, 8719–8730 (2022)

31. Li, Q., Diao, Y., Chen, Q., He, B.: Federated learning on non-iid data silos: an experimental study. arXiv preprint arXiv:2102.02079 (2021)

32. Li, X., Huang, K., Yang, W., Wang, S., Zhang, Z.: On the convergence of fedavg on non-iid data (2019). https://doi.org/10.48550/ARXIV.1907.02189. arxiv.org/abs/1907.02189

33. Lin, C.C., Yang, C.M.: Heartbeat classification using normalized RR intervals and wavelet features. In: 2014 International Symposium on Computer, Consumer and Control, pp. 650–653. IEEE (2014)
34. Ling, C.X., Li, C.: Data mining for direct marketing: problems and solutions. In: KDD, vol. 98, pp. 73–79 (1998)
35. Mariappan, P.M., Raghavan, D.R., Aleem, S.H.A., Zobaa, A.F.: Effects of electromagnetic interference on the functional usage of medical equipment by 2g/3g/4g cellular phones: a review. J. Adv. Res. **7**(5), 727–738 (2016)
36. McKinney, S.M., et al.: International evaluation of an AI system for breast cancer screening. Nature **577**(7788), 89–94 (2020)
37. McMahan, B., Moore, E., Ramage, D., Hampson, S., Arcas, B.A.: Communication-efficient learning of deep networks from decentralized data. In: Artificial Intelligence and Statistics, pp. 1273–1282. PMLR (2017)
38. For the Advancement of Medical Instrumentation, A.: Testing and reporting performance results of cardiac rhythm and st segment measurement algorithms: American National Standard 2013. ANSI/AAMI EC **57**, 2012 (2013)
39. Min, S., et al.: Bag of tricks for electrocardiogram classification with deep neural networks. In: 2020 Computing in Cardiology, pp. 1–4 (2020). https://doi.org/10.22489/CinC.2020.328
40. Moody, G.B., Mark, R.G.: The impact of the MIT-BIH arrhythmia database. IEEE Eng. Med. Biol. Mag. **20**(3), 45–50 (2001)
41. Mori, J., Teranishi, I., Furukawa, R.: Continual horizontal federated learning for heterogeneous data (2022). https://doi.org/10.48550/ARXIV.2203.02108. arxiv.org/abs/2203.02108
42. Müller, H., Holzinger, A., Plass, M., Brcic, L., Stumptner, C., Zatloukal, K.: Explainability and causability for artificial intelligence-supported medical image analysis in the context of the european in vitro diagnostic regulation. New Biotechnol. **70**, 67–72 (2022)
43. Murat, F., Yildirim, O., Talo, M., Baloglu, U.B., Demir, Y., Acharya, U.R.: Application of deep learning techniques for heartbeats detection using ECG signals-analysis and review. Comput. Biol. Med. **120**, 103726 (2020). https://doi.org/10.1016/j.compbiomed.2020.103726. https://www.sciencedirect.com/science/article/pii/S0010482520301104
44. Natarajan, A., et al.: A wide and deep transformer neural network for 12-lead ECG classification. In: 2020 Computing in Cardiology, pp. 1–4 (2020). https://doi.org/10.22489/CinC.2020.107
45. Ookura, S., Mori, H.: An efficient method for wind power generation forecasting by LSTM in consideration of overfitting prevention. IFAC-PapersOnLine **53**(2), 12169–12174 (2020)
46. Panch, T., Mattie, H., Celi, L.A.: The "inconvenient truth" about AI in healthcare. NPJ Dig. Med. **2**(1), 1–3 (2019)
47. Perez Alday, E.A., Gu, A.S.A.: Classification of 12-lead ECGs: the physionet/computing in cardiology challenge 2020. Physiol. Meas. (2020). https://doi.org/10.1088/1361-6579/abc960. https://moody-challenge.physionet.org/2020/papers/
48. Rajkumar, A., Ganesan, M., Lavanya, R.: Arrhythmia classification on ECG using deep learning. In: 2019 5th International Conference on Advanced Computing & Communication Systems (ICACCS), pp. 365–369. IEEE (2019)
49. Raza, A., Tran, K.P., Koehl, L., Li, S.: Designing ECG monitoring healthcare system with federated transfer learning and explainable AI. Knowl.-Based Syst. **236**, 107763 (2022)

50. Rocher, L., Hendrickx, J.M., De Montjoye, Y.A.: Estimating the success of re-identifications in incomplete datasets using generative models. Nat. Commun. **10**(1), 1–9 (2019)
51. Rohmantri, R., Surantha, N.: Arrhythmia classification using 2D convolutional neural network. Int. J. Adv. Comput. Sci. Appl. **11**(4), 201–208 (2020)
52. Rosychuk, R.J., Mariathas, H.H., Graham, M.M., Holroyd, B.R., Rowe, B.H.: Geographic clustering of emergency department presentations for atrial fibrillation and flutter in Alberta, Canada. Acad. Emerg. Med. **22**(8), 965–975 (2015)
53. da S. Luz, E.J., Schwartz, W.R., Cámara-Chávez, G., Menotti, D.: ECG-based heartbeat classification for arrhythmia detection: a survey. Comput. Methods Prog. Biomed. **127**, 144–164 (2016). https://doi.org/10.1016/j.cmpb.2015.12.008. https://www.sciencedirect.com/science/article/pii/S0169260715003314
54. Sahoo, S., Kanungo, B., Behera, S., Sabut, S.: Multiresolution wavelet transform based feature extraction and ECG classification to detect cardiac abnormalities. Measurement **108**, 55–66 (2017)
55. Serhani, M.A., El Kassabi, H.T., Ismail, H., Nujum Navaz, A.: ECG monitoring systems: review, architecture, processes, and key challenges. Sensors **20**(6), 1796 (2020)
56. Sheller, M.J., Reina, G.A., Edwards, B., Martin, J., Bakas, S.: Multi-institutional deep learning modeling without sharing patient data: a feasibility study on brain tumor segmentation. In: Crimi, A., Bakas, S., Kuijf, H., Keyvan, F., Reyes, M., van Walsum, T. (eds.) BrainLes 2018. LNCS, vol. 11383, pp. 92–104. Springer, Cham (2019). https://doi.org/10.1007/978-3-030-11723-8_9
57. Tang, R., Luo, J., Qian, J., Jin, J.: Personalized federated learning for ECG classification based on feature alignment. Secur. Commun. Netw. **2021**, 1–9 (2021)
58. Van Panhuis, W.G., et al.: A systematic review of barriers to data sharing in public health. BMC Public Health **14**(1), 1–9 (2014)
59. Wang, F., Casalino, L.P., Khullar, D.: Deep learning in medicine-promise, progress, and challenges. JAMA Int. Med. **179**(3), 293–294 (2019)
60. Wang, H., et al.: Attack of the tails: yes, you really can backdoor federated learning (2020). https://doi.org/10.48550/ARXIV.2007.05084. arxiv.org/abs/2007.05084
61. Wodschow, K., Bihrmann, K., Larsen, M.L., Gislason, G., Ersbøll, A.K.: Geographical variation and clustering are found in atrial fibrillation beyond socioeconomic differences: a Danish cohort study, 1987–2015. Int. J. Health Geogr. **20**(1), 1–10 (2021)
62. Yang, Q., Liu, Y., Chen, T., Tong, Y.: Federated machine learning: concept and applications. ACM Trans. Intell. Syst. Technol. (TIST) **10**(2), 1–19 (2019)
63. Yang, Q., Liu, Y., Chen, T., Tong, Y.: Federated machine learning: concept and applications. ACM Trans. Intell. Syst. Technol. (TIST) **10**(2), 12 (2019). https://doi.org/10.48550/ARXIV.1902.04885. arxiv.org/abs/1902.04885
64. Zhang, M., Wang, Y., Luo, T.: Federated learning for arrhythmia detection of non-iid ECG. In: 2020 IEEE 6th International Conference on Computer and Communications (ICCC), pp. 1176–1180. IEEE (2020)
65. Zhao, Z., et al.: Adaptive lead weighted resnet trained with different duration signals for classifying 12-lead ECGs. In: 2020 Computing in Cardiology, pp. 1–4 (2020). https://doi.org/10.22489/CinC.2020.112
66. Zhao, Z., et al.: Adaptive lead weighted resnet trained with different duration signals for classifying 12-lead ECGs. In: 2020 Computing in Cardiology, pp. 1–4. IEEE (2020)

67. Zhu, Z., et al.: Classification of cardiac abnormalities from ECG signals using se-resnet. In: 2020 Computing in Cardiology, pp. 1–4 (2020). https://doi.org/10.22489/CinC.2020.281

68. Zisou, C., Sochopoulos, A., Kitsios, K.: Convolutional recurrent neural network and lightgbm ensemble model for 12-lead ecg classification. In: 2020 Computing in Cardiology, pp. 1–4 (2020). https://doi.org/10.22489/CinC.2020.417

An Adaptive, Energy-Efficient DRL-Based and MCMC-Based Caching Strategy for IoT Systems

Aristeidis Karras[1]($\boxtimes$)(iD), Christos Karras[1](iD), Ioannis Karydis[2](iD), Markos Avlonitis[2](iD), and Spyros Sioutas[1](iD)

[1] Computer Engineering and Informatics Department, University of Patras, 26504 Patras, Greece
{akarras,c.karras,sioutas}@ceid.upatras.gr
[2] Department of Informatics, Ionian University, 49100 Corfu, Greece
{karydis,avlon}@ionio.gr

Abstract. The Internet of Things (IoT) has seen remarkable growth in recent years, but the data volatility and limited energy resources in these networks pose significant challenges. In addition, traditional quality of service metrics like throughput, latency, packet delay variation, and error rate remain important benchmarks. In this work, we explore the application of Markov Chain Monte Carlo (MCMC) methods to address these issues by designing efficient caching policies. Without the necessity for prior knowledge or context, MCMC methods provide a promising alternative to traditional caching schemes and existing machine learning models. We propose an MCMC-based caching strategy that can improve both cache hit rates and energy efficiency in IoT networks. Additionally, we introduce a hierarchical caching structure that allows parent nodes to process requests from several edge nodes and make autonomous caching decisions. Our experimental results indicate that the MCMC-based approach outperforms both traditional and other ML-based caching policies significantly. For environments where file popularity changes over time, we propose an MCMC-based adaptive caching solution. This solution detects shifts in popularity distribution using clustering and cluster similarity metrics, leading to an MCMC adaptation process. This adaptability further enhances the efficiency and effectiveness of our caching scheme, reducing training time and improving overall performance.

Keywords: Internet of Things · Deep Reinforcement Learning · MCMC Methods · Edge Cache · Cache Memory · IoT Systems · Energy-Efficiency

1 Introduction

In the era of the Internet of Things (IoT), rapid data proliferation and increased demand for high-speed, reliable connections necessitate smarter networking

I. Chatzigiannakis and I. Karydis (Eds.): ALGOCLOUD 2023, LNCS 14053, pp. 66–85, 2024.
https://doi.org/10.1007/978-3-031-49361-4_4

strategies. Caching, especially edge caching, has emerged as an effective solution for mitigating network congestion and improving response times by allowing edge nodes to store frequently requested files. However, traditional caching methods such as Least Frequently Used (LFU) and Least Recently Used (LRU) are insufficient in addressing the multifaceted challenges of IoT networks. These challenges arise from the dynamic nature of data, limited energy resources, and the vast scale and complexity of these networks, which intricately complicate decision-making processes.

Recent advancements in artificial intelligence and machine learning have introduced innovative solutions to these challenges. Deep Reinforcement Learning (DRL), a subfield of machine learning, offers a promising approach to solve complex caching problems without requiring extensive prior network knowledge or explicit feature definitions. Nonetheless, addressing IoT-specific constraints, such as data freshness and energy limitations, calls for a more tailored solution. This paper thus introduces a pioneering application of Markov Chain Monte Carlo (MCMC) methods and DRL to devise a novel, energy-efficient caching strategy specifically designed for IoT networks.

Our proposed approach incorporates a unique hierarchical architecture that captures region-specific popularity distributions, providing a more practical and robust solution. In the following sections, we delve deeper into the technical details of our model, illustrating its superior performance through a comprehensive suite of experimental results.

The structure of the rest paper is as follows. In Sect. 2, we offer a detailed examination of previous works. Section 3 presents the problem formulation of our approach to framing the IoT caching problem as a Markov decision process (MDP), wherein we establish the state and reward function for DRL training, mindful of the lifespan of IoT data. Section 4 details our utilization of the proximal policy optimization solver to resolve the MDP problem, emphasizing the incorporation of both MCMC and DRL methods. Section 5 showcases a spectrum of experimental results, highlighting the superior performance of our proposed caching strategy compared to traditional techniques. Section 6 summarizes the further extensions, and applications of the proposed caching strategies in the context of cloud computing. Finally, Sect. 7 brings together our insights and provides a concluding summary of the study.

2   Background and Related Work

Edge caching has emerged as an innovative technology that utilizes edge nodes (e.g., base stations or user devices) to be a part of the caching architecture, thereby drastically reducing the response time and load on the backhaul link [24]. Traditional caching strategies, such as Least Frequently Used (LFU) and Least Recently Used (LRU), despite their effectiveness in conventional settings, have shown limitations when applied to the IoT environments [21,33,44], and especially in scenarios addressing risks and vulnerabilities closely related to climate change (e.g. flood risk, risk of fire, erosion, landslides and landslides).

Given the rising interest in artificial intelligence and machine learning, Reinforcement Learning (RL) has gained considerable attention for its potential to address these complex problems. More specifically, Deep Reinforcement Learning (DRL), which combines deep learning and RL, has shown remarkable potential in addressing problems with enormous searching spaces without the need for prior knowledge about network features [45]. The application of DRL to caching problems has been explored in different scenarios, such as Content Delivery Networks (CDNs) [28,44], mobile networks [13], and Internet of Things (IoT) networks [11,15,23,36]. However, many of these works have not sufficiently addressed the unique constraints of IoT systems, particularly the limited data lifetime and energy constraints [11,12,15,23,35,36,43].

Several studies have focused on the role of multiple edge nodes in caching, either through non-cooperative or cooperative caching schemes [15,35,36,43]. For example, cooperative caching schemes involving multiple nodes exchanging information with each other or with a central server have shown promising results [15,43]. A recent study by Wang et.al. [35] utilized a federated deep reinforcement learning method for cooperative edge caching, achieving performance on par with the centralized DRL approach but with significantly reduced performance degradation.

Despite these advancements, a critical challenge unique to IoT networks remains underexplored - the issue of data freshness, a consequence of periodic data generation and limited data lifespan in IoT networks. This has not been adequately addressed in the previous works [11,12,15,43]. In light of these considerations, the focus of our study is to develop an adaptive, energy-efficient DRL and MCMC-based caching strategy. This novel approach aims to comprehensively address these specific challenges in IoT systems, placing special emphasis on ensuring data freshness while operating within the stringent energy constraints of IoT devices.

2.1 Caching in IoT Systems: Fundamentals, Analysis, and Opportunities

Fundamentals of Caching in IoT Systems: IoT, with its array of connected devices, generates vast amounts of data. Caching plays an essential role in enhancing the efficiency of data access, reducing latency, and optimizing network traffic. It involves storing frequently accessed data closer to the devices to expedite future access. However, caching in IoT is not without its challenges. Given the distributed nature of IoT, determining what, where, and how long to cache data becomes intricate. The limited storage and computational capabilities of many IoT devices further complicate caching strategies.

Caching significantly enhances the efficiency and performance of Internet of Things (IoT) systems. Some fundamental aspects of caching aspects of caching in these systems:

- **Hierarchical Caching Systems:** Hierarchical caching in edge networks, especially within 5G small cells, aids smart industrial applications and connected cars. Such systems support multiple applications concurrently, though managing shared resources remains challenging [8].

- **Named Data Networking (NDN) and In-network Caching:** NDN offers a networking architecture that suits the application-centric nature of IoT systems. Integral to NDN is in-network caching, enhancing data accessibility and reducing both content retrieval delay and network traffic [3].

- **Digital Twin Edge Networks (DITEN):** Integrating mobile/multi-access edge computing (MEC) with digital twin (DT) enhances network performance and cuts down on communication, computation, and caching expenses. Within DITENs, the state of the network undergoes consistent monitoring, enabling centralized, efficient networking [31].

- **Optical Networks on Chip (ONoC):** Increased on-chip processing requirements in IoT systems, driven by advancements in 5G, IoT, and data centers, benefit from ONoC. ONoC's efficacy is contingent on the efficiency of optical routers [30].

- **Information-Centric Networking (ICN):** Envisioned as a next-generation Internet architecture, ICN prioritizes content-centric design. It has the potential to accelerate expansive IoT deployment by ensuring enhanced performance, scalability, and security [26].

- **Collaborative Edge Computing (CEC) and Trustworthiness:** CEC, an extension of various edge paradigms, caters to latency-sensitive, computation-heavy applications in edge-centric networks. Trust among CEC participants is pivotal, with blockchain-empowered frameworks like BlockEdge ensuring collaborative service security [37].

Comparative Analysis: Several techniques have been proposed for IoT caching, each with its own merits and demerits. For instance, traditional methods like LRU might be simplistic and efficient but can be suboptimal for IoT's dynamic environment. On the other hand, advanced methods like DRL-based strategies adapt to changing environments but might come with higher computational overheads. Emerging techniques, though less explored, such as federated learning for caching, show promise by leveraging the distributed nature of IoT while ensuring data privacy. A comprehensive understanding requires a deep dive into each technique, comparing their suitability for specific IoT scenarios.

Research Gaps and Opportunities: While significant progress has been made, certain challenges remain unaddressed. For instance, ensuring data freshness in caches, considering the periodic data generation in IoT, hasn't been explored thoroughly. The incorporation of energy efficiency with caching strategies, especially for battery-operated IoT devices, is another understudied area. These gaps present rich opportunities for future research. The confluence of IoT with other emerging technologies, like edge computing or blockchain, can also lead to innovative caching strategies that are yet to be explored.

Data Freshness in IoT Systems: In the context of IoT, data freshness pertains to the temporal relevance of the cached data. As IoT devices frequently generate and transmit data, ensuring that the cached data is up-to-date becomes crucial for accurate and timely decision-making. Data freshness is especially essential in scenarios like health monitoring or real-time surveillance where stale data can lead to undesired consequences. However, maintaining data freshness in caching poses challenges. Given the sporadic and voluminous data generation in IoT, devising strategies to periodically update caches without overwhelming the network or draining device resources is intricate.

Energy Constraints in IoT Devices: IoT ecosystems are populated by a multitude of devices, many of which are battery-operated with limited energy reserves. These constraints necessitate energy-efficient operations, including caching. Every caching decision, from data storage to retrieval, consumes energy. The challenge is to optimize these decisions such that they not only improve data access but also prolong device lifetime. This necessitates caching strategies that are cognizant of the energy profile of IoT devices and can adapt to their energy constraints.

Cooperative Caching in IoT Systems: Cooperative caching refers to a strategy where multiple nodes (devices or servers) collaborate to store and retrieve cached data. In IoT scenarios, where devices are often spatially distributed and possess limited storage, cooperative caching can be a game-changer. By allowing devices to fetch data from nearby caches rather than a distant server, it can drastically reduce latency and network congestion. While the idea is promising, its implementation in IoT is non-trivial. Factors like device heterogeneity, network topology, and data access patterns influence cooperative caching decisions. Several works have ventured into this domain, exploring algorithms and protocols to realize efficient cooperative caching in IoT systems.

2.2   State-of-the-Art (SOTA) Caching Techniques in IoT Systems

Recent research has delved into various caching methods designed for the complexities of IoT systems. Bando et al. offer mechanisms tailored for single-level storage systems capable of supporting a vast array of IoT devices [5]. Asmat et al. present the Central Control Caching (CCC) approach, aiming at energy conservation and reduction in access times [4]. Khodaparas et al. introduce a software-defined caching strategy, capitalizing on Content-Centric Networking (CCN) to enhance latency metrics and optimize resource deployment, also minimizing transmission intermediaries [18]. Moreover, Nasehzadeh et al. employ deep reinforcement learning to devise a caching policy designed to elevate cache hit rates, economize on energy, and account for the limited data lifespan typical of IoT networks [22].

More specialized strategies have been developed to address the complex challenges essential to the IoT domain. Hongda Wu et al. investigate the integration of deep reinforcement learning in enhancing IoT caching, underscoring notable advancements in cache hit rates and energy optimization [38]. Jingjing Yao et al. emphasize the significance of caching within IoT gateways, positing that the strategic placement of frequently accessed IoT data at these points optimizes direct user accessibility [40]. The user-centric paradigm is further exemplified by Akhtari Zameel et al., who propose a context-aware caching mechanism to optimize content delivery based on user-specific criteria [42]. Complementing this, Khodaparas et al. present a cooperative caching strategy, achieving a commendable 40% enhancement in cache hit rates and expedited content access [19].

State-of-the-art caching techniques have emerged as a pivotal research focus in IoT systems, primarily in response to the considerable and varied data generated by IoT devices. These techniques strategically place data to minimize bandwidth usage and latency, thereby facilitating access for end devices. An overview of these methods includes:

- **Edge Caching**: Implementing data storage at the network edge to minimize latency and preserve bandwidth [10].
- **Federated Edge Intelligence with Edge Caching Mechanisms**: This study explores the integration of Edge Caching and Bayesian Optimization to enhance the performance and efficiency of IoT Systems [16]. Additionally, strategies such as adaptive communication and gradient sparsification are applied to further refine the algorithm's effectiveness in federated learning scenarios. In essence, this approach utilizes edge caching to minimize communication overhead and applies Bayesian optimization for pragmatic hyperparameter tuning, thereby improving performance and reducing communication costs in federated learning contexts.
- **Collaborative Filtering**: Employing artificial intelligence to predict forthcoming requests from IoT devices by proactively caching relevant data, reducing latency, and improving user experience [10].
- **Structural Caching**: This technique is employed for stream reasoning, it caches data based on the respective data stream's structure, improving system efficiency, and expressivity [6].
- **Bandwidth-Aware Routing Scheme**: Focused on congestion control in MANETs, it strategically caches data by monitoring residual bandwidth capacity and queue space, preventing potential congestion [1].

Such strategies and methods can be further integrated with technologies such as fog computing and SDN-IoT architectures, significantly IoT systems' operational efficiency and sustainability [14,41].

2.3   Reinforcement Learning in Caching

Reinforcement Learning (RL) has emerged as a crucial mechanism for enhancing content delivery and caching efficiency in mobile networks, addressing various complexities and challenges in mobile caching contexts. For example, a study in vehicular edge computing (VEC) employed asynchronous federated and deep reinforcement learning (CAFR) to accurately predict widespread content and determine optimal cooperative caching locations, considering the constrained caching capacity of roadside units (RSUs) [39]. Additionally, a comprehensive survey outlined and classified RL-augmented mobile edge caching solutions, demonstrating insights across several network frameworks such as fixed cellular, fog, cooperative, vehicular, and aerial networks, and categorizing them based on networking architecture and optimization aims [25].

The application of RL extends to enabling computation offloading and enhancing task caching, especially in multi-user and multi-task Mobile Edge Computing (MEC) systems. Employing multi-agent deep reinforcement learning, one investigation modelled a multi-user multi-server task caching scenario, converting the task caching issue into a nonlinear integer programming challenge to streamline computation offloading in 5G MEC [9]. Further, research exploring Device-to-Device (D2D) supported heterogeneous collaborative edge caching incorporated an attention-weighted federated deep reinforcement learning (AWFDRL) model. This approach employed federated learning to enhance the training efficiency of the Q-learning network while managing the constraints of limited computing and storage capacities [34].

In the following model, merging RL and cross-layer network coding (CLNC) addressed challenges by effectively pre-loading requested content to local caches and ensuring its delivery to users in a downlink fog-radio access network (F-RAN) with D2D communications [2]. Adaptive mechanisms within RL were also illuminated in research that proposed a distributed resources-efficient Federated Proactive Caching (FPC) policy. Employing an adaptive FPC (AFPC) algorithm, it combined deep reinforcement learning (DRL) and employed mechanisms of client selection and local iteration number decisions to improve content caching efficiency and mitigate resource consumption [27]. Consequently, RL emerges as an essential mechanism in effectively addressing the challenges existing in optimizing caching and content delivery within mobile networks.

2.4   Deep Reinforcement Learning for IoT Caching

Deep Reinforcement Learning (DRL) serves as a key methodology in formulating effective caching policies within Internet of Things (IoT) networks. Notably, DRL demonstrates its capacity to adapt to heterogeneous environments with scarce prior knowledge, showcasing its suitability for IoT systems characterized by transient data and restricted energy resources [20,38,40].

One explicit application of DRL in IoT caching addresses the joint caching and computing service placement (JCCSP) problem, specifically for sensing-data-driven IoT applications. Within this context, dedicated caching functions (CFs) are necessitated to cache crucial sensing data, ensuring the Quality of Service (QoS) for applications in an edge-enabled IoT system [7].

To address the JCCSP problem, a policy network, constructed using the encoder-decoder model, is formulated. This network manages challenges related to the varying sizes of JCCSP states and actions, which arise from different numbers of CFs associated with applications. Initially, an on-policy reinforce-based method is utilized for training the policy network. Subsequently, an off-policy training strategy, grounded on the twin-delayed (TD) deep deterministic policy gradient (DDPG), is implemented to enhance training efficacy and experience utilization [7].

Moreover, DRL-based caching approaches have been developed aiming to increase the cache hit rate and reduce energy usage in IoT networks, while also taking into account critical aspects such as data freshness and the constrained lifespan of IoT data [20,38,40]. These strategies employ hierarchical architectures to deploy edge caching nodes within IoT networks and define the caching problem as a Markov Decision Process. The goal is to minimize the long-term aggregated cost expectation, while simultaneously considering the average Age of Information (AoI) of users and the energy expenditure of sensors. To address this challenge, actor-critic-based caching algorithms are applied [20,36].

In conclusion, DRL-based caching methodologies have demonstrated efficacy in significantly improving IoT network performance, achieved through judicious reduction of energy consumption, enhancement of cache hit rate, and minimization of average end-to-end delay [20,36,38,40].

3   Problem Formulation

In this section, we re-define our caching problem as a Partially Observable Markov Decision Process (POMDP) and detail its components, namely, the design of state, action, and reward function. In addition to the freshness feature of transient data in the IoT system, we incorporate energy efficiency considerations into our problem formulation, which is primarily based on Deep Reinforcement Learning (DRL) and Markov Chain Monte Carlo (MCMC) techniques [17,32].

3.1   Partially Observable Markov Decision Process Modeling

At each time step n, a POMDP is symbolized by the tuple:

$$s_n, a_n, p(s_{n+1}|s_n, a_n), r_n, \Omega_n, \Omega_{n+1} \tag{1}$$

where $s_n \in S$ denotes the current state, $a_n \in A$ the chosen action, $p(s_{n+1}|s_n, a_n) \in P(S, A)$ the probability distribution for the next state given the current state and action, r_n is the reward evaluating the action's effectiveness, Ω_n represents the observation at current state, and Ω_{n+1} at the next state.

In the context of IoT systems, due to variable network conditions and device states, the full system state is not always observable, hence our transition from MDP to POMDP. To counter the partial observability, we maintain a belief state, b_n, a probability distribution over all possible states, which is updated based on the observation and action at each time step.

Similar to MDP, we aim to maximize the expected cumulative reward as defined in the equation,

$$G_n = \sum_{\tau=0}^{T} \gamma^\tau r_{n+\tau} \tag{2}$$

and to find the optimal policy π^*, which maximizes the expected cumulative reward,

$$\pi^* = \arg\max_\pi E\left[G_n \mid \pi\right] \tag{3}$$

Value function $V_\pi(b_n)$ and action-value function $Q_\pi(b_n, a_n)$ are defined in our POMDP model, but instead of being functions of the state s_n, they are functions of the belief state b_n.

3.2   State, Action, and Reward Incorporating Energy-Efficiency

In the context of IoT systems, due to variable network conditions and device states, the full system state is not always observable, hence our transition from MDP to POMDP. To counter the partial observability, we maintain a belief state, b_n, a probability distribution over all possible states, which is updated based on the observation and action at each time step.

Similar to MDP, we aim to maximize the expected cumulative reward as defined in the equation,

– Energy Consumption of Cache Memory: The energy consumption of each cached file, $E_{cache}(f_i)$, can be modeled as the sum of energy used for receiving, storing, and delivering the file. This can be mathematically represented as:

$$E_{cache}\ (f_i) = E_{rec}\ (f_i) + E_{store}\ (f_i) + E_{del}\ (f_i)\,, \tag{4}$$

where $E_{rec}(f_i)$, $E_{store}(f_i)$, and $E_{del}(f_i)$ represent the energy consumed for receiving, storing, and delivering the file f_i respectively.
– Adaptive Caching Decision: The adaptive caching decision can be represented as a probability value $\pi(a|b_n, E_{cache})$, which indicates the chance of taking action a given the belief state b_n and the energy status E_{cache}. The optimal adaptive caching policy can be formulated as:

$$\pi^*\ (a \mid b_n, E_{cache}\ ) = \arg\max_\pi E\left[G_n \mid \pi, E_{cache}\ \right] \tag{5}$$

where $E[G_n|\pi, E_{cache}]$ is the expected cumulative reward considering the energy efficiency of the caching strategy.
– Energy-Efficient Reward Function: We modify the reward function to reflect the energy consumption as a penalty. For each file in the cache memory that expires without being accessed at least once, a negative reward (penalty) is given, considering both its freshness and energy consumption.

$$r_{i,\ expire}\ = \left[\operatorname{sign}\left(k_i - 0.5\right) - 1\right] \times C_1 - C_2 \times E_{cache}\ (f_i)\,, \tag{6}$$

where C_1 is the freshness penalty coefficient, and C_2 is the energy consumption penalty coefficient.
– Energy-Efficient Q-Function: We adjust the action-value function, or Q-function, to accommodate the energy consumption. The new Q-function, $Q_\pi(b_n, a_n, E_{cache})$, is the expected cumulative reward starting from the belief

state b_n, taking action a_n, considering the energy consumption E_{cache}, and following the policy π after that. We can express it as:

$$Q_\pi(b_n, a_n, E_{\text{cache}}) =$$

$$\sum_{b_{n+1} \in B} p(b_{n+1} \mid b_n, a_n) \left[r_n + \gamma \sum_{a_{n+1} \in A} \pi(a_{n+1} \mid b_{n+1}, E_{\text{cache}}) Q_\pi(b_{n+1}, a_{n+1}, E_{\text{cache}}) \right]$$

(7)

A comprehensive energy-efficient adaptive DRL-based and MCMC-based caching strategy for IoT Systems as follows:

Define the comprehensive adaptive caching strategy $\Sigma = (A, E_{\text{cache}}, \pi, Q)$ where A is the action space, E_{cache} is the energy consumed by the cache memory, π is the adaptive caching decision policy, and Q is the energy-efficient Q-function.

First, we express the energy consumption of cache memory E_{cache} as a function of action a, denoted as $E_{\text{cache}} = E(a)$.

Next, we incorporate this into the adaptive caching decision policy as:

$$\pi^*(a \mid b_n, E(a)) = \arg\max_\pi E[G_n \mid \pi, E(a)].$$

(8)

Then, we reformulate the energy-efficient reward function to consider the energy consumption of each action, denoted as:

$$r_{i,\text{expire}} = [\text{sign}(k_i - 0.5) - 1] \times C_1 - C_2 \times E(a.$$

(9)

Finally, we adjust the energy-efficient Q-function to incorporate the energy consumption of each action, denoted as:

$$Q_\pi(b_n, a_n, E(a)) = \sum_{b_{n+1} \in B} p(b_{n+1} \mid b_n, a_n)$$

$$\left[r_n + \gamma \sum_{a_{n+1} \in A} \pi(a_{n+1} \mid b_{n+1}, E(a_{n+1})) Q_\pi(b_{n+1}, a_{n+1}, E(a_{n+1})) \right].$$

(10)

Therefore, the combined equation for this framework (strategy) can be represented as:

$$\Sigma = \left(A, E(a), \pi^*(a \mid b_n, E(a)) = \arg\max_\pi E[G_n \mid \pi, E(a)], Q_\pi(b_n, a_n, E(a)) = \sum_{b_{n+1} \in I} \right.$$

(11)

Equation 11 incorporates the key components of our proposed strategy and represents a comprehensive mathematical formulation for an adaptive, energy-efficient DRL-based and MCMC-based caching strategy for IoT Systems.

4 Methodology

In this section, we propose a novel energy-efficient variant of the Actor-Critic (AC) models, specifically the Proximal Policy Optimization (PPO) algorithm [29]. The PPO algorithm is an advancement over the Trust Region Policy Optimization (TRPO) algorithm, designed to inherit its data efficiency and reliability while circumventing the need for second-order optimizations.

Our algorithm, named PPO-based Energy-Efficient Caching Strategy 1, is based on the AC method. Two distinct neural networks, termed the actor (θ) and critic (θ_v), are employed to concurrently approximate the policy and value function. The actor network decides the action to take, i.e., the caching decision, while the critic network assesses this action, calculating the value function $V_{\pi_\theta}(s_n; \theta_v)$ based on the energy consumption of the cache memory and the potential energy savings from the caching decision.

Algorithm 1. PPO-based Energy-Efficient Caching Strategy

Require: Initial neural network parameters for actor and critic (θ, θ_v), initial cache state s_0, energy consumption function $E(a)$, discount factor γ

Ensure: Optimal policy π_θ that minimizes the total energy consumption of the caching system while ensuring the system's QoS requirements

1: **for** iteration $= 1, 2, \ldots$ **do**
2:    Collect a set of trajectories $T = \{\tau_j\}$ by running the policy π_θ in the environment for T steps, while considering energy consumption $E(a)$ for each action
3:    Estimate advantage values $\hat{A}_1, \ldots, \hat{A}_T$ considering energy consumption $E(a)$ and the effect on caching decisions
4:    Calculate the rewards and compute $\hat{G}_1, \ldots, \hat{G}_T$, incorporating the energy-efficient reward function $r_{i,\text{expire}}$
5:    Optimize surrogate loss w.r.t. θ using stochastic gradient ascent with Adam: $\theta \leftarrow \arg\max_\theta L_{\text{clip}}(\theta)$
6:    Fit value function by regression on mean squared error using stochastic gradient descent: $\theta_v \leftarrow \arg\min_{\theta_v} L_{\text{VF}}$, where $L_{\text{VF}} = \frac{1}{|T|} \sum_{\tau \in D} \sum_{n=0}^{T} (V_{\theta_v}(s_n) - \hat{G}_n)^2$
7: **end for**

In the proposed Markov Chain Monte Carlo (MCMC)-based Energy-Efficient Caching Strategy 2, we utilize the statistical sampling method to make optimal caching decisions that minimize energy consumption. This technique exploits the probabilistic nature of Markov chains and Monte Carlo simulations to optimize the state transition, i.e., caching decisions, while considering energy efficiency.

The MCMC approach offers a robust and adaptive mechanism to handle the dynamism and uncertainties inherent in IoT systems. It iteratively samples states from a stationary distribution and uses these to guide the caching strategy. The MCMC-based caching strategy involves transitioning from the current state (cache configuration) to a new state in a way that progressively reduces energy consumption, navigating towards the optimal caching decision. This energy-efficient caching strategy performs state transition based on a carefully crafted energy-aware reward function. The reward function is designed to penalize high energy consumption and reward energy-saving actions, thereby guiding the MCMC sampler towards energy-efficient caching decisions. Thus, the MCMC-based strategy provides a powerful tool for realizing energy-efficient caching in IoT systems.

Algorithm 2. MCMC-based Energy-Efficient Caching Strategy

Require: Initial cache state s_0, energy consumption function $E(a)$, discount factor γ, number of iterations N

Ensure: A sequence of states representing an energy-efficient caching strategy that minimizes the total energy consumption of the caching system while ensuring the system's QoS requirements

1: Initialize current state $s = s_0$ and initial action $a = a_0$
2: **for** iteration $= 1, 2, ..., N$ **do**
3:     Propose a new action a' from a proposal distribution $q(a'|a)$
4:     Calculate acceptance probability α using the energy-efficient Q-function $Q_\pi(b_n, a_n, E(a))$
5:     Draw a random number u from Uniform$(0, 1)$
6:     **if** $u < \alpha$ **then**
7:         Update $a = a'$ and update state s according to action a'
8:     **else**
9:         Remain in current state with action a
10:    **end if**
11:    Update cache strategy based on new state and action
12: **end for**

The complexity of the PPO-based algorithm is influenced by the size of the neural networks used (denoted as P) and the number of trajectories per iteration (denoted as T). Generally, the computational complexity is approximately $O(TP)$. The Metropolis-Hastings MCMC-based algorithm, in contrast, primarily depends on the number of iterations it performs (denoted as N). Thus, its computational complexity can be considered as $O(N)$.

5   Simulation and Experimental Results

5.1   Simulation Interface and Setup

To evaluate the performance of the proposed MCMC-based Energy-Efficient Caching Strategy in comparison to other caching methods, we conducted a simulation using a hierarchical IoT caching structure. The simulation consists of one parent node, two edge nodes, and one hundred IoT devices, each producing a single type of file with a unique ID and a randomly assigned lifetime sampled from a uniform distribution. The popularity distribution of the files follows Zipf's law, with a skewness factor α characterizing the distribution.

We conducted experiments with 24 different settings, combining four request rate values (w) ranging from 0.5 to 2.0 requests per time step and six values of the popularity skewness factor α ranging from 0.7 to 1.2. The popularity distributions are unknown to the MCMC-based Energy-Efficient Caching Strategy, as they are used solely for generating requests in the simulations. Each request is assumed to be fulfilled before the corresponding user leaves the network.

Comparison Methods: In our evaluation, we compare the performance of the proposed MCMC-based Energy-Efficient Caching Strategy with two well-known conventional caching strategies: Least Recently Used (LRU) and Least Frequently Used (LFU) algorithms. Additionally, we implement an existing DRL-based caching method with a different reward function from ours, denoted as DRL, to observe the effects of our proposed reward function.

- LRU: In the LRU algorithm, files are ranked based on their recent usage, and when the cache is full, the least recently used file is replaced with the new file.
- LFU: Similar to LRU, the LFU algorithm ranks cached items based on the frequency of their requests. When the cache is full, the file with the least frequency of requests is replaced by the new file.
- DRL: This existing DRL-based caching method considers the freshness of files in its reward function. It differs from our proposed MCMC-based Energy-Efficient Caching Strategy in terms of the reward function design.

5.2   Experimental Results

In this Section, we evaluate our two proposed algorithmic schemes against state-of-the-art caching techniques. In particular, we access our method against Least Frequently Used (LFU), Least Recently Used (LRU), and Adopting deep reinforcement learning (DRL) methods. The aim is to identify which algorithmic choice has the best cache hit rate and at the same time the lowest energy consumption.

Figure 1(a) shows the performance of four different caching methods: LFU, LRU, DRL, and our proposed PPO approach. The performance is measured in terms of both cache hit rates and energy efficiency, plotted against time intervals. The objective is to visualize how each method responds to increasing time demands and to assess which method performs optimally under such conditions. We hypothesize that the PPO method will outperform the others due to its advanced learning capabilities. As per the skewness α, the results are shown in Fig. 1(b).

The plot demonstrates our hypothesis: the PPO method outperforms LFU, LRU, and even DRL methods in terms of both cache hit rate and energy efficiency. As the time interval increases, PPO maintains a steady and high-performance level, highlighting its robustness and reliability under varying demands. This performance difference accentuates the potential of the PPO method in enhancing caching processes and optimizing system performance. Our future work will focus on refining the PPO method and investigating its potential in other application areas.

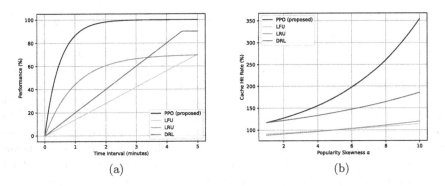

Fig. 1. (a) Cache Hit rate vs varying request rates w (b) Hit rates vs popularity skewness α.

As the popularity skewness α increases, PPO outperforms the other three methods, achieving the highest cache hit rates. The rapid increase in the PPO curve signifies its superior adaptability to a skewed distribution, where a small set of objects is highly popular. On the other hand, LFU, LRU, and DRL show lower rates, highlighting their limitations in such scenarios. This comparison emphasizes the strength of PPO in handling highly skewed distributions, making it an attractive method for improving cache hit rates in systems with similar characteristics.

As we further explore the performance of the four caching strategies, two crucial parameters come to the fore: the request rates (w) and the popularity skewness (α). Both these factors can significantly impact the energy consumption of the caching mechanisms, which is a critical aspect in energy-sensitive systems. We present a comparative analysis of energy consumption across different request rates and popularity skewness in Fig. 2.

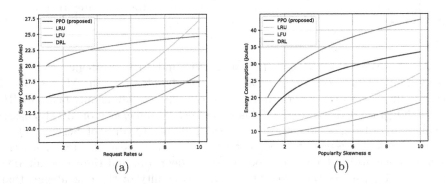

Fig. 2. (a) Energy consumption vs request rates w (b) Energy consumption vs popularity skewness α.

The plots in Fig. 2 highlight the superior performance of the Proximal Policy Optimization (PPO) method in terms of energy efficiency. In the first plot, we observe that as the request rate (w) increases, PPO maintains the lowest energy consumption followed closely by the Deep Reinforcement Learning (DRL) method. On the other hand, the Least Recently Used (LRU) and Least Frequently Used (LFU) display higher energy consumption. The second plot emphasizes the robustness of PPO and DRL under varying levels of popularity skewness (α). They show a considerably slower rise in energy consumption with increasing skewness compared to LRU and LFU. These observations underscore the effectiveness of reinforcement learning-based strategies like PPO and DRL in managing cache resources efficiently while ensuring energy conservation.

Lastly, the following set of graphs (Fig. 3) provides an in-depth look at the comparative performance of various caching strategies, including the newly proposed MCMC-based Energy-Efficient Caching Strategy. The comparison spans across two major performance indicators - energy consumption and cache hit rate - with the number of iterations serving as the common parameter. It is essential to consider these metrics while designing a cache management strategy, as they directly impact the overall system performance.

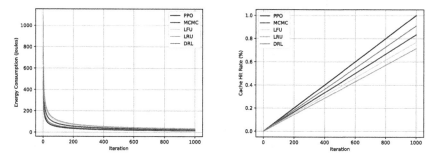

Fig. 3. Evolution of Energy Consumption and Cache Hit Rate over Iterations for Different Caching Strategies.

As observed from the graphs, while LFU and LRU strategies have relatively higher energy consumption and lower cache hit rates, the MCMC-based method displays superior performance in these aspects, falling only behind DRL and PPO (proposed) strategies. This underlines the efficiency of MCMC-based caching in utilizing system resources and fulfilling Quality of Service (QoS) requirements. Moreover, it is evident that with an increase in iterations, the energy consumption for all methods tends to decrease, and the cache hit rate increases. This shows the inherent learning capability of these strategies that adapt over time, enhancing their performance. Specifically, the PPO algorithm exhibits the highest cache hit rate and lowest energy consumption, emerging as the most effective caching strategy amongst the lot.

6   Futher Extensions

The proposed PPO-based Energy-Efficient Caching Strategy 1 and MCMC-based Energy-Efficient Caching Strategy 2 outlined in the paper offer valuable contributions to the field of IoT systems. However, their implications and potential applications extend beyond the realm of IoT networks and can be further extended to the domain of cloud computing. By integrating these caching strategies into cloud computing architectures, numerous benefits can be realized, enhancing performance, scalability, and energy efficiency.

Cloud computing environments are characterized by their distributed nature, involving data centers and edge nodes responsible for storing and processing vast amounts of data. The incorporation of the PPO-based and MCMC-based caching strategies into cloud computing frameworks can have a transformative impact. One key area of improvement lies in cache hit rates. By applying the reinforcement learning and Monte Carlo methods embedded in these strategies, cache hit rates can be significantly enhanced within cloud computing architectures. By intelligently caching frequently accessed data and optimizing cache eviction policies, the proposed strategies enable faster data retrieval, reduced latency, and improved overall response times for cloud-based applications.

Energy efficiency is vital in cloud computing and can greatly benefit from these caching strategies. By effectively managing data storage and retrieval, these strategies optimize energy consumption in cloud infrastructures. Also, they minimize unnecessary data transfers, reduce idle resource usage, and employ adaptive caching policies, resulting in significant energy savings. This enhances the sustainability and cost-effectiveness of cloud computing systems.

Dynamic workload patterns and varying data popularity are common challenges in cloud computing. The adaptive nature of the PPO-based and MCMC-based caching strategies enables them to effectively address these challenges. By continuously monitoring and adapting cache contents based on evolving data popularity and access patterns, these strategies ensure that the most relevant and frequently accessed data remains readily available, improving cache hit rates and system performance in dynamic cloud environments. The integration of these caching strategies also offers benefits in terms of reducing network congestion and optimizing resource utilization. By caching data at edge nodes and distributing content closer to end-users, the strategies mitigate the strain on central cloud infrastructure and alleviate network congestion. This leads to improved scalability, reduced network strain, and enhanced user experiences, as data can be retrieved and processed more efficiently.

Ultimately, the proposed caching Strategies 1, 2 have significant implications for cloud computing infrastructures and can greatly enhance their performance, efficiency, and scalability. These strategies find wide applicability in various cloud computing use-cases, such as content delivery networks (CDNs), edge computing, data centers, and distributed systems. Furthermore, by applying these strategies, cloud providers can effectively distribute the load on network infrastructure, optimize the data transfer, and ensure high-quality service delivery, resulting in improved user experiences and enhanced resource utilization.

7   Conclusions and Future Work

In this work, we have introduced a novel MCMC-based caching strategy tailored for the distinctive needs of IoT networks, focusing on the critical issues of data volatility and limited energy resources. This innovative strategy has successfully proven to improve the cache hit rates and enhance energy efficiency, benchmarking significant advancements over traditional caching schemes such as LFU and LRU, as well as other ML-based caching policies.

Our experimental results demonstrated the superiority of the MCMC-based approach, showing the impressive capabilities of our method in environments where file popularity changes over time. The MCMC-based adaptive caching solution introduced in this paper has been adept at detecting shifts in popularity distribution and triggering an efficient MCMC adaptation process, thereby drastically reducing training time and improving overall performance. In addition, we have presented a novel hierarchical caching structure that offers autonomous decision-making for parent nodes processing queries from multiple edge nodes. This innovative architecture enables a practicable capture of region-specific popularity distributions, thereby strengthening our caching strategy.

There are numerous directions for future research and development based on the current results. The algorithms could be modified to include more dynamic and complex network scenarios, such as those with mobile nodes or nodes with variable resources. This would necessitate additional algorithmic layers of adaptability and responsiveness. It would be beneficial to investigate how the MCMC-based approach could be combined with other AI-based methodologies, such as Deep Neural Networks or Genetic Algorithms, in order to improve its performance. These methods may offer additional capabilities, including enhanced non-linear data management and enhanced global policy optimizations. Ultimately, it is crucial to evaluate the performance of the proposed approach in real-world IoT environments and Cloud-based applications, which would provide additional insight into its strengths and weaknesses as well as valuable feedback for future improvements. In conclusion, this paper presents two novel caching strategies that represent a significant advance in IoT networking. On the other hand, there exists an unrealized potential, which promises future developments.

Acknowledgments. The financial support of the European Union and Greece (Partnership Agreement for the Development Framework 2014–2020) under the Regional Operational Programme Ionian Islands 2014–2020 for the project "Laertis" is gratefully acknowledged.

References

1. Akhtar, N., Khan, M.A., Ullah, A., Javed, M.Y.: Congestion avoidance for smart devices by caching information in manets and iot. IEEE Access **7**, 71459–71471 (2019)
2. Al-Abiad, M.S., Hassan, M.Z., Hossain, M.J.: A joint reinforcement-learning enabled caching and cross-layer network code in f-ran with d2d communications. IEEE Trans. Commun. **70**(7), 4400–4416 (2022)

3. Alduayji, S., Belghith, A., Gazdar, A., Al-Ahmadi, S.: Pf-clustercache: popularity and freshness-aware collaborative cache clustering for named data networking of things. Appl. Sci. **12**(13) (2022). https://doi.org/10.3390/app12136706. https://www.mdpi.com/2076-3417/12/13/6706

4. Asmat, H., Ullah, F., Zareei, M., Khan, A., Mohamed, E.M.: Energy-efficient centrally controlled caching contents for information-centric internet of things. IEEE Access **8**, 126358–126369 (2020). https://doi.org/10.1109/ACCESS.2020.3008193

5. Bando, Y., et al.: Caching mechanisms towards single-level storage systems for internet of things. In: 2015 Symposium on VLSI Circuits (VLSI Circuits), pp. C132–C133 (2015). https://doi.org/10.1109/VLSIC.2015.7231352

6. Bonte, P., Turck, F.D., Ongenae, F.: Bridging the gap between expressivity and efficiency in stream reasoning: a structural caching approach for IoT streams. Knowl. Inf. Syst. **64**(7), 1781–1815 (2022)

7. Chen, Y., Sun, Y., Yang, B., Taleb, T.: Joint caching and computing service placement for edge-enabled IoT based on deep reinforcement learning. IEEE Internet Things J. **9**(19), 19501–19514 (2022)

8. Coutinho, R.W.L., Boukerche, A.: Modeling and analysis of a shared edge caching system for connected cars and industrial IoT-based applications. IEEE Trans. Ind. Inf. **16**(3), 2003–2012 (2020). https://doi.org/10.1109/TII.2019.2938529

9. Elgendy, I.A., Zhang, W.Z., He, H., Gupta, B.B., Abd El-Latif, A.A.: Joint computation offloading and task caching for multi-user and multi-task mec systems: reinforcement learning-based algorithms. Wirel. Netw. **27**(3), 2023–2038 (2021)

10. Gupta, D., Rani, S., Ahmed, S.H., Verma, S., Ijaz, M.F., Shafi, J.: Edge caching based on collaborative filtering for heterogeneous ICN-IoT applications. Sensors **21**(16), 5491 (2021)

11. He, X., Wang, K., Huang, H., Miyazaki, T., Wang, Y., Guo, S.: Green resource allocation based on deep reinforcement learning in content-centric IoT. IEEE Trans. Emerg. Top. Comput. **8**(3), 781–796 (2018)

12. He, X., Wang, K., Xu, W.: QoE-driven content-centric caching with deep reinforcement learning in edge-enabled IoT. IEEE Comput. Intell. Mag. **14**(4), 12–20 (2019)

13. He, Y., Zhao, N., Yin, H.: Integrated networking, caching, and computing for connected vehicles: a deep reinforcement learning approach. IEEE Trans. Veh. Technol. **67**(1), 44–55 (2017)

14. Jazaeri, S.S., Asghari, P., Jabbehdari, S., Javadi, H.H.S.: Toward caching techniques in edge computing over SDN-IoT architecture: a review of challenges, solutions, and open issues. Multimedia Tools Appl. 1–67 (2023)

15. Jiang, W., Feng, G., Qin, S., Liu, Y.: Multi-agent reinforcement learning based cooperative content caching for mobile edge networks. IEEE Access **7**, 61856–61867 (2019)

16. Karras, A., Karras, C., Giotopoulos, K.C., Tsolis, D., Oikonomou, K., Sioutas, S.: Federated edge intelligence and edge caching mechanisms. Information **14**(7), 414 (2023)

17. Karras, C., Karras, A., Avlonitis, M., Sioutas, S.: An overview of MCMC methods: from theory to applications. In: Maglogiannis, I., Iliadis, L., Macintyre, J., Cortez, P. (eds.) IFIP International Conference on Artificial Intelligence Applications and Innovations, pp. 319–332. Springer, Heidelberg (2022). https://doi.org/10.1007/978-3-031-08341-9_26

18. Khodaparas, S., Benslimane, A., Yousefi, S.: A software-defined caching scheme for the internet of things. Comput. Commun. **158**, 178–188 (2020)

19. Khodaparas, S., Yousefi, S., Benslimane, A.: A multi criteria cooperative caching scheme for internet of things. In: ICC 2019–2019 IEEE International Conference on Communications (ICC), pp. 1–6 (2019). https://doi.org/10.1109/ICC.2019. 8761546

20. Lai, L., Zheng, F.C., Wen, W., Luo, J., Li, G.: Dynamic content caching based on actor-critic reinforcement learning for IoT systems. In: 2022 IEEE 96th Vehicular Technology Conference (VTC2022-Fall), pp. 1–6. IEEE (2022)

21. Meddeb, M., Dhraief, A., Belghith, A., Monteil, T., Drira, K.: How to cache in ICN-based IoT environments? In: 2017 IEEE/ACS 14th International Conference on Computer Systems and Applications (AICCSA), pp. 1117–1124. IEEE (2017)

22. Nasehzadeh, A., Wang, P.: A deep reinforcement learning-based caching strategy for internet of things. In: 2020 IEEE/CIC International Conference on Communications in China (ICCC), pp. 969–974 (2020). https://doi.org/10.1109/ICCC49849. 2020.9238811

23. Nath, S., Wu, J.: Deep reinforcement learning for dynamic computation offloading and resource allocation in cache-assisted mobile edge computing systems. Intell. Conv. Netw. **1**(2), 181–198 (2020)

24. Niesen, U., Shah, D., Wornell, G.W.: Caching in wireless networks. IEEE Trans. Inf. Theory **58**(10), 6524–6540 (2012)

25. Nomikos, N., Zoupanos, S., Charalambous, T., Krikidis, I.: A survey on reinforcement learning-aided caching in heterogeneous mobile edge networks. IEEE Access **10**, 4380–4413 (2022)

26. Nour, B.: ICN communication optimization for Internet of Things. Ph.D. thesis, Beijing Institute of Technology (2020)

27. Qiao, D., Guo, S., Liu, D., Long, S., Zhou, P., Li, Z.: Adaptive federated deep reinforcement learning for proactive content caching in edge computing. IEEE Trans. Parallel Distrib. Syst. **33**(12), 4767–4782 (2022)

28. Sadeghi, A., Wang, G., Giannakis, G.B.: Deep reinforcement learning for adaptive caching in hierarchical content delivery networks. IEEE Trans. Cogn. Commun. Netw. **5**(4), 1024–1033 (2019)

29. Schulman, J., Wolski, F., Dhariwal, P., Radford, A., Klimov, O.: Proximal policy optimization algorithms. arXiv preprint arXiv:1707.06347 (2017)

30. Sutar, A., Gaikwad, S., Bhadani, R., Dere, A., Domb, R., Malve, S.: Comparison and loss analysis of efficient optical routers. In: 2023 International Conference for Advancement in Technology (ICONAT), pp. 1–4 (2023). https://doi.org/10.1109/ ICONAT57137.2023.10080535

31. Tang, F., Chen, X., Rodrigues, T.K., Zhao, M., Kato, N.: Survey on digital twin edge networks (diten) toward 6G. IEEE Open J. Commun. Soc. **3**, 1360–1381 (2022)

32. Vlachou, E., Karras, C., Karras, A., Tsolis, D., Sioutas, S.: EVCA classifier: a MCMC-based classifier for analyzing high-dimensional big data. Information **14**(8) (2023). https://doi.org/10.3390/info14080451. https://www.mdpi.com/ 2078-2489/14/8/451

33. Wang, S., Zhang, X., Zhang, Y., Wang, L., Yang, J., Wang, W.: A survey on mobile edge networks: convergence of computing, caching and communications. IEEE Access **5**, 6757–6779 (2017)

34. Wang, X., Li, R., Wang, C., Li, X., Taleb, T., Leung, V.C.: Attention-weighted federated deep reinforcement learning for device-to-device assisted heterogeneous collaborative edge caching. IEEE J. Sel. Areas Commun. **39**(1), 154–169 (2020)

35. Wang, X., Wang, C., Li, X., Leung, V.C., Taleb, T.: Federated deep reinforcement learning for internet of things with decentralized cooperative edge caching. IEEE Internet Things J. **7**(10), 9441–9455 (2020)
36. Wei, Y., Yu, F.R., Song, M., Han, Z.: Joint optimization of caching, computing, and radio resources for fog-enabled IoT using natural actor-critic deep reinforcement learning. IEEE Internet Things J. **6**(2), 2061–2073 (2018)
37. Wu, B., Xu, K., Li, Q., Ren, S., Liu, Z., Zhang, Z.: Toward blockchain-powered trusted collaborative services for edge-centric networks. IEEE Netw. **34**(2), 30–36 (2020)
38. Wu, H., Nasehzadeh, A., Wang, P.: A deep reinforcement learning-based caching strategy for IoT networks with transient data. IEEE Trans. Veh. Technol. **71**(12), 13310–13319 (2022). https://doi.org/10.1109/TVT.2022.3199677
39. Wu, Q., Zhao, Y., Fan, Q., Fan, P., Wang, J., Zhang, C.: Mobility-aware cooperative caching in vehicular edge computing based on asynchronous federated and deep reinforcement learning. IEEE J. Sel. Topics Signal Process. **17**(1), 66–81 (2022)
40. Yao, J., Ansari, N.: Caching in dynamic IoT networks by deep reinforcement learning. IEEE Internet Things J. **8**(5), 3268–3275 (2020). https://doi.org/10.1109/JIOT.2020.3004394
41. Zahmatkesh, H., Al-Turjman, F.: Fog computing for sustainable smart cities in the IoT era: caching techniques and enabling technologies-an overview. Sustain. Urban Areas **59**, 102139 (2020)
42. Zameel, A., Najmuldeen, M., Gormus, S.: Context-aware caching in wireless IoT networks. In: 2019 11th International Conference on Electrical and Electronics Engineering (ELECO), pp. 712–717 (2019). https://doi.org/10.23919/ELECO47770.2019.8990647
43. Zhang, Y., et al.: Cooperative edge caching: a multi-agent deep learning based approach. IEEE Access **8**, 133212–133224 (2020)
44. Zhong, C., Gursoy, M.C., Velipasalar, S.: A deep reinforcement learning-based framework for content caching. In: 2018 52nd Annual Conference on Information Sciences and Systems (CISS), pp. 1–6. IEEE (2018)
45. Zhu, H., Cao, Y., Wang, W., Jiang, T., Jin, S.: Deep reinforcement learning for mobile edge caching: review, new features, and open issues. IEEE Netw. **32**(6), 50–57 (2018)

Real-Time Leakage Zone Detection in Water Distribution Networks: A Machine Learning-Based Stream Processing Algorithm

Domenico Garlisi[1,3]([✉]) [iD], Gabriele Restuccia[1,3] [iD], Ilenia Tinnirello[1,3] [iD],
Francesca Cuomo[2,3] [iD], and Ioannis Chatzigiannakis[2,3] [iD]

[1] University of Palermo, Palermo, Italy
{domeico.garlisi,gabriele.restuccia,ilenia.tinnirello}@unipa.it
[2] University of Rome "La Sapienza", Rome, Italy
{francesca.cuomo,ioannis.chatzigiannakis}@uniroma1.it
[3] CNIT Parma, Parma, Italy

Abstract. This work presents LEAKSTREAM, a novel approach for detecting leakages in water distribution networks by leveraging the power of clustering and stream processing techniques, combined with advanced machine learning approaches. Given the critical importance of efficient water management and the significant economic and environmental consequences of undetected leaks, it is crucial to develop innovative strategies that can accurately and promptly identify anomalies within distribution networks.

Our proposed method focuses on an algorithm that creates clusters of nodes in the water distribution network, taking into account their spatial proximity and hydraulic characteristics. We employ stream processing to efficiently handle large-scale real-time data generated from meters installed at consumer locations throughout the network.

The results of our study indicate that the proposed leakage detection algorithm effectively employs a generalization technique to detect events not included in the training data. We show performance in terms of precision and loss in the case of 75 different leakages positions in a water distribution network which extends in an area of 7×3.5 *sq km*. Furthermore, its capacity to process data at the edge and in real-time enables prompt responses and mitigation measures, thereby reducing the overall impact of leaks on both the environment and infrastructure.

Our results attain an average accuracy of detecting and localizing the zone of the leakages of about 98.6% when leakages are not present during the training of the ML models.

Keywords: WDN · water supply system · IoT · leakage detection · stream processing · k-means clustering · LoRaWAN · neural network

I. Chatzigiannakis and I. Karydis (Eds.): ALGOCLOUD 2023, LNCS 14053, pp. 86–99, 2024.
https://doi.org/10.1007/978-3-031-49361-4_5

1   Introduction

Worldwide water consumption is consistently increasing, with demand growing annually. Additionally, considering the issue of climate change, the globe is confronted with an anticipated 40% water deficit by 2030 [18]. For this reason, the optimization and digitalization of Water Distribution Networks (WDNs) are becoming key objectives in our modern society.

In recent years, the increasing availability of data from water meter sensors, coupled with advancements in data processing and Machine Learning (ML) techniques, has provided new opportunities for enhancing leakage detection capabilities. Data-driven approaches can significantly improve conventional methods by providing more accurate, timely, and scalable solutions. Moreover, emerging IoT Low Power Wide Area Network (LPWAN) technologies, together with ML solutions, can help monitor water consumption and automatically detect leakages. In this paper, we leverage stream processing combined with IoT and ML to deploy a smart and innovative leakage detection method in a WDN. Indeed, most of the current smart WDNs solutions just collect measurements from the smart meters and send the data to the cloud servers, in order to execute the intended analyses, in a centralised way.

This paper proposes LEAKSTREAM, a new solution to improve monitoring, leak management and prediction by exploiting stream processing capabilities in LPWAN networks. We will consider data-driven methodologies for detecting leakages in WDNs, focusing on innovative strategies that utilize real-time data from utility meters, clustering techniques, and advanced ML algorithms. Our approach supposes to use common IoT water sensors placed at the utility consumers, used to measure user water consumption and ML algorithms to process the data directly at the edge of the network in order to detect leakages. Our solution is a Supervised Classification problem where we attempt to predict if there is a leakage in a zone of the WDN. We propose a methodology to detect leakage events in a distributed way by running ML algorithms at the edges of the communication network, and we use k-means clustering and neural network models for leakage identification. Finally, we present case studies that demonstrate the practical benefits and effectiveness of data-driven approaches in a simulated scenario that reproduces a real-world WDN. The innovative aspects of this work are the following:

1. We present and validate a learning-based for smart WDN, named LEAK-STREAM, which leverages the measurements of user utility demand and pressure to detect leakages in WDN.
2. We propose an original algorithm, encompassing WDN and IoT network scenarios, including a stream processing framework. The algorithm extracts *"zones"* using clustering techniques and feeds measured data to train ML models. The trained model is able to generalize the WDN structure and detect the presence of leakages in the zone, even in the case of untrained ones.
3. We assess the robustness of LEAKSTREAM under different placements of the leakage positions that were not present during the training phase.

Our source code mostly uses the Python programming language, and each of those parts is available in a public repository [1]. In order to assess our results we use a simulation tool specifically tailored to match a WDN structure and collect the desired hydraulic measurements. Finally, we publicly released the dataset and the code implementation of the designed algorithm to allow repeatability and provide a performance benchmarking [1].

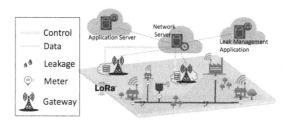

Fig. 1. LoRaWAN and WDN network architecture.

As shown in Fig. 1, a WDN consists of a series of interconnected links and nodes. Links represent pipes, while nodes comprise junctions, tanks, or reservoirs. Junctions are points that also function as demand points within the WDN. Tanks and reservoirs supply the hydraulic resources to the system, with tanks being finite water sources and reservoirs being infinite sources.

Due to the nature of WDNs, leakage characteristics tend to produce a similar impact in other collected measurements when positions are near. The goal of the proposed method is to detect leakages using only data collected from utility meters, without relying on flow sensors placed along pipes to monitor internal hydraulic flows. Instead, we put the focus on monitoring hydraulic flows that exclusively exit from the network as utility sources (demand at the junction). This view is justified by the current trend where any utility will be served from a smart meter in the near future [14].

Specifically, LEAKSTREAM works in two steps: i) first use k-means to cluster the WDN junctions in groups or zone with similar features and ii) use a Neural Network to classify the zone based on the correctness of the dynamic flow as affected or not by leakage. The defined model is supported by current literature in [15] and [16]. The authors established a fixed node merge threshold to combine nodes exhibiting similar leakage traits in order to improve classifier accuracy. Differently, we consider fewer features, introduce stream processing and simplify the ML model.

Selected Wireless Network Technology. There is no one-size-fits-all wireless technology for leakage detection, with different solutions being better suited for various use cases. IoT chips with low power consumption and long-distance communication capability are ideal for these purposes. Three trends in communication have been identified: WiFi-based networks, cellular networks, and LPWAN networks. LPWAN devices are expected to dominate the field [11]. However, it faces potential scalability issues in large-scale scenarios. This study targets the LoRaWAN technology [17] and proposes to address scalability issues by enabling real-time analysis and processing of the vast amounts of data generated by connected devices within the network edge. By streamlining data processing, the network can achieve improved performance and better resource allocation, consequently addressing the challenges associated with large-scale deployments.

As shown in Fig. 1, the LoRaWAN architecture relies on a star-of-star topology, where End Devices (EDs) connect with one or more Gateways (GWs) that forward packets to the Network Server (NS) and eventually to the corresponding IoT applications server. According to the considered scenario, LoRaWAN EDs are deployed in the WDN to collect data from junction nodes (water demand). Moreover, we leverage NebulaStream [23], an IoT stream-processing framework to enable processing data at the edge, with the aim of reducing the latency and the traffic on the backhaul [4]. This latter part is represented in Fig. 1 where the resources processing happens at the gateways controlled by the NS, which also plays a role in the remote processing coordinator. The rest of the paper is organized as follows. The related work is in Sect. 2. In Sect. 3 we detail the proposed leakage detection approach. The learning architecture, which represents the STREAMLEAK building blocks and the experimental setup is presented in Sect. 4, including the details of the stream processing design. Finally, the performance of the proposed approach is evaluated in Sect. 5. Conclusions are drawn in Sect. 6.

2 Related Work

As for data-driven leakage detection techniques for WDNs the most widely used approaches in the literature are prediction-classification methods [25]. One notable study by [16] focuses on leak localization in WDNs using Bayesian classifiers. The authors provide a technique that takes into account sensor noise, leak size uncertainty and demand uncertainty to calibrate the probability density functions for pressure residuals. Using case studies from the Hanoi and Nova Icaria networks, they show how a Bayesian classifier operates in locating leaks in real-time.

Another approach presented by [5] addresses leakage zone identification in WDNs through an iterative method based on machine learning. To find leakage zones, Authors use a combination of k-means clustering and a random forest classifier. Through iterations, the method refines the identification process, reduces the number of candidate leakage zones, and selects the minimum number of sensors for training the model. Different approaches, such as Support Vector Machines (SVMs), Long short-term memory (LSTM) recurrent neural network [21], k-NN classifiers or multi-layer neural networks have been investigated in [8] and [20], respectively. Convolutional neural networks (CNN) can be used to learn the different pressure residual maps [12]. Moreover, K-means clustering was used to divide the network into different k zones based on the pressure residual matrix generated by the hydraulic model [24]. Most of the time these

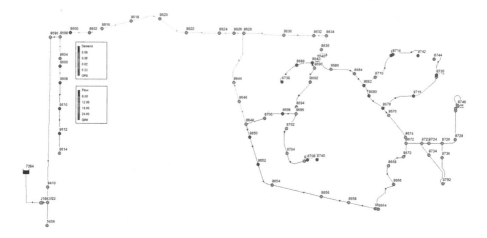

Fig. 2. Considered WDN branch with 75 junctions and 1 reservoir (junctions and flow measurements).

methods can not generalize the presence of leakage not considered during the training phase [9].

To consider the implementation of water leakage detection in a real WDN scenario, we face a high volume of data reaching the application server, which can be considered as a Big Data system. In LoRaWAN technology, k-means has been already used for profiling operations, in order to group devices according to their characteristics and position [19]. Cloud-based systems do not fully exploit IoT capabilities and present bottlenecks, while Fog-based solutions may lack resources when dealing with Big Data. Emerging distributed approaches balance processing operations by reducing data at the edge and performing more expensive computations in the cloud. This is achieved through mapping functions that aggregate local data and send only the results upstream. A large set of software frameworks have been designed or extended for dealing with this paradigm, among which Hadoop 2.0 [10], Spark [22] and Flink [3]. These frameworks are similar in terms of functionalities for optimizing the query process. NebulaStream is an example of a novel data processing platform that addresses heterogeneity, unreliability and scalability challenges in IoT systems. It includes an inference operator used from LEAKSTREAM to support edge processing.

3   Leakage Detection Problem

In our WDN hydraulic model we analyze the water flow using the Hardy-Cross method [6] that assumes that the water flow follows a distribution pattern where every junction adheres to the principle of continuity. The continuity equation dictates that the algebraic sum of flow rates in pipes converging at a node, along with any external flows, must be zero. To better formulate the concept, we used pre-defined network model offered by Open Water Analytics's community public

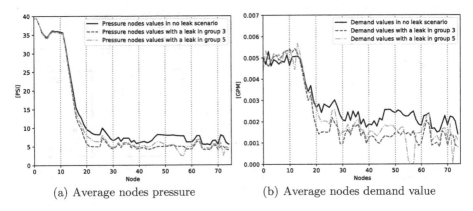

(a) Average nodes pressure   (b) Average nodes demand value

Fig. 3. Average pressure in Pound per square inch [PSI] (a) and demand value in Gallons per minute [GPM] (b) of 75 WDN nodes in three different scenarios, one without leakage (line) and two with leakage at different positions (dashed lines).

repository [2]. Specifically, we considered the sub-networks shown in Fig. 2. The network provides $n = 75$ junctions and $m = 1$ reservoirs. Each node is configured with a specific *base demand* pattern which represents the water request of the user during the whole simulation changing at a step size of an hour and evenly distributed in range. In WDNs, base demand and satisfied water requests are two distinct concepts related to the amount of water needed and the amount of water that can be successfully supplied to the consumers. In summary, while base demands represent the foreseen water consumption by users in a WDN, satisfied water request reflects the actual amount of water provided to them, taking into account the network's capacity and available resources and is labelled as demand value. In the network representation of Fig. 2, we can see that, for a specific measurement interval, two color scales are used to plot nodes demand values (color of the circle marker), and pipes flow (color of the nodes connection segment). The reservoir is positioned on the left side of the network (element with 7384 identifiers), with flow primarily moving from left to right. As we move further away from the reservoir, the total demand value and pressure at the junctions decrease due to the demand from left-side junctions. Figure 3 illustrates the average pressure and Fig. 3(b)) the demand values experienced at each node in our selected network, respectively. The black line represents the measured values when no leaks are present in the network, with nodes sorted by their position relative to the reservoir; farther nodes perceive lower pressure and lower demand value. The two dashed lines demonstrate the impact of the presence of two leaks, respectively. It can be observed that the average pressure increases as the position moves closer to the reservoir. The vertical dashed line provides cluster or zone separation.

In the outlined scenario, where flow balance cannot be achieved due to the lack of intermediate pipe sensors, leakages might not be detected by utility meter devices if the pipes operate under high pressure and the leakage effects are negli-

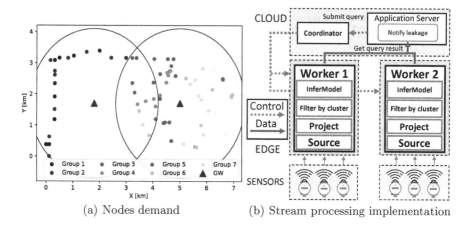

(a) Nodes demand   (b) Stream processing implementation

Fig. 4. Map of the nodes and GWs position, nodes are coloured according to the selected clustering, GWs are provided together with the coverage area (a). Example of deployed operators that implement LEAKSTREAM on GWs workers.

gible. Consequently, the proposed approach focuses on establishing a ML model that captures the physical hydraulic inner properties governing the flow within the zone where only part of the base demand is satisfied. LEAKSTREAM considers clusters of nodes where leakage presence produces a similar effect independently from its position in the cluster. Thus, rather than considering multiple leakage positions to train the ML model, we consider the effect of a generic leakage in the network and we train the ML model to recognize it.

The approach first requires the creation of clusters of nodes according to the proximity position of the network and to the trend of the two features' pressure and demand value on the cluster nodes. Furthermore, these features are used to train the model. We assumed that leaks occur only at a pipe of the network and we expect to create a model for each cluster.

We use the Water Network Tool for Resilience (WNTR) simulator [13] in order to generate our desired hydraulic data. WNTR is a Python package designed to simulate the WDN. WNTR is based on EPANET (US Environmental Protection Agency water NETwork), which is an open source software to model hydraulic and quality dynamics of a WDN [26]. It takes into account the topological structure of the pipeline system along with a set of initial conditions (e.g. pipe diameter) and rules of how the system is operated so that it can compute flows and pressures throughout the network for a specific period of time. The simulator can add leaks to the network using a leak model [7].

4   LEAKSTREAM: Distributed Leakage Detection

Our proposed approach relies on different entities. We use WNTR to generate a suitably large dataset to train and assess our ML model. The simulator generates a complete trace, with the status of each node and pipe over time. We then extract a subset of generated data (`timestamp, nodeID, demand_value, pressure, position`), together with the actual status of nodes, and use that to train the ML model whose input is the total set of measurements in a period of time, and whose output is a vector with the status `leakage/no-leakage` of each cluster.

In Fig. 4(a) we show the 2D data position of the clustering of the nodes extracted by the k-means algorithm, nodes belonging to the same cluster are represented with the same color. We employ Elbow and Silhouette Methods to find the best k number of clusters. Both are based on empirical methods where inter and intra-clustering node similarity functions are applied to evaluate better k value. We pick a range of candidate values of k, then apply k-Means clustering using each of the values of k to extract the best number of clusters that is $k = 7$. Algorithm features include average demand value and pressure rather than the node's position, for this reason, in the figure, nodes belonging to the same cluster are not properly in proximity.

We integrate a Supervised Classification model in which we try to predict if there is a leakage on the cluster. Using a classical approach, we have been able to build a feature matrix $\mathbf{X}$ and an output vector $\mathbf{y}$, suitable for being used for training and testing ML algorithms. We extract our training set (X $matrix$) with the following features: `demand_value, pressure and position` measured in the network cluster (Cartesian coordinates are considered for the position). Since this is a classification problem, our test set (y $vector$) contains just the Boolean `has_leak` field, reporting if that specific cluster is currently affected by a leak in some moment. We designed that the classifier takes as input features a matrix with $n \times t$ rows, and 4 columns, where n is the number of nodes present in the cluster and t the number of collected measures for each node in the considered time period. The classifier output is a vector with t number of elements that reports the prediction value for each reading interval. According to the provided input, the model can detect leakages at different intervals of time.

For the model definition, we consider a Neural Network with a densely connected hidden layer, a dropout layer to reduce overfitting, and an output sigmoid layer that returns the probability of a cluster being a leakage. We select 40 neurons for the hidden layer, evaluated by the 4×10, the features and average nodes per cluster respectively. Looking at the data distribution, for the training phase, we suppose that measures are collected hourly over a time period of 2 months, half part without leakage and half part with a single leakage with an average lost water flow rate of 0.05 GPM. We remark that the goal of the proposed approach is to use a single leakage position for each cluster to create a model able to generalize leakage detection at any position. To recreate the infer models we use 8 training dataset of 30 days, 7 with the presence of leakage and one without leakage. For each of the 7 leakage examined scenarios, we configure leakage position in proximity of a selected cluster node. For each cluster model we merge together the dataset without leakage and the dataset with the leakage. Finally, the dataset include $10,080$ observations obtained from $7 cluster \cdot 24 hours \cdot 30 days \cdot 2 scenario$, only 720 of them positive samples $24hours \cdot 30days$, they represent the observation of the cluster with leakage for one of the 2 scenarios. The ML model is fed with cluster aggregate data in a window time of 1 h and The result is a setup where positive examples contain a very low attendance rate. The produced dataset results are unbalanced with a value of 7.1% (720 : 10,080) of positive samples. Notice that the model is fitted using a batch size of 2048 samples which ensures that each batch has a good chance of containing a few positive samples. If the batch size was too small, they would likely have no leakage event to learn from. Thus, we set the output layer's bias to help with initial convergence.

The application of the model has been compared in terms of accuracy on the cluster leakage classification. Accuracy values are calculated after the fitting and prediction phases and after the confusion matrices generation. Specifically, to generate the confusion matrix, we extract the *True Positives (TP)*, *True Negatives (TN)*, *False Positives (FP)* and *False Negatives (FN)* values. False negatives and false positives are samples that were incorrectly classified. True negatives and true positives are samples that were correctly classified. Finally, accuracy is the percentage of examples correctly classified ($Accuracy = (TP + TN)/(TP + TN + FP + FN)$).

4.1   Stream Processing

LEAKSTREAM aims to reduce leakage detection latency by processing data at the edge and decreasing the amount of data transmitted over the network backhaul, thereby minimizing link latency to the central server. Different from the classical cloud paradigm, where data is gathered centrally for processing in a batch way. We propose to use sensor-fog-cloud scheme, which enables dynamic allocation of data stream processing across nodes from source to cloud. In this section, we present the implementation of the LEAKSTREAM algorithm based on the sensor-fog-cloud approach. In particular, we implement this approach in the *NebulaStream* platform [23].

According to the selected network topology, we find the best suitable GWs position to collect monitoring data. The considered GWs positions are shown in Fig. 4(a) (triangular markers are the nodes) together with the coverage area (represent by big blue circles). According to the coverage area, each GW is able to receive only a subset of the total WDN measurements.

NebulaStream allows the implementation of distributed queries by means of workers running on edge. As shown in Fig. 4(b), workers are responsible for moving the data flow hierarchically from source to sink, including the data sources, and applying different operators before forwarding the results in the output stream towards another worker or a data sink. The framework also includes a coordinator, running on the cloud, which exposes an interface for responding to external queries. The coordinator is responsible for the workload allocation on workers and query processing, taking into account the node capabilities and network topology. For the LoRaWAN network, we consider the resource capabilities present in the GWs as our edge layer. The GWs run a proxy agent and use it to feed the worker source. The activation by personalization method is configured in the LoRaWAN network to access the monitored information normally ciphered in the LoRaWAN protocol.

In our case, the Application Server implementing the scheme sends query requests to the NebulaStream coordinator by means of a REST interface. The coordinator orchestrates the execution of the query, according to the distributed availability of data and returns a result to the microservice by a message broker protocol. Queries are implemented by considering the NebulaStream available operators.

In Fig. 4(b), we depict blocks structure of our implementation, with a total of 2 workers (one for each GW). The figure also shows the operators that have been identified for data pre-processing and for supporting the algorithm. In the edge layer, the *source* operator connects the data stream and the *projection* operator for selecting a sub-group of data packet fields. Thus, the figure shows the *filter* operator, which is responsible for extracting all data referring to the same cluster and the infer model operator. The latter facilitates an inference procedure on the incoming data stream, requiring a pre-trained TensorFlow model provided through a function parameter. Lastly, at the cloud layer, classification results from network zones or clusters are consolidated. Subsequently, these results are forwarded to the application server, which is responsible for initiating the leakage alarm trigger. Finally, we also report the query, whose implementation in Java is summarized in the following code.

```
1   // Provide input parameter
2   String CLUSTER = ARG_PAR_1
3   List FEATURES_LIST = ARG_PAR_2
4   //create stream and select subset of fields
5   Query stream = new Query().from("WDN_STREAM")
6   stream.from(gatewaystream).project(FEATURES_LIST)
7       .filter(CLUSTER)
8       .inferModel(Objects.requireNonNull(
9           InferModel.class.getResourceAsStream("/model.tflite")))
10          .on(attribute(FEATURES_LIST)
11          .as(attribute("leakage_prediction", BasicType.FLOAT32));
12      .sink(new MQTTSink());
```

Four phases can be clearly distinguished in the code, it clarifies the concept of stream processing, by specifying the chain of operations: i) connecting to the main data stream and extracting relevant fields (FEATURES) from data (rows 6); ii) filter packets sent by the EDs at a given cluster (row 7); iii) the infermodel operator is applied by considering the TensorFlow lite saved model (row 9, 10 and 11); iv) finally, the sink operation is provided (row 12).

5 Performance Evaluation

One of the key objectives of the suggested method is to generalize the leakage position by inferred leakage at the clusters. The goal of LEAKSTREAM is to perform a TensorFlow model for each cluster. In this section, we report the evaluation performance of the suggested method when varying leakage positions. For each cluster model, we merge together the dataset without leakage and the dataset with leakage, finally, we split it into the train, validation, and test sets. The validation set is used during the model fitting to evaluate the loss and create TensorFlow model. The test set is used at the end to evaluate how the model generalizes to new data. This is especially important with imbalanced datasets where overfitting is a significant concern from the lack of training data.

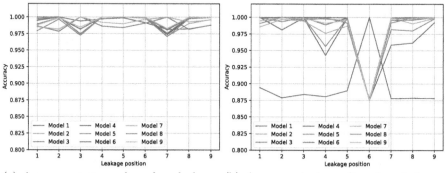

(a) Accuracy test results when leakages move around cluster 3

(b) Accuracy test results when leakages move around cluster 4

Fig. 5. Accuracy results of 9 models to infer leakage at different positions for cluster 3 (a) and cluster 4 (b). Models are trained by considering leakage position in all the cluster.

We note that when generating the training dataset, LEAKSTREAM considers a single leakage. To assess the impact of the chosen leakage position on the performance of the cluster model, Fig. 5 displays the accuracy of 9 different models (represented by different lines) in detecting the presence of 9 leakages located at 9 distinct positions within the same cluster. Each model has been trained by moving a single leakage around the pipes cluster. Specifically, Fig. 5(a) refers to cluster 3, and Fig. 5(b) refers to cluster 4 of the provided WDN. As can be noticed, the accuracy exceeds 95% in most of the cases. Clearly, system performance depends on the selected leakage position; for instance, in Fig. 5(b), model 6 achieves an accuracy above 90% for all considered leakages positions except position 6, where the accuracy is 100% since this position was used to create the training and validation set of this model.

As demonstrated above, the choice of leakage position for the model creation can influence the final performance of the generated model, making it crucial to define an evaluation method for selecting the leakage position. LEAKSTREAM computes the leakage position by starting from the cluster's centre of gravity and finding the nearest pipe where the leakage is set. In case of no WDN topology information are accessible, LEAKSTREAM treats real collected demand value

Table 1. Average performance results at the different clusters in case of a dataset of time duration of two months. The first two columns report loss and accuracy, while the remaining 4 columns summarize the actual vs. predicted labels, where values are percentages of TN, FP, FN and TP with respect to the total number of observations.

Cluster	Loss	Accuracy [%]	No leakage detected (TN)[%]	No leakage Incorrectly Detected (FP) [%]	Leakage Incorrectly Detected (FN) [%]	Leakage detected (TP) [%]
1	0.046	**99.730**	93.609	0.200	0.070	6.120
2	0.034	**98.344**	92.178	1.656	0.000	6.166
3	0.014	**99.785**	93.658	0.122	0.093	6.128
4	0.036	**99.223**	93.707	0.081	0.696	5.517
5	0.143	**97.971**	93.725	0.049	2.158	4.066
6	0.069	**97.672**	93.213	0.475	1.853	4.458
7	0.158	**97.260**	93.272	0.501	2.298	3.929
Average	**0.071**	**98.569**	**93.338**	**0.441**	1.024	**5.198**

and pressure trend as reference behaviours and generates a dataset with leakage events by using the general curve fitting method. To assess a complete performance evaluation of LEAKSTREAM, we train models using a dataset where, for each cluster, the leakage is positioned near the pipe closest to the centre of gravity. During testing, ten different leakage positions are considered based on the nodes' proximity. As for the model generalization we take into account a complete scenario where leakages that were not present during the training phases are added to the WDNs. To this aim, we consider 75 additional test set. We set the leakage position in proximity to each node present in the cluster. Table 1 presents the accuracy outcomes of this case study, taking again into account the previous 7 clusters. The first two columns report loss and average accuracy for each cluster, while the remaining 4 columns summarize the actual vs. predicted labels, where values are reported as percentages of TN, FP, FN and TP with respect to the total number of observations. As noticed from the table, the lower performance of 97.67% and 97.26% are obtained from clusters 6 and 7, although the average accuracy for the other clusters is more than 98.5%. Evidently, the models' performance decreases, especially when clusters are far from the hydraulic source, this is the situation of clusters 5, 6 and 7. Indeed, according to the trend of demand value and pressure, in these clusters, the nodes perceive more fluctuation which makes the detection of the model difficult. However, the precision is nevertheless maintained at a good level for all the clusters.

Finally, we note that for extremely complicated networks, performance can be maintained at a high level by developing many models that work in a subpart of the WDN as more simply separated districts.

6   Conclusion

This paper introduces LEAKSTREAM, an innovative solution that enhances monitoring, leak management, and prediction in water distribution networks

(WDNs) by leveraging stream processing within LPWAN networks, specifically focusing on LoRaWAN. The system utilizes IoT-based water sensors and machine learning algorithms to detect leaks at the network edge. The proposed method has been demonstrated to be robust and capable of identifying leaks even with incomplete or inaccurate information about the collected measurements from the entire WDN. Through simulations, the approach achieved an average accuracy of 99.2% for detecting nearby leakages and 97.6% for identifying leaks farther away from the hydraulic source. Furthermore, this approach does not rely on having complete knowledge of the WDN's topology and only requires data from normal smart meter operation behaviour.

Acknowledgment. This work was supported by the University of Palermo FFR 2023 (FONDO FINALIZZATO ALLA RICERCA DI ATENEO). This work was partially supported by the H2020 ELEGANT project (Grant agreement ID: 957286) and by the European Union under the Italian National Recovery and Resilience Plan (NRRP) of NextGenerationEU, partnership on "Telecommunications of the Future" (PE00000001 - program "RESTART") in the WITS (Watering IoTs) focused project.

References

1. LEAKSTREAM.   https://github.com/domenico-garlisi/LEAKSTREAM. Accessed 07 July 2023
2. OpenWaterAnalytics. https://raw.githubusercontent.com/OpenWaterAnalytics/ epanet-example-networks/master/epanet-tests/large
3. Alexandrov, A., et al.: The stratosphere platform for big data analytics. VLDB J. **23**(6), 939–964 (2014). https://doi.org/10.1007/s00778-014-0357-y
4. Amaxilatis, D., Chatzigiannakis, I., Tselios, C., Tsironis, N., Niakas, N., Papadogeorgos, S.: A smart water metering deployment based on the fog computing paradigm. Appl. Sci. **10**(6), 1965 (2020). https://doi.org/10.3390/app10061965
5. Chen, J., Feng, X., Xiao, S.: An iterative method for leakage zone identification in water distribution networks based on machine learning. Struct. Health Monit. **20**(4), 1938–1956 (2021)
6. Cross, H.: Analysis of flow in networks of conduits or conductors. Technical report. University of Illinois at Urbana Champaign, College of Engineering... (1936)
7. Crowl, D.A., Louvar, J.F.: Chemical Process Safety: Fundamentals with Applications. Pearson Education, London (2001)
8. Ferrandez-Gamot, L., et al.: Leak localization in water distribution networks using pressure residuals and classifiers. IFAC-PapersOnLine (2015). https://doi.org/10. 1016/j.ifacol.2015.09.531. 9th IFAC Symposium on Fault Detection, Supervision andSafety for Technical Processes SAFEPROCESS 2015
9. Garlisi, D., Restuccia, G., Tinnirello, I., Cuomo, F., Chatzigiannakis, I.: Leakage detection via edge processing in LoRaWAN-based smart water distribution networks. In: 2022 18th International Conference on Mobility, Sensing and Networking (MSN), pp. 223–230. IEEE (2022)
10. Ghemawat, S., Gobioff, H., Leung, S.T.: The google file system. In: Proceedings of the Nineteenth ACM Symposium on Operating Systems Principles, SOSP '03, pp. 29–43. Association for Computing Machinery, New York (2003). https://doi.org/ 10.1145/945445.945450

11. Islam, M.R., Azam, S., Shanmugam, B., Mathur, D.: A review on current technologies and future direction of water leakage detection in water distribution network. IEEE Access **10**, 107177–107201 (2022). https://doi.org/10.1109/ACCESS.2022.3212769

12. Javadiha, M., Blesa, J., Soldevila, A., Puig, V.: Leak localization in water distribution networks using deep learning. In: 2019 6th International Conference on Control, Decision and Information Technologies (CoDIT), pp. 1426–1431. IEEE (2019)

13. Klise, K.A., Bynum, M., Moriarty, D., Murray, R.: A software framework for assessing the resilience of drinking water systems to disasters with an example earthquake case study. Environ. Model. Softw. **95**, 420–431 (2017)

14. Randall, T., Koech, R.: Smart water metering technology for water management in urban areas. Water eJ **4**, 1–14 (2019)

15. Soldevila, A., Blesa, J., Tornil-Sin, S., Duviella, E., Fernandez-Canti, R., Puig, V.: Leak localization in water distribution networks using a mixed model-based/data-driven approach. Control. Eng. Pract. **55**, 162–173 (2016). https://doi.org/10.1016/j.conengprac.2016.07.006

16. Soldevila, A., Fernandez-Canti, R.M., Blesa, J., Tornil-Sin, S., Puig, V.: Leak localization in water distribution networks using bayesian classifiers. J. Process Control **55**, 1–9 (2017)

17. Sornin, N., Y.A.E.A.: LoRaWAN 1.1 Specification (2017). https://lora-alliance.org/resource-hub/lorawantm-specification-v11

18. Urama, K.E.A.: Options for decoupling economic growth from water use and water pollution: a report of the water working group of the UNEP international resource panel (2016)

19. Valtorta, J.M., Martino, A., Cuomo, F., Garlisi, D.: A clustering approach for profiling LoRaWAN IoT devices. In: Chatzigiannakis, I., De Ruyter, B., Mavrommati, I. (eds.) AmI 2019. LNCS, vol. 11912, pp. 58–74. Springer, Cham (2019). https://doi.org/10.1007/978-3-030-34255-5_5

20. Verde, C., Torres, L.: Modeling and Monitoring of Pipelines and Networks. Springer, Cham (2017)

21. Wang, X., Guo, G., Liu, S., Wu, Y., Xu, X., Smith, K.: Burst detection in district metering areas using deep learning method. J. Water Resour. Plan. Manag. **146**(6), 04020031 (2020)

22. Zaharia, M., Chowdhury, M., Franklin, M.J., Shenker, S., Stoica, I.: Spark: Cluster computing with working sets. In: Proceedings of the 2nd USENIX Conference on Hot Topics in Cloud Computing, HotCloud'10, p. 10 (2010)

23. Zeuch, S., et al.: The nebulastream platform: data and application management for the internet of things. In: Conference on Innovative Data Systems Research (CIDR) (2020)

24. Zhang, Q., Wu, Z.Y., Zhao, M., Qi, J., Huang, Y., Zhao, H.: Leakage zone identification in large-scale water distribution systems using multiclass support vector machines. J. Water Resour. Plan. Manag. **142**(11), 04016042 (2016)

25. Wan, X., Kuhanestani, P.K., Farmani, R., Keedwell, E.: Literature review of data analytics for leak detection in water distribution networks: a focus on pressure and flow smart sensors. J. Water Resour. Plan. Manage. **148**(10), 03122002 (2022)

26. Liu, J., Guoping, Y.: Iterative methodology of pressure-dependent demand based on EPANET for pressure-deficient water distribution analysis. J. Water Resour. Plan. Manage. **139**, 34–44 (2013). https://doi.org/10.1061/(ASCE)WR.1943-5452.0000227

Multi-agent Reinforcement Learning-Based Energy Orchestrator for Cyber-Physical Systems

Alberto Robles-Enciso[1]([⊠])(iD), Ricardo Robles-Enciso[2](iD),
and Antonio F. Skarmeta[1](iD)

[1] University of Murcia, 30100 Murcia, Murcia, Spain
{alberto.roblese,skarmeta}@um.com
[2] Technical University of Cartagena, 30202 Cartagena, Murcia, Spain
ricardo.roblese@edu.upct.es

Abstract. To reach a low-emission future it is necessary to change our behaviour and habits, and advances in embedded systems and artificial intelligence can help us. The smart building concept and energy management are key points to increase the use of renewable sources as opposed to fossil fuels. In addition, Cyber-Physical Systems (CPS) provide an abstraction of the management of services that allows the integration of both virtual and physical systems. In this paper, we propose to use Multi-Agent Reinforcement Learning (MARL) to model the CPS services control plane in a smart house, with the aim of minimising, by shifting or shutdown services, the use of non-renewable energy (fuel generator) by exploiting solar production and batteries. Moreover, our proposal is able to dynamically adapt its behaviour in real time according to the current and historical energy production, thus being able to address occasional changes in energy production due to meteorological phenomena or unexpected energy consumption. In order to evaluate our proposal, we have developed an open-source smart building energy simulator and deployed our use case. Finally several simulations are evaluated to verify the performance, showing that the reinforcement learning solution outperformed the heuristic-based solution in both power consumption and adaptability.

Keywords: Internet of Things · cyber-physical system · Edge Computing · reinforcement learning · energy orchestration

1 Introduction

In the last few decades, embedded computing technology has advanced dramatically, greatly simplifying the deployment of sensors and devices among us. The successful adoption of embedded systems in our society brings new paradigms such as Cloud Computing, Internet of Things and Edge Computing. In addition, the increase in the intelligence of devices, with the aim of enabling them to operate independently, is leading to the development of new intelligence systems [21,27].

I. Chatzigiannakis and I. Karydis (Eds.): ALGOCLOUD 2023, LNCS 14053, pp. 100–114, 2024.
https://doi.org/10.1007/978-3-031-49361-4_6

One of the approaches of increasing interest in Industry 4.0 is cyber-physical systems [19]. Cyber-physical systems (CPS) are computer control systems that deeply integrate computation and physical components to provide an abstraction of control components [4,9,29]. The integration of CPS in smart systems facilitates the optimisation of power consumption [17], which makes them particularly useful for the design of zero-energy buildings [3] and smart-grids.

Energy management is a fundamental aspect of all intelligent systems, in order to reduce carbon emissions [7]. It is also important to increase the use of renewable energy sources rather than fossil fuels, either by increasing the installation of clean energy sources or by shifting consumption from fossil to clean production schedules.

The aim of this work is the intelligent energy management of a smart building [6,10], as it is an important objective of the European energy strategy [11]. Among the artificial intelligence methods, Reinforcement Learning (RL) approaches are widely used as a machine learning control technique [16]. There are several proposals in the literature that use reinforcement learning to manage energy consumption by shifting energy consumption [15,30] to reduce the final consumption [14], battery usage [1,8,18] or price [13], some of them even use fuzzy reasoning techniques [2,31] and user-preference rules [5].

Nevertheless, there is no proposal that combines both CPS and RL for the energy management and optimisation of a zero-energy isolated house with fixed, shiftable and optional energy consumptions associated with different services. Therefore, the main contributions of this work as the following:

- We designed a smart home use case with a set of services deployed, which are both virtual services and associated with physical devices.
- We propose a control system for CPSs based on reinforcement learning that responds to the status of power generation in real time.
- We develop an open-source dynamic and extensible smart-building energy simulator to deploy our proposal.
- The performance of the proposal is compared with a dummy and greedy alternative, showing that the proposed solution is superior in performance and flexibility to the other algorithms.

The rest of the paper is organized as follows. In Sect. 2 we introduce the energy orchestrator with its main components. In Sect. 3 we present our approaches to energy management. Then, in Sect. 4 we evaluate the proposed algorithm and present the results. Finally, the conclusions and future work are drawn in Sect. 5.

2   Energy Orchestrator

Our proposed system consists of an isolated house that has no external energy sources (grid) and therefore relies on solar panels, batteries and a generator. Energy management is crucial to avoid draining the batteries overnight and to take advantage of peak solar generation, therefore we design a control plane for the services that will adjust the status of the services according to energy production and consumption. The control plane is deployed over the system as a service orchestrator focusing on energy management.

The services managed by the orchestrator are both virtual (*video streaming*) and physical (*fridge, pool pump*) services, and are therefore modelled as cyber-physical services with a defined power consumption per hour (*Wh*) and an execution rule (*on/off timetable and maximum run time*).

In addition, CPS services can be separated into two groups depending on whether the orchestrator manages them intelligently. The Non-Manageable services are those that the orchestrator cannot dynamically control their operation, so it is restricted to control their on/off switching according to their defined daily execution schedule (*execution rule*). On the contrary, manageable services are those that the orchestrator can manage intelligently, shutting them down when needed (*low energy or unexpected load*) and shifting their execution (*peak solar generation*) according to the service priority and energy status.

Furthermore, the orchestrator also considers the existence of unexpected events that make energy supply more complex and force to take actions to reduce or shift energy consumption. For example, unexpected events can be the reduction of solar production on cloudy days, the punctual connection of a high power demand device to the system's power grid or the complete draining of the batteries. Figure 1 summarises the proposed system components and some example services.

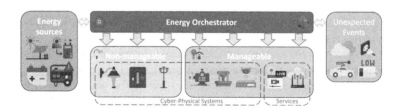

Fig. 1. Proposed System

3 Proposed Approaches

In this section we present our energy orchestrator approaches. Figure 2 provides an overview of the architecture of the proposed control algorithms. The energy orchestrator receives every minute information about the state of energy generation and consumption of the services provided by the simulator or real-world sensors. At each information update the orchestrator generates a set of events that it sends to the control plane where the main interface of the service controller receives it.

The service controller will collect event information and then make control decisions on the services in each timeslot according to the behaviour of the specific controller implementation. Timeslots are user-defined time intervals, e.g. 60 min, where the control algorithm will only collect information for decision making at the beginning of the next timeslot. In the following subsections we will explain the proposed methods in detail.

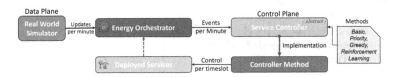

Fig. 2. Orchestrator architecture

3.1 Basic Approach

The most basic service orchestration algorithm we propose is the Basic method, which is limited to keep the services always on according to their execution rules. Therefore, in each timeslot the controller will iterate through the list of deployed services and for each of them check its execution rule to determine if it can be switched on or not.

This method is neither practical nor efficient but it provides an upper bound on the bad performance of the methods that we will use for comparison with other solutions in the results section. Furthermore, this method can be seen as a comparison with an ordinary scenario where there is no service orchestrator and the services execution rules are controlled by standard plug-in time switches.

3.2 Greedy Approach

A common technique for solving computational problems are Greedy algorithms, which are based on the use of heuristics to directly determine sub-optimal solutions. The major advantage of these methods is that they require little computational resources and execution time to achieve local solutions that are often very close to the optimal solution.

As an alternative and more dynamic approach to the previous one we have designed an algorithm that activates or deactivates services by comparing their heuristic value with the heuristic value of the environment. Consequently, in each timeslot the algorithm will determine the heuristic value of the environment and the heuristic value of each service to compare them and turn off all services that have a value below the environment value. The heuristic value of the environment is defined as a threshold given by the square of the inverse battery level. On the other hand, the value of each service is defined as the product of a constant, the square root of its priority, and the power of eight of its consumption relative to the battery. The complete control process for each service is detailed in 1.

Algorithm 1: Greedy Algorithm per Service

Parameters: daily minimum battery level percentage mB, trade-off constant C, priority of the service p, power consumption of the service pC and the total battery storage capacity bC

1 **begin**
2   **for** *each timeslot t* **do**
3       $threshold \leftarrow (100 - mB)^2$
4       $heuristic \leftarrow C * \sqrt{p} * (1 - (pC/bC))^8$
5   **if** *heuristic < threshold* **then**
6 | Turn off the service
7   **else**
8 | Turn on the service
9   **end**
10   Wait until the end of the time slot
11   **end**
12 **end**

3.3   Reinforcement Learning Approach

As seen in the literature [22,28], one of the most promising artificial intelligence methods for dynamic control of autonomous systems is reinforcement learning, which has been shown to be much more effective than other AI and heuristics approaches [12,20] in real-time control system. Therefore, we propose to use multi-agent reinforcement learning to design the CPS service orchestrator. Thus, each service will run an RL agent that will make control decisions locally to optimise a global reward.

RL agents are implemented as a Q-Leaning model-free algorithm, so each of them will store a Q-table that will be updated based on local rewards, status and actions. At each control time step of an episode, the agent will decide a control action ($a_t \in A = \{0,1\}$), whether to turn off (*action 0*) or turn on (*action 1*) the service in for that time step. The decision will depend on the environment, which is based on the battery percentage, the minimum daily battery percentage and the realtime energy available, calculated as the difference between energy production and energy consumption in Wh.

Classical Q-Learning algorithms require a finite state space, so it is necessary to discretize continuous values of the environment before using them. The discretisation process of the state parameters is summarised in Fig. 3.

The learning process uses a Q-Value table to store and query the value of the Q-function for each state and action. When an action is performed, the new Q-Value in the table is updated according to the following one-step Q update formula:

$$Q(s_t, a_t) = (1 - \alpha)\, Q(s_t, a_t) + \alpha\, (C_t + \gamma \min_a Q(s_{t+1}, a)) \tag{1}$$

The reward obtained after the execution of an action is a piecewise function of two elements that depends on the action taken, the parameters of the service

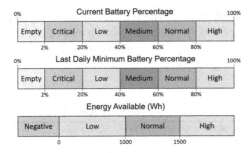

Fig. 3. Discretisation of state parameters

and also on the new state of the environment. Thereby, the reward of service "**s**" at time "**t**" is is formulated as the following weighted sum between the service priority (S_p), the current operating time (S_{rt}), the waiting time (S_{wt}), the remaining battery level (B_t), the min. daily battery level (B_t^m) and the generator usage (G_t):

$$
C_t = \begin{cases} \beta_2 S_{wt} - \beta_4 B_t^m & a = 0 \\ \beta_0 S_p + \beta_1 S_{rt} + \beta_2 S_{wt} + \beta_3 B_t + \beta_4 B_t^m + \beta_5 G_t & a = 1 \end{cases} \tag{2}
$$

where each β_x is the trade-off constant for each parameter.

The control policy follows a decay ε-greedy approach, thus the best action, the one with the higher Q-Value, will only be selected if a random number e is greater than or equal to ε, otherwise the action is chosen randomly from the set of feasible actions. Since the policy is *decay*, the value of ε will be reduced by the simulation time (*to one-tenth per week*) and the priority of the service (*higher priority higher reduction*).

Regarding the workflow of the method, the control process divides the operating time into slots of fixed duration. In the first minute of each timeslot, the decision-making algorithm is executed for the current state of the environment, after that the algorithm waits until the last minute of the timeslot to determine the reward for the action taken based on the average state of the waiting time. This control loop is repeated by each agent continuously until the end of the simulation. Figure 4 illustrates the described behaviour.

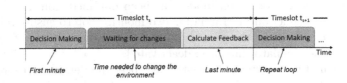

Fig. 4. Timeslot structure of the RL control process

Therefore, each agent will run the RL algorithm independently and synchronised with the global timeslots to update at the end of each one the local reward of its actions. The proposed multi-agent solution based on decay ε-greedy Q-Learning is shown in Algorithm 2.

Algorithm 2: Decay ε-greedy Q-Learning Algorithm

Parameters: discount factor γ, learning rate α, exploration rate ε and weighting parameters β

1 **begin**
2   **for** *each timeslot t* **do**
3   Observe actual state s_t
4   Determine feasible action set A' from A
5        $e \leftarrow$ random number from $[0,1]$
6        $\varepsilon' \leftarrow \varepsilon \div S_p(1 + \frac{simulationMinute}{1120})$
7   **if** $e < \varepsilon'$ **then**
8            $a_t \leftarrow$ randomly select an action from A'
9   **else**
10          $a_t \leftarrow \arg \min_{a \in A'} Q(s_t, a)$
11   **end**
12   Execute energy management action a_t
13   Wait for next feedback step
14   Observe new state s_{t+1}
15   Calculate reward C_t by (2)
16   Update $Q(s_t, a_t)$ according to (1)
17   **end**
18 **end**

---

4 Simulations Results and Discussion

In this section the performance of the proposed solution is analyzed using the results of a smart house simulator. The detailed simulation results are available in our GitHub repository [23] and the source code of the simulator implemented is also available in our Github repository [24].

4.1 Simulation Setup

To verify our proposal, we have configured the aforementioned simulator to emulate a house with different energy sources and a set of CPS services. The characteristics of the house are summarised in Table 1 and the parameters of the reinforcement learning algorithm are shown in Table 2.

The solar energy production model has been obtained from a real dataset of solar energy production in Murcia for two months [26] To ensure a fair comparison between methods, the procedural option to randomly modify the solar generation in the simulator has been deactivated.

In addition, two unexpected events have been implemented to verify the performance of the methods in critical situations. The first one consists of simulating cloudy weather for the first four days so the solar output drops to 80%. The second one simulates the occasional switch-on during 10:30 to 12:00 of a high-consumption device (1.2kWh and 1.8kWh).

Table 1. Characteristics of the simulated house

Parameter	Value
Simulated Time	25 d
Procedural data generation	Disabled
Battery capacity	7000 Wh
Solar peak production	2200 W
Cloudy days	First 4 d
Cloudy solar production	80% of sunny days
Unexpected load days	4th, 13th, 17th and 22nd
Unexpected load (kWh)	1.2, 1.2, 1.8 and 1.8
Unexpected load time	During 10:30 a.m. and 12:00 p.m

Table 2. Reinforcement learning algorithm parameters

Parameter / RL Algorithm	Single
Timeslot	60m
Learning rate α	0.2
Discount factor γ	0.8
Initial ε	0.2
Initial Q-Value (Off, On)	0 and 50
Value of β_x	50, 0.02, −0.01, −40, −200, −2000

Table 3. CPS services deployed

Service	Smart	Priority	Load	Rule
Fence lights	No	–	15 Wh	8pm-8am
Facade lights	No	–	10 Wh	8pm-8am
Fridge	No	–	120 Wh	All time
CCTV DVR	Yes	10	20 Wh	All time
Internet	Yes	8	40 Wh	All time
Pool Pump	Yes	4	600 Wh	9am-5pm (max 3h)
Streaming Services	Yes	2	30 Wh	All time
Fountain	Yes	1	35 Wh	9am-3pm

Finally, to demonstrate the behaviour of the energy orchestrator, a set of CPS services, both manageable and unmanageable, are deployed. Table 3 lists the deployed services showing the consumption and run rules for each of them.

4.2   Tested Methods

Using the simulator, we have obtained a complete set of data about the performance of the orchestrator and the energy consumption and production for 25 d. We have tested three control algorithms for the orchestrator, the first one called "**Basic**" does not perform any intelligent control of the services, it only turns on and off the services according to its running rules. The second is a **Greedy** method that is based on comparing the value of a dynamic heuristic that depends on the state of the environment with the heuristic value of each service, in case the service has a lower value it is turned off.

Lastly, the third one is the multi-agent **RL** algorithm explained before which dynamically decides whether to turn services off or on at each timeslot (subject to execution rules). Due to the nature of RL algorithms, the agent needs to gradually learn the best actions to take based on the rewards. For this reason, the algorithm requires repeating the simulation several times (saving the Q-tables) to progressively converge to the best policy. In our scenario the simulation had to be repeated five times in order to obtain the best solution.

4.3   Experimental Results and Analysis

The most important metrics to consider when evaluating each method are the average daily percentage of execution of each service (relative to its maximum time) and the final energy consumption of the generator, since using the generator is considered exceptional and should be avoided as much as possible. Table 4 shows the performance of each method in the simulator according to the parameters mentioned above.

Table 4. Performance of methods

	Basic	Greedy	RL	RL5
CCTV DVR	100%	100%	99.8%	100%
Internet	100%	100%	100%	100%
Pool Pump	100%	72.0%	88%	70.7%
Streaming Services	100%	100%	100%	99.2%
Fountain	100%	49.3%	98.7%	99.3%
Generator (Watts)	*20180*	*7502*	*14680*	*7335*

As shown in the table, the Dummy method represents the worst possible performance as it keeps all services on, therefore the generator consumption result of this method serves as the upper bound of the methods to be compared.

On the other hand, the Greedy method offers superior final performance concerning the consumption of the generator and by keeping the services on as much as possible. This is due to the use of dynamic heuristics that change according to the energy state, shutting down all services that have a lower value. Thus, when solar production is low or the battery reaches critical levels, the lowest priority services with the highest consumption are preferentially switched off (e.g. pool pump). The disadvantage of this method is the low dynamism, as the trade-off between priority, consumption, execution time and energy status is manually defined and does not easily adapt to changes in the system.

In contrast, the method based on reinforcement learning is completely flexible as it continuously adapts to changes and does not need to define any heuristics beforehand. The drawback is the need to repeat several times its execution (episodes) until the algorithm converges (learns) to the optimal solution. For that reason, in the table are shown to compare the result of the simulation with the initial RL method (without knowledge) and the result after running the simulation 5 times keeping the Q-tables of each agent.

As can be seen, the method without initial knowledge hardly turns off the services as it does not yet know the most appropriate actions to take, which leads to a high generator consumption. On the contrary, the trained method achieves the best solution as its generator usage is the lowest while keeping the services on as much as possible. The proposed method not only adapts in real time to unexpected events, it is also able to shift the execution of scheduled services to the hours of highest solar production or to the hours it estimates to be the most suitable.

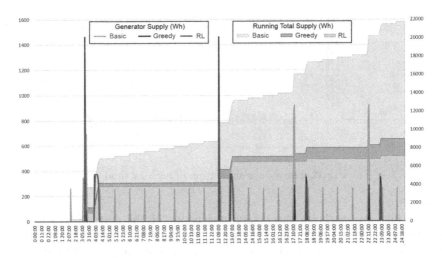

Fig. 5. Comparison of generator usage of each method

To graphically summarise the comparison between the methods according to their generator usage, Fig. 5 shows the punctual and the aggregate usage of the generator in Wh during the simulation execution.

The Dummy method uses the generator continuously every night as the batteries run out of energy. However, the Greedy method reduces the use of the generator only to occasions where unexpected consumption occurs. Similarly, the RL method only uses the generator when the energy production is not sufficient due to unexpected consumption, but it also manages to minimise the use of the generator by shifting or limiting the execution time of the energy-intensive services.

Figure 6 shows a detailed comparison of each method in a three-day segment of the simulation, where the behaviour of each algorithm in different situations can be more precisely appreciated. Each graph in the figure shows the consumption of the active services in each hour (timeslot) combined with the battery level (per mille) and the energy consumption (Wh).

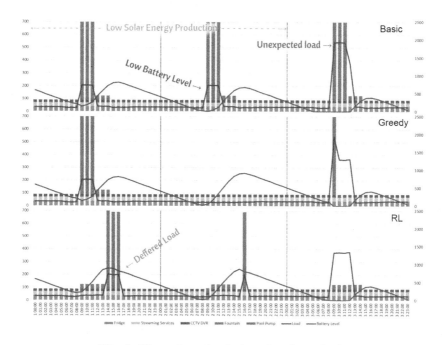

Fig. 6. Three days simulation of each method

The first graph shows the default behaviour of the system, in which the services are turned on according to their execution rules, causing the system to run out of energy during peak hours on both the second and third days. Also, on the third day, an unexpected consumption of 1.2 kWh occurs.

The second graph shows how the Greedy method detects the low battery status of the second day in order not to turn on any services with low priority. In addition, during the unexpected consumption on the third day it also turns off the low priority services to save energy.

The last graph shows how the RL algorithm is able to dynamically adapt the execution of the services to reduce the use of the generator while maximising the running time. One of the most important results of the proposed method is the shift of the pool pump service to the period of highest battery level and solar production. Also, the partial turn-on of the pump service in case of detecting a low energy production level or total turn-off in case of unexpected high consumption proves the proper adaptive behaviour of the algorithm.

And finally, the complete simulation result of 25 d is shown in Fig. 7 in the same format as the previous figure. Both the Greedy and the RL methods avoid the continuous discharge of the batteries due to the unexpected load, but the RL approach constantly demonstrates its adaptive behaviour by shifting the energy consumption of some services or performing partial or intermittent power cycles when the energy conditions is critical.

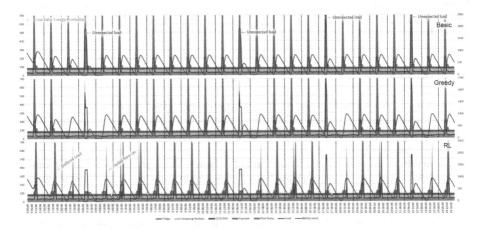

Fig. 7. Twenty-five days simulation of each method

5   Conclusion and Future Work

This paper proposes the design of a smart house service orchestrator intending to reduce the use of non-renewable energy. The energy orchestrator manages services modelled as Cyber-Physical System and we propose to use of a multi-agent reinforcement algorithm to intelligently and dynamically control the energy usage of the services. Therefore, we formulate the environment and the management of each CPS service as independent Q-Learning agents that will perform actions and receive feedback on each timeslot.

To verify the performance of the proposed method, an open-source simulator is also developed in which a particular scenario is deployed to compare the proposed solution with a heuristic-based and a dummy-based one.

The experimental results show that our proposed method is superior to the heuristic-based and also achieves the intended autonomous and dynamic behaviour without any guidance. In addition, the source code of the simulator and the results of the simulations are available in our GitHub repository for verification and reproducibility of the results.

However, we consider that the performance of our proposal can be improved using neural networks (DQL) to overcoming the Q-Leaning limitations such as a low number of states and discrete variables. Furthermore, the architecture of the orchestrator could be enhanced to provide a passive knowledge transfer model following the multi-layer RL proposal of our previous work on tasks offloading in edge computing [25].

Acknowledgements. This work was supported by the FPI Grant 21463/FPI/20 of the Seneca Foundation in Region of Murcia (Spain) and partially funded by FLUIDOS project of the European Union's Horizon Europe Research and Innovation Programme under Grant Agreement No. 101070473 and the ONOFRE project (Grant No. PID2020-112675RB-C44) funded by MCIN/AEI/10.13039/501100011033.

References

1. Abedi, S., Yoon, S.W., Kwon, S.: Battery energy storage control using a reinforcement learning approach with cyclic time-dependent markov process. Inter. J. Electrical Power Energy Syst. **134**, 107368 (2022). https://doi.org/10.1016/j.ijepes.2021.107368
2. Alfaverh, F., Denai, M., Sun, Y.: Demand response strategy based on reinforcement learning and fuzzy reasoning for home energy management. IEEE Access (2020). https://doi.org/10.1109/ACCESS.2020.2974286
3. Belussi, L., et al.: A review of performance of zero energy buildings and energy efficiency solutions. J. Building Eng. **25**, 100772 (2019). https://doi.org/10.1016/j.jobe.2019.100772
4. Cao, K., Hu, S., Shi, Y., Colombo, A.W., Karnouskos, S., Li, X.: A survey on edge and edge-cloud computing assisted cyber-physical systems. IEEE Trans. Industr. Inf. **17**(11), 7806–7819 (2021). https://doi.org/10.1109/TII.2021.3073066
5. Chen, S.J., Chiu, W.Y., Liu, W.J.: User preference-based demand response for smart home energy management using multiobjective reinforcement learning. IEEE Access **9**, 161627–161637 (2021). https://doi.org/10.1109/ACCESS.2021.3132962
6. Farzaneh, H., Malehmirchegini, L., Bejan, A., Afolabi, T., Mulumba, A., Daka, P.P.: Artificial intelligence evolution in smart buildings for energy efficiency. Applied Sci. **11**(2) (2021). https://doi.org/10.3390/app11020763
7. Gielen, D., Boshell, F., Saygin, D., Bazilian, M.D., Wagner, N., Gorini, R.: The role of renewable energy in the global energy transformation. Energ. Strat. Rev. **24**, 38–50 (2019). https://doi.org/10.1016/j.esr.2019.01.006
8. Kell, A.J.M., McGough, A.S., Forshaw, M.: Optimizing a domestic battery and solar photovoltaic system with deep reinforcement learning. CoRR abs arXiv:2109.05024 (2021)
9. Khujamatov, K., Reypnazarov, E., Khasanov, D., Akhmedov, N.: Networking and computing in internet of things and cyber-physical systems. In: 2020 IEEE 14th International Conference on Application of Information and Communication Technologies (AICT), pp. 1–6 (2020). https://doi.org/10.1109/AICT50176.2020.9368793

10. Kumar, A., Sharma, S., Goyal, N., Singh, A., Cheng, X., Singh, P.: Secure and energy-efficient smart building architecture with emerging technology iot. Comput. Commun. **176**, 207–217 (2021). https://doi.org/10.1016/j.comcom.2021.06.003

11. Kylili, A., Fokaides, P.A.: European smart cities: the role of zero energy buildings. Sustain. Urban Areas **15**, 86–95 (2015). https://doi.org/10.1016/j.scs.2014.12.003

12. Lee, H., Song, C., Kim, N., Cha, S.W.: Comparative analysis of energy management strategies for hev: dynamic programming and reinforcement learning. IEEE Access **8**, 67112–67123 (2020). https://doi.org/10.1109/ACCESS.2020.2986373

13. Li, Y., Wang, R., Yang, Z.: Optimal scheduling of isolated microgrids using automated reinforcement learning-based multi-period forecasting. IEEE Trans. Sustainable Energy **13**(1), 159–169 (2022). https://doi.org/10.1109/TSTE.2021.3105529

14. Liu, Y., Zhang, D., Gooi, H.B.: Optimization strategy based on deep reinforcement learning for home energy management. CSEE J. Power Energy Syst. **6**(3), 572–582 (2020). https://doi.org/10.17775/CSEEJPES.2019.02890

15. Lu, R., Hong, S.H., Yu, M.: Demand response for home energy management using reinforcement learning and artificial neural network. IEEE Trans. Smart Grid **10**(6), 6629–6639 (2019). https://doi.org/10.1109/TSG.2019.2909266

16. Mason, K., Grijalva, S.: A review of reinforcement learning for autonomous building energy management. Comput. Elect. Eng. **78**, 300–312 (2019). https://doi.org/10.1016/j.compeleceng.2019.07.019

17. Mazumder, S.K., Kulkarni, A., Sahoo, E.A.: A review of current research trends in power-electronic innovations in cyber-physical systems. IEEE J. Emerging Selected Topics Power Electronics **9**(5), 5146–5163 (2021). https://doi.org/10.1109/JESTPE.2021.3051876

18. Mbuwir, B.V., Ruelens, F., Spiessens, F., Deconinck, G.: Battery energy management in a microgrid using batch reinforcement learning. Energies **10**(11) (2017). https://doi.org/10.3390/en10111846

19. Mosterman, P., Zander, J.: Industry 4.0 as a cyber-physical system study. Softw. Syst. Modeling **15** (2016). https://doi.org/10.1007/s10270-015-0493-x

20. Nazib, R.A., Moh, S.: Reinforcement learning-based routing protocols for vehicular ad hoc networks: a comparative survey. IEEE Access **9**, 27552–27587 (2021). https://doi.org/10.1109/ACCESS.2021.3058388

21. Radanliev, P., De Roure, D., Van Kleek, M., Santos, O., Ani, U.P.D.: Artificial intelligence in cyber physical systems. AI & Soc. **36** (2021). https://doi.org/10.1007/s00146-020-01049-0

22. Recht, B.: A tour of reinforcement learning: The view from continuous control. ArXiv arXiv:1806.09460 (2019)

23. Robles-Enciso, A.: MA-RL CPS Simulations results (2022). https://github.com/alb1183/MARL-CPS-results/tree/main/Conference

24. Robles-Enciso, A.: Sim-PowerCS Simulator (2022). https://github.com/alb1183/Sim-PowerCS/tree/Conference

25. Robles-Enciso, A., Skarmeta, A.F.: A multi-layer guided reinforcement learning-based tasks offloading in edge computing. Comput. Netw. **220**, 109476 (2023). https://doi.org/10.1016/j.comnet.2022.109476

26. Robles-Enciso, R.: Personal Weather Station - Casa Ruinas - IALGUA2 (2022). https://www.wunderground.com/dashboard/pws/IALGUA2

27. Schranz, M., et al.: Swarm intelligence and cyber-physical systems: concepts, challenges and future trends. Swarm Evol. Comput. **60**, 100762 (2021). https://doi.org/10.1016/j.swevo.2020.100762

28. Schreiber, T., Netsch, C., Baranski, M., Müller, D.: Monitoring data-driven reinforcement learning controller training: a comparative study of different training strategies for a real-world energy system. Energy Build. **239**, 110856 (2021). https://doi.org/10.1016/j.enbuild.2021.110856

29. Serpanos, D.: The cyber-physical systems revolution. Computer **51**(3), 70–73 (2018). https://doi.org/10.1109/MC.2018.1731058

30. Xu, X., Jia, Y., Xu, Y., Xu, Z., Chai, S., Lai, C.S.: A multi-agent reinforcement learning-based data-driven method for home energy management. IEEE Trans. Smart Grid **11**(4), 3201–3211 (2020). https://doi.org/10.1109/TSG.2020.2971427

31. Zhou, S., Hu, Z., Gu, W., Jiang, M., Zhang, X.P.: Artificial intelligence based smart energy community management: a reinforcement learning approach. CSEE J. Power Energy Syst. **5**(1), 1–10 (2019). https://doi.org/10.17775/CSEEJPES.2018.00840

Clustering-Based Numerosity Reduction for Cloud Workload Forecasting

Andrea Rossi[1]([✉])[iD], Andrea Visentin[2][iD], Steven Prestwich[2][iD],
and Kenneth N. Brown[2][iD]

[1] SFI CRT in Artificial Intelligence, University College Cork, Cork, Ireland
`a.rossi@cs.ucc.ie`
[2] School of Computer Science, University College Cork, Cork, Ireland
`andrea.visentin@ucc.ie`, {`s.prestwich,k.brown`}`@cs.ucc.ie`

Abstract. Finding smaller versions of large datasets that preserve the same characteristics as the original ones is becoming a central problem in Machine Learning, especially when computational resources are limited, and there is a need to reduce energy consumption. In this paper, we apply clustering techniques for wisely selecting a subset of datasets for training models for time series prediction of future workload in cloud computing. We train Bayesian Neural Networks (BNNs) and state-of-the-art probabilistic models to predict machine-level future resource demand distribution and evaluate them on unseen data from virtual machines in the Google Cloud data centre. Experiments show that selecting the training data via clustering approaches such as Self Organising Maps allows the model to achieve the same accuracy in less than half the time, requiring less than half the datasets rather than selecting more data at random. Moreover, BNNs can capture uncertainty aspects that can better inform scheduling decisions, which state-of-the-art time series forecasting methods cannot do. All the considered models achieve prediction time performance suitable for real-world scenarios.

Keywords: Cloud Computing · Workload Prediction · Clustering · Bayesian Neural Network · Deep Learning

1 Introduction

As many companies are migrating their services to the cloud, the demand for resources in cloud computing platforms is continuously growing, with a market size of USD 545.8 billion in 2022 and expected to grow to USD 1,240.9 billion by 2027 [26]. To make more efficient use of limited resources, predicting near-term demand is becoming ever more important. Providers aim to maximise their profit while correctly predicting customers' requests and managing resources efficiently while limiting the environmental impact of CO_2 emissions and pollution [1].

Time series prediction of future workload in cloud computing has been widely studied for more than twenty years [8,10,11,42]. Recent research has shifted to

I. Chatzigiannakis and I. Karydis (Eds.): ALGOCLOUD 2023, LNCS 14053, pp. 115–132, 2024.
https://doi.org/10.1007/978-3-031-49361-4_7

probabilistic forecasts to provide a more comprehensive picture and to help resource scheduler decisions [27,28]. Time series probabilistic forecast allows providers to consider uncertainty and noise while guaranteeing high accuracy.

The emergence of Deep Learning (DL) and Big Data has introduced new approaches for enhancing the ability to generalize using large datasets to train more sophisticated and precise prediction models [6,38]. However, when computational resources for training Deep Learning (DL) models are limited, it is important to carefully select the data used for training. The goal is to find a smaller subset of the original dataset that retains its characteristics. This allows a model to be trained with the same accuracy as when using a larger dataset but with reduced energy consumption and faster training time. Unsupervised clustering[1] has been proven to be a powerful tool for dividing workload datasets into several groups and training independent forecasting models for each of them [13,49].

In this paper, we use clustering approaches to group workload datasets into groups that share similar patterns. Then, we select a subset of datasets from each cluster for training DL probabilistic predictive models to accurately and jointly forecast CPU and memory usage demand distributions and compare it to a random selection of the non-clustered training sets. We analyse the performance of a Hybrid Bayesian Neural Network (HBNN) [38], and state-of-the-art predicting models DeepAR [40] by Amazon and Temporal Fusion Transformer (TFT) [23] by Google.

From the output probability distribution, we compute confidence intervals. We use their upper bounds to estimate the total predicted resources needed to meet the demand with a level of confidence and relate it to the percentage of correctly predicted requests. We evaluate the predictive methods using 29-day load datasets of 2,500 machines from a Google Cloud cell [48].

In particular, our contributions in this paper are as follows:

- We investigate the performance of state-of-the-art time series forecasting architectures such as DeepAR and TFT that, to the best of our knowledge, are applied for the first time in the context of cloud workload prediction.
- We provide an analysis and comparison of a wide range of clustering methods suitable for dealing with cloud workload time series.
- We show how a clustering approach leverages the prediction capabilities of DL probabilistic forecasting models, offering a trade-off between accuracy and limited computational resource. An accurate selection of training datasets allows a provider to reach the same accuracy in less than half the time, requiring less than half the datasets.
- We preprocess the datasets and make them available for reproducibility.

The rest of the paper is organized as follows. Section 2 describes the background and related work in this field. In Sect. 3, we describe the forecasting models. Section 4 presents the experimental results based on a real-world Google Cloud trace. Finally, Sect. 5 concludes the paper and discusses future work.

---

[1] To avoid confusion, we will use 'cluster' to refer to a subcollection of data identified in the workload trace files, and 'cell' to refer to a collection of computational nodes.

2   Background and Related Work

In this section, we discuss the problem of data reduction, specifically on the clustering approaches in this paper, with a focus on cloud computing applications.

2.1   Data Reduction

There are several methods for data reduction, including feature selection, numerosity reduction, and dimensionality reduction [47]. These methods aim to obtain a smaller version of the dataset while preserving its information value. In workload forecasting in Cloud Computing, feature selection is difficult due to a lack of information in unlabelled workload traces [2], and dimensionality reduction techniques can lack explainability [37].

This work focuses on numerosity reduction, which aims to reduce the number of training samples. Coresets are a popular approach for reducing training data, but their formation can be complex [15]. Simple random sampling [46] is an easy way to reduce training data size, but it does not guarantee that all possible patterns are selected. Stratified sampling [31] overcomes this problem by dividing samples into subgroups before sampling, but identifying the relevant characteristics or attributes that define the subgroups (strata) in cloud workload traces is generally hard due to lack of information [2], so it is difficult to apply it directly to the problem.

2.2   Unsupervised Clustering

Clustering is an unsupervised method that aims to divide a set of unlabeled data items into uniform groups or *clusters*. The goal is to create clusters where points are most similar within the group and least similar to those in other groups. K-Means is a method that partitions the dataset into K clusters by minimizing the sum of the squared distances between the data points and their centroids.

Time series can be seen as data in high-dimensional spaces where each timestamp is a feature. However, time series can suffer from the curse of dimensionality [5], where the increase in distance measurement negatively impacts distance-based algorithms such as K-means clustering. Many approaches have been proposed to deal with time series clustering.

Principal Component Analysis. Principal Component Analysis (PCA) is one of the most popular statistical methods for reducing dataset dimensionality [32,45]. The data are transformed linearly into a new orthogonal coordinate system with fewer dimensions that preserves most of the variance of the original data. Due to its high interpretability, especially when data are mapped into two dimensions to identify clusters of correlated data points, it became a popular tool in time series analysis [21,22]. PCA can be used to reduce the dimensionality of the time series before applying K-Means.

Variational Recurrent Auto-Encoder. The Variational Recurrent Auto-Encoder (VRAE) is a model that maps time series data to a latent vector representation of probability distribution in an unsupervised fashion [12]. It combines the representation learning power of a variational auto-encoder with the ability of recurrent neural networks to deal with sequential data. The network's parameters are learned by jointly optimizing the sum of the Kullback-Leibler divergence between the distribution learned in the latent space and a Gaussian distribution plus the reconstruction error. The variational component of the VRAE can handle larger time series data without slowing down the learning process. This model has been widely applied in anomaly detection and forecasting time series applications [33,50] and can be used to reduce the dimensionality of time series and apply K-Means on the latent space.

Self-Organising Maps. A Self-Organizing Map (SOM) or Kohonen map is an unsupervised machine learning technique introduced by Kohonen [18]. It is an artificial neural network trained with competitive learning to create a lower-dimensional representation of the input data. The objective of the training is to convert an input space into a two-dimensional map space. SOMs are inspired by the brain map for visual and sensory information and can produce a map as a method for dimensionality reduction that is a nonlinear generalization of PCA. SOMs can be used as a clustering technique and have been widely applied in time series contexts, including forecasting applications [4,9,41].

Dynamic Time Warping. In the context of time series, the centroid can be computed as the arithmetic mean of each timestamp of all the time series grouped into a cluster. However, Euclidean distance has often been proven less effective and accurate than elastic metrics [29,30]. A popular one is the Dynamic Time Warping (DTW) [34], which can handle time series of different lengths and is invariant to dilation in time. DTW Barycenter Averaging (DBA) is used [35] as the distance metric. DTW offers the opportunity to apply the K-Means algorithm directly to the time series data at the cost of extra complexity. It has been used in various time series applications, including sensor-based signal classification in healthcare [44] and forecasting [24,36,49].

3   Workload Prediction Models

Our aim is to help a resource manager to configure available computational resources by using an estimation of the future demand for resources from a predictive model based on the historical workload data.

For the purposes of this paper, we have narrowed our analysis to three DL probabilistic forecasting models outlined in this section. This decision was made due to the significant computational resources required for extensive experimentation. However, we believe these models are sufficient to validate our results.

HBNN. A Bayesian Neural Network (BNN) is a type of neural network with probabilistic weights optimized using Bayes-by-backprop [7]. A variation of BNN, called Hybrid BNN (HBNN), only has a Bayesian last layer as a trade-off between training time and epistemic uncertainty modelling [19], i.e. the uncertainty due to the small size of the datasets or the lack of knowledge of the model parameters [16]. This model has been successfully used for workload prediction in cloud computing [38]. The full model includes a 1D convolution layer, two Long Short-Term Memory (LSTM) layers, and three dense layers, with only the last layer being Bayesian. The output layer is two Gaussian distributions for CPU and memory demand forecasts. The loss function is the negative log-likelihood, and the model captures aleatory uncertainty due to the noise in the input data. The network is implemented using Keras and TensorFlow Probability libraries.

DeepAR. DeepAR is a time series probabilistic forecasting model using auto-regressive RNNs proposed by Amazon [40]. It is trained on one or more target time series produced by the same or related processes. The model approximates these processes and uses them to forecast the evolution of the target time series. The model estimates the parameters of a Gaussian distribution to produce a probabilistic forecast and is trained by minimizing the log-likelihood function via the Adam algorithm. The model is implemented using the PyTorch Forecasting library with hyperparameter optimization using Optuna. The output of the models consists of seven quantiles of the distribution from which the mean and standard deviation of the Gaussian distribution are calculated.

Temporal Fusion Transformer. Temporal Fusion Transformer (TFT) is an attention-based Deep Neural Network designed by Google for time series forecasting [23]. It can be applied to multi-horizon forecasting and includes components such as an LSTM encoder-decoder layer and a variable selection network for feature selection. The multi-head attention mechanism highlights the most relevant parts of the input window for prediction. The network is optimized using quantile loss as the loss function and is jointly optimized using multiple time series from different distributions. TFT has outperformed DeepAR in electricity demand and traffic forecasting applications. The output of the models consists of seven quantiles of the distribution from which the mean and standard deviation of the Gaussian distribution are calculated.

4   Experiments

The studies in this section investigate the effectiveness of using clustering-based training data selection for cloud workload prediction. The optimal number of clusters for each clustering technique is determined experimentally, and a subset of datasets is selected randomly or with representatives from each cluster. This subset is used to train predictive models, with the number of datasets varied to compare the models in terms of Mean Squared Error (MSE) and Mean Absolute

Error (MAE). The models are also compared based on confidence intervals to evaluate the quality of probabilistic forecasts, and runtime performance and energy saving are evaluated.

Dataset. The machine-level workload datasets used in the experiments come from the real-world Google Cloud Trace 2019 [48], which records resource utilization of tasks for 29 d on eight cells worldwide. The data is compiled from the Instance Usage table of Google trace using Google BigQuery, with missing records ignored and average CPU and memory demand aggregated in 5-minute intervals, similarly to [14, 20].

The datasets are used to train Deep Learning models to predict future resource demand. Each dataset has 8352 data points, with CPU and memory burden multiplied by a weight proportional to the run time period inside the window, as done in [17, 38]. The distribution of the datasets is Gaussian, and the time series are stationary according to the Augmented Dickey-Fuller test.

Experimental Setup. The experiments were conducted using Ubuntu 20.04, a 2.60GHz Intel®Xeon®Gold 6240 CPU, and a 48 GB NVIDIA Quadro RTX 8000 GPU, using historical workload data from Google Cloud Trace 2019. The workload is predicted for a time interval of 10 min ahead, which is sufficient for most applications [3, 25]. The datasets are split into training and test sets, with the first 80% (23 d) of each dataset used for training and the remaining 20% (6 d) used for evaluation. An exhaustive hyperparameter search is conducted to find the best hyperparameters for the Deep Learning models. More details on the implementation, hyperparameters, and clustering techniques can be found in the open-source GitHub repository[2].

Clustering Evaluation. This section describes the evaluation of clustering, where the exact number of clusters is unknown. The performance of the algorithm is evaluated by varying the number of clusters, K. The elbow curve method [43] is a popular method for finding the best K, based on the distortion score, which is the sum of squared distances of points from cluster centres. As K increases, the distortion score decreases, but overfitting can occur. The elbow curve method selects K where there is an elbow in the distortion curve. The Silhouette score [39] confirms the results of the elbow method.

The methods used to select the datasets are as follows:

- **Random**: The Random method selects training datasets randomly without using clustering methods.
- **PCA**: The PCA method reduces the dimension of the datasets using the first two principal components and applies K-Means to the latent space, with the best K found to be 7 using the elbow method.

---

[2] https://github.com/andreareds/clustered-reduction-cloud-workload.

- **VRAE**: The VRAE method trains a VRAE algorithm to minimize reconstruction error and uses the encoder to reduce dataset dimensionality, with K-Means applied to the encoded space and the best K found to be 5.
- **SOM**: The SOM method trains multiple SOMs with varying map sizes and selects the best size using the elbow method, with the best configuration found to be a 2×3 map with 6 clusters.
- **DTW**: The DTW method applies DTW directly on the workload datasets based on the DBA distance function, with resampling used to reduce computation cost and the best K found to be 4.

Clusters are computed using the first 80% of each dataset to avoid leakage in forecasting, while the last 20% is used as the test set.

Point Estimate Accuracy. After clustering the time series, a certain number of datasets L are selected to train the predictive models, with dimensionality reduction used for clustering only. As a baseline, L datasets are randomly selected among all available ones, while when the series are clustered, an equal number of datasets are selected for each cluster such that the total number is L. The models are trained by varying L between 50 and 2000 and tested on datasets not used for training. The first evaluation is in terms of MSE and MAE, computed with respect to the mean of the predicted Gaussian distribution.

We plot the MSE of the memory prediction for DeepAR and TFT for all the clustering approaches by varying the number of datasets (whose scale is logarithmic) in Fig. 1. From the plot, we can see that once the number of datasets increases sufficiently, all the approaches, including the baseline, converge to similar metrics values. However, the clustering approaches allow the models to reach the same performance with much less data and, consequently, fewer computational resources compared to a random selection of the datasets. In Table 2 in Appendix A, we list the results in terms of MSE and MAE for all clustering approaches for the models trained with 500, 1000 and 2000 datasets.

Experiments show that, independently of the clustering techniques used for training, the HBNN has an MSE and MAE at least five times higher than the ones conducted by the state-of-the-art methods DeepAR and TFT. This is because the HBNN is a much simpler network, incapable of learning patterns from several time series, compared to more complex architectures. DeepAR and TFT achieve similar performance in MSE and MAE for all the considered clustering techniques for both CPU and memory demand.

While TFT previously outperformed DeepAR in electricity demand and traffic forecasting [23], for our cloud prediction, it is not possible to conclude which is the best DL model. We believe it is due to the absence of covariates of the resource demand to train the model, an essential component used by the variable selection network of the TFT.

From these experiments, we can see how all the clustering-based selection techniques significantly boost the performance of DeepAR and TFT compared to a random selection of the training data when increasing the number of training datasets, showing the benefits of clustering the datasets before training when the computational resources are limited. For example, DeepAR-Random reaches 0.014 with 1,000 training datasets, while DeepAR-DTW requires only 200 datasets to reach the same MSE. Moreover, DeepAR-Random trained with 1,000 datasets has an CPU and memory MSE 7% and 14% higher than the respective MSEs achieved by DeepAR-DTW.

On the contrary, HBNN does not benefit much from a clustered selection of the training datasets. DTW and SOM are the best approaches among all the clustering techniques. This is because DTW has been designed for dealing with time series, while the other approaches are more general and data structure independent. Instead, PCA and VRAE achieve an unsatisfactory score from a point estimate point of view for DeepAR and TFT because the clustering is not applied directly to the time series but to the learned latent space. However, these dimensionality reduction approaches seem more effective for simpler models such as HBNN. This is likely because HBNN is a simpler model compared to DeepAR and TFT, with the best clustering method being dependent on the predictive models utilized.

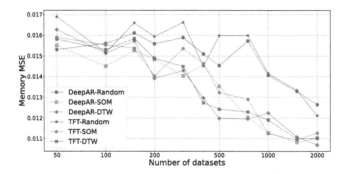

Fig. 1. MSE comparison of DeepAR and TFT for the memory demand. DTW and SOM are the best clustering-based selection approaches and allow the models to achieve the same MSE with fewer training datasets compared to a random selection. When the number of datasets is high, the MSE of all the approaches converge. The x-axis is in a logarithmic scale.

Confidence Intervals Evaluation. In this section, we evaluate the forecasting models with the metrics defined in [38]. This evaluation aims to assess the prediction's quality if we want to exploit the prediction for resource allocation and virtual machine provisioning problems. Given the mean and the standard deviation of a Gaussian distribution, we can compute confidence intervals of the prediction and quantify the number of predicted resources based on the upper bound (UB) of the confidence interval to compare the predictive models.

The considered metrics are as follows:

– **Success Rate (SR)**: the percentage of correctly predicted requests, i.e. the percentage of actual requests that are within the UB of the prediction.

– **Overprediction (OP)**: the percentage of overprediction computed as the difference between the UB of the confidence interval and ground truth for those predictions which exceed the real demand of resources.
– **Underprediction (UP)**: the percentage of underprediction computed as the difference between ground truth and the UB of the confidence interval for those predictions which are below the real demand of resources.

There are important differences between HBNN and state-of-the-art models. HBNN reaches an SR very close to the target confidence level (2% points above the target), while DeepAR and TFT are over 15% points below. This can be seen graphically in Fig. 2, where we measure the SR with a training size of 1000 datasets while varying the confidence level of the predicted probability distribution of memory for the best clustering approaches and the baseline. This is due to the predicted standard deviation of the model. The numerical results are listed in Table 3 in Appendix B. While the Bayesian layer of the HBNN is capable of modelling the epistemic uncertainty of the prediction and the uncertainty of the prediction is quantified by the magnitude of the standard deviation, DeepAR and TFT are overconfident in the prediction, with a much lower standard deviation, capable of modelling only the noise of the data. A similar discussion can be extended to the UP because this metric is related to the percentage of unmatched requests, with a portion of those much lower for the HBNN compared to the other two methods, making it more reliable for high Quality of Service (QoS) applications. Interestingly, the UP of the CPU demand is lower for DeepAR and TFT, meaning that the upper bound of the prediction is quite close to the ground truth. For this reason, the prediction requires further processing to improve its performance. On the other hand, a high standard deviation makes the UB of the prediction much higher, thus increasing the OP, which is up to 5 times lower for DeepAR and TFT compared to the HBNN.

Regarding the clustering approaches, as in the previous results on the point estimate accuracy, DTW and SOM approaches are the best clustering methods to select the datasets for training, with a better SR, OP and UP of up to 6% compared to a random selection of the datasets for state-of-the-art method. The HBNN, again, is not benefiting much from a clustering-based selection. The differences between the clustering methods decrease as the number of datasets used in training increases.

When we use the majority of the datasets in training, it does not matter whether the datasets are selected randomly or via a clustering approach. This can be seen in Fig. 3 for the OP of memory for DeepAR and TFT models while varying the number of datasets. This proves that when a high amount of data is available, an accurate selection of training data that considers different patterns, i.e. different distributions of the training input, is essential to achieve a good trade-off between performance and computational cost. DTW and SOM are the clustering approaches which reduce both the UP and OP for both DeepAR and TFT models, confirming that time series-based clustering approaches are more suitable for grouping similar datasets according to their patterns.

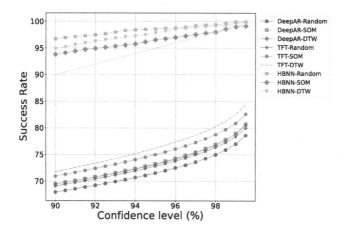

Fig. 2. Memory SR comparison of DeepAR, TFT and HBNN as a function of the confidence level with models trained with 1000 datasets. The model is the most accurate when the curve is closest to the line $y = x$. DTW and SOM-based selections improve the SR compared to the random selection of datasets.

Runtime Performance Analysis. Another critical aspect of the predictive models in Cloud Computing applications is related to the runtime performance, which is critical for the deployability of the models in real-world scenarios. We are interested in measuring both the time necessary to train a model and the time to make a prediction once the model is trained.

First, we measure the training time of the models while using the selected datasets from the clusters. We plot the training time by varying the number of training datasets L in Fig. 4. We consider the average training time, which is affected by the amount of input data and not by how its selection is performed. Increasing the number of training datasets, i.e. the training data, increases the time for the model to converge, with some fluctuations whose causes include the random initialization of the network and the batch order fed in the backpropagation optimization. However, from the plot, it is clear that DeepAR converges two times faster, independently of the clustering approach used.

The Bayesian layer is much slower to train because of the reparametrization trick applied in each epoch, and it scales poorly compared to the state-of-the-art methods, which have been designed to be jointly trained with multiple time series. Moreover, the libraries used to implement HBNN and state-of-the-art methods are different, with Keras slower than PyTorch.

If we relate the training time to the accuracy, we can see that clustering approaches allow us to reach the same performance with a much lower number of training datasets. As a result, to achieve the same MSE, a random selection requires many more datasets, compared to training based on clustering approaches, with reduced computational cost and, consequently, energy-saving. Table 1 lists the time-saving in percentage. This is computed as the difference in

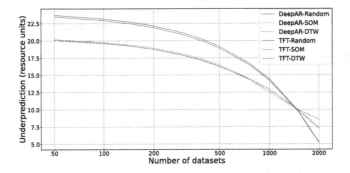

Fig. 3. Memory OP comparison of DeepAR and TFT. If DTW and SOM are applied, a much lower number of datasets is required to get the same OP compared to a random selection of the datasets. The x-axis is in a logarithmic scale.

training time between the random selection of the datasets and the best clustering approach used to train the model, where the cluster-based model achieves at least the same MSE accuracy.

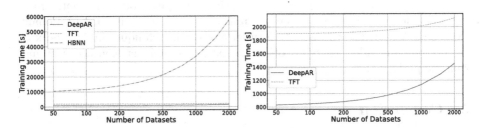

Fig. 4. Training time curve as a function of the number of datasets. On the left, all three models are plotted. On the right, we plot only DeepAR and TFT to show the differences between the two models. The training time increases when we increase L, but TFT grows slower when the number of datasets increases, compared to the other methods. The x-axis is in a logarithmic scale.

We also measure the inference time of HBNN, DeepAR and TFT to predict one sample. All the DL models are fast, with 0.1 ms required for prediction using the HBNN. DeepAR takes 2.16 ms, while TFT requires 20.10 ms. The differences depend on the complexity of the architecture. Although the inference time among the three models is significantly different, with the HBNN 200 times faster than the TFT, it is on the order of ms, negligible compared to the 10 min ahead forecast. Inference time is also independent of the clustering approach because once the model is trained, the time depends only on the number of parameters and the complexity of the network.

Table 1. Time saving for all the models trained with the best clustering approach w.r.t. a random selection of the training datasets, with the baseline trained using 2000, 1500 and 1000 datasets. The training size of the clustering is selected as the minimum size required to achieve an MSE less or equal to the MSE achieved by the baseline.

Training Size Baseline	Model	CPU		Memory	
		Training Size Clustering	Time Saving (%)	Training Size Clustering	Time Saving (%)
2000	HBNN	200	75.63	400	67.23
	DeepAR	400	34.82	500	32.65
	TFT	500	8.48	500	8.49
1500	HBNN	200	69.15	400	58.51
	DeepAR	200	31.75	300	29.31
	TFT	400	6.41	500	5.83
1000	HBNN	100	65.22	300	50.73
	DeepAR	200	22.26	200	22.26
	TFT	200	4.80	500	3.00

Therefore, with similar performance in terms of point estimate accuracy and the considerations on the confidence intervals computed from the predicting probability distributions, DeepAR is preferable to the TFT because both the training time and the inference time are lower.

For the clustering algorithms, SOM is the fastest method under both training and inference time, while the training phase for DTW is computationally expensive. We include runtime performance of these techniques in Appendix C.

We can conclude that SOM offers the best trade-off between accuracy and runtime performance.

5   Conclusion

Resource demand prediction is a challenging task for cloud computing managers. An accurate training data reduction is necessary when computational resources are limited and to reduce energy consumption.

This paper analyses the accuracy of forecasting models in predicting future demand distribution of CPU and memory in the latest Google Cloud Trace, comparing state-of-the-art models with BNNs that capture prediction uncertainty.

Clustering algorithms are applied to aggregate datasets with similar patterns and select good representatives among available datasets, reducing training time compared to random selection. Results show that clustering-based selection achieves the same accuracy with fewer data and time series clustering methods such as DTW and SOMs are more effective. Confidence intervals are computed from the output distribution to relate prediction confidence to the rate of correctly predicted requests. State-of-the-art methods achieve better point estimate accuracy but are often overconfident.

At the same time, HBNN can quantify epistemic uncertainty, providing a trade-off between accuracy and successful resource requests, but allocating more resources. The models' runtime performance is analysed for practical deployment in real-world scenarios, with the DeepAR method trained with datasets selected with SOMs offering the best trade-off between cost and accuracy.

In future work, we will extend the clustering algorithms for dealing with time series and extend these to a multi-step ahead prediction. Finally, the aim is to use the predictions in resource allocation algorithms to preconfigure the machine in cloud cells in advance, providing a high QoS level.

Acknowledgments. This publication has emanated from research supported in part by Science Foundation Ireland under Grant Nos. 18/CRT/6223 and 12/RC/2289-P2, by the EU Horizon projects Glaciation (GA No. 101070141) and TAILOR (GA No. 952215), and the Google Cloud Research Credits program with the award GCP203677602.

A   Point Estimate Accuracy Results

Table 2 shows the MSE and MAE for CPU and memory demand prediction with $L = 500$, $L = 1000$ and $L = 2000$ for all predicted models trained with the clustering techniques.

Table 2. MSE and MAE for CPU and memory demand with different training sizes (500, 1000 and 2000). In bold, for each model, the best clustering technique.

| Model | Clustering | Training Size 500 | | | | Training Size 1000 | | | | Training Size 2000 | | | |
| | | CPU | | Memory | | CPU | | Memory | | CPU | | Memory | |
		MSE	MAE	MSE	MAE	MSE	MAE	MSE	MAE	MSE	MAE	MSE	MAE
HBNN	Random	0.13	0.291	0.103	0.255	**0.085**	**0.229**	0.12	0.278	0.075	0.217	0.079	**0.212**
	PCA	**0.098**	**0.253**	0.122	0.274	0.09	0.233	0.073	0.216	**0.071**	0.217	**0.071**	0.215
	VRAE	0.158	0.314	0.099	0.253	0.157	0.27	0.081	0.228	0.073	**0.215**	0.081	0.231
	SOM	0.114	0.271	0.124	0.281	0.163	0.319	0.107	0.257	0.082	0.22	0.085	0.226
	DTW	0.106	0.259	**0.07**	**0.21**	0.125	0.283	**0.07**	**0.206**	0.078	0.228	0.081	0.219
DeepAR	Random	**0.014**	**0.094**	0.015	0.091	0.014	0.093	0.014	0.09	0.015	0.097	0.013	0.082
	PCA	0.026	0.13	0.014	0.088	0.025	0.126	0.014	0.088	0.013	0.088	**0.011**	**0.077**
	VRAE	0.024	0.124	0.016	0.095	0.014	0.095	0.014	0.09	0.014	0.094	0.013	0.081
	SOM	**0.014**	0.096	0.014	0.088	0.017	0.103	**0.011**	**0.08**	**0.012**	**0.085**	**0.011**	0.079
	DTW	0.022	0.12	**0.012**	**0.082**	**0.013**	**0.09**	0.012	0.083	0.013	0.089	**0.011**	0.078
TFT	Random	0.02	0.114	0.016	0.096	0.014	0.093	0.014	0.09	0.014	0.097	0.012	0.084
	PCA	0.024	0.124	0.014	0.088	0.021	0.116	0.013	0.086	0.013	0.087	**0.011**	**0.078**
	VRAE	0.016	0.101	0.015	0.092	0.014	0.094	0.015	0.093	0.014	0.094	0.013	0.082
	SOM	0.017	0.104	0.013	0.087	0.017	0.103	**0.011**	**0.08**	**0.012**	**0.085**	**0.011**	0.08
	DTW	**0.014**	**0.094**	**0.012**	**0.084**	**0.012**	**0.089**	0.012	0.082	0.013	0.089	**0.011**	0.079

B   Confidence Intervals Evaluation Results

We display numerical results for SR, OP and UP in Table 3 using 500 and 1000 datasets in training for HBNN, DeepAR and TFT models for a 95% confidence interval. Under these metrics, a clustering-based selection improves the performance compared to training with a random selection of the datasets, with DTW and SOM performing best overall, especially for state-of-the-art probabilistic methods.

Table 3. CPU and Memory demand prediction statistics (Success Rate, Overprediction and Underprediction in percentage) of HBNN, DeepAR and TFT with 500 and 1000 training datasets at 95% confidence. In bold, for each model, the best clustering technique.

Training size	Model	Clustering	CPU			Memory		
			SR (%)	OP (%)	UP (%)	SR (%)	OP (%)	UP (%)
500	HBNN	Random	98.06	220.67	**19.38**	99.85	**125.11**	5.08
		PCA	98.83	179.26	27.99	99.19	136.20	10.79
		VRAE	98.29	180.61	23.17	98.91	151.32	11.30
		SOM	**97.62**	220.24	64.51	**98.15**	140.13	16.38
		DTW	98.25	**173.61**	27.02	98.92	140.82	9.88
	DeepAR	Random	72.65	42.86	18.60	74.61	29.66	16.42
		PCA	71.88	43.85	18.92	74.22	29.29	15.10
		VRAE	72.49	40.71	18.45	74.66	29.66	15.92
		SOM	76.28	**35.08**	16.05	77.44	**25.74**	11.97
		DTW	**76.85**	38.90	**15.94**	**77.63**	26.55	**11.42**
	TFT	Random	72.56	42.9	18.85	75.45	30.35	16.36
		PCA	72.84	45.56	19.24	76.04	29.83	15.25
		VRAE	73.72	41.91	18.47	76.92	30.62	16.22
		SOM	78.42	**36.75**	16.22	**80.81**	27.55	11.81
		DTW	**78.43**	39.70	**15.96**	80.09	**27.27**	11.08
1000	HBNN	Random	98.35	139.93	**10.30**	99.49	**80.99**	**2.57**
		PCA	98.54	170.5	22.25	99.08	130.48	3.82
		VRAE	98.53	125.04	12.82	98.98	105.31	2.75
		SOM	**97.64**	141.81	37.20	**98.33**	90.05	6.41
		DTW	98.29	**123.46**	12.94	99.44	100.14	4.78
	DeepAR	Random	73.94	33.63	14.00	75.88	23.38	12.61
		PCA	73.23	42.07	17.43	75.65	28.26	14.19
		VRAE	73.81	33.55	14.64	75.94	24.58	12.85
		SOM	77.74	**27.86**	**12.28**	78.83	**20.55**	9.18
		DTW	**78.28**	32.59	12.75	**79.05**	22.33	**9.17**
	TFT	Random	73.85	33.73	14.20	76.77	23.92	12.60
		PCA	74.14	43.95	17.74	77.44	28.86	14.37
		VRAE	75.03	34.65	14.65	78.21	25.46	13.15
		SOM	**79.84**	**29.34**	**12.43**	**82.23**	**22.13**	9.09
		DTW	79.82	33.38	12.76	81.55	22.98	**8.90**

C   Clustering Runtime Performance

We measure the fitting and prediction time of the four clustering approaches. Each technique includes a different training procedure. PCA includes reducing the feature space and computing the K-Means on the top of the latent space. Similarly, VRAE consists of the joint training of the encoder and decoder, the encoder is then used to map the time series to a latent space, and K-Means is applied on top of it. SOM requires the training of the neurons of the map that will be used for the prediction. Finally, the DTW is comparable to the K-Means algorithms, with a different distance metric which is computationally more expensive. We list the time performance in Table 4.

Table 4. Fitting and inference time of the clustering approaches. In bold, the best fitting and inference time.

Clustering Method	Fitting Time [s]	Inference Time [s]
PCA	158.6	0.965
VRAE	185.6	1.744
SOM	**7.8**	**0.177**
DTW	2010.7	0.682

References

1. Achar, S.: Cloud computing: toward sustainable processes and better environmental impact. J. Comput. Hardware Eng. (JCHE) **1**(1), 1–9 (2022)
2. Ali, S.M., Kecskemeti, G.: SeQual: an unsupervised feature selection method for cloud workload traces. J. Supercomput. **79**, 15079–15097 (2023). https://doi.org/10.1007/s11227-023-05163-w
3. Baldan, F.J., Ramirez-Gallego, S., Bergmeir, C., Herrera, F., Benitez, J.M.: A forecasting methodology for workload forecasting in cloud systems. IEEE Trans. Cloud Comput. **6**(4), 929–941 (2016)
4. Barreto, G.A.: Time Series Prediction with the Self-Organizing Map: A Review. In: Hammer, B., Hitzler, P. (eds) Perspectives of Neural-Symbolic Integration. Studies in Computational Intelligence, vol 77. Springer, Berlin, Heidelberg (2007). https://doi.org/10.1007/978-3-540-73954-8_6
5. Bellman, R.: Dynamic programming. Science **153**(3731), 34–37 (1966)
6. Bi, J., Li, S., Yuan, H., Zhou, M.: Integrated deep learning method for workload and resource prediction in cloud systems. Neurocomputing **424**, 35–48 (2021)
7. Blundell, C., Cornebise, J., Kavukcuoglu, K., Wierstra, D.: Weight uncertainty in neural network. In: International Conference on Machine Learning, pp. 1613–1622. PMLR (2015)
8. Calheiros, R.N., Masoumi, E., Ranjan, R., Buyya, R.: Workload prediction using ARIMA model and its impact on cloud applications' QoS. IEEE Trans. Cloud Comput. **3**(4), 449–458 (2014)
9. Cherif, A., Cardot, H., Boné, R.: SOM time series clustering and prediction with recurrent neural networks. Neurocomputing **74**(11), 1936–1944 (2011)
10. Di, S., Kondo, D., Cirne, W.: Host load prediction in a Google compute cloud with a Bayesian model. In: SC'12: Proceedings of the International Conference on High Performance Computing, Networking, Storage and Analysis, pp. 1–11. IEEE (2012)
11. Dinda, P.A., O'Hallaron, D.R.: Host load prediction using linear models. Clust. Comput. **3**(4), 265–280 (2000)

12. Fabius, O., Van Amersfoort, J.R.: Variational recurrent auto-encoders. arXiv preprint arXiv:1412.6581 (2014)
13. Gao, J., Wang, H., Shen, H.: Machine learning based workload prediction in cloud computing. In: 2020 29th International Conference on Computer Communications and Networks (ICCCN), pp. 1–9. IEEE (2020)
14. Herbst, N.R., Huber, N., Kounev, S., Amrehn, E.: Self-adaptive workload classification and forecasting for proactive resource provisioning. Concurrency Comput. Pract. Experience 26(12), 2053–2078 (2014)
15. Huang, L., Sudhir, K., Vishnoi, N.: Coresets for time series clustering. Adv. Neural. Inf. Process. Syst. 34, 22849–22862 (2021)
16. Hüllermeier, E., Waegeman, W.: Aleatoric and epistemic uncertainty in machine learning: an introduction to concepts and methods. Mach. Learn. 110(3), 457–506 (2021)
17. Janardhanan, D., Barrett, E.: CPU workload forecasting of machines in data centers using LSTM recurrent neural networks and ARIMA models. In: 2017 12th International Conference for Internet Technology and Secured Transactions (ICITST), pp. 55–60 (2017)
18. Kohonen, T.: The self-organizing map. Proc. IEEE 78(9), 1464–1480 (1990)
19. Kristiadi, A., Hein, M., Hennig, P.: Being Bayesian, even just a bit, fixes overconfidence in relu networks. In: International Conference on Machine Learning, pp. 5436–5446. PMLR (2020)
20. Kumar, J., Singh, A.: An efficient machine learning approach for virtual machine resource demand prediction. Int. J. Adv. Sci. Technol. 123, 21–30 (2019)
21. Lakhina, A., Crovella, M., Diot, C.: Diagnosing network-wide traffic anomalies. ACM SIGCOMM Comput. Commun. Rev. 34(4), 219–230 (2004)
22. Li, H.: Multivariate time series clustering based on common principal component analysis. Neurocomputing 349, 239–247 (2019)
23. Lim, B., Arık, S.Ö., Loeff, N., Pfister, T.: Temporal fusion transformers for interpretable multi-horizon time series forecasting. Int. J. Forecast. 37(4), 1748–1764 (2021)
24. Malarya, A., Ragunathan, K., Kamaraj, M.B., Vijayarajan, V.: Emerging trends demand forecast using dynamic time warping. In: 2021 IEEE 22nd International Conference on Information Reuse and Integration for Data Science (IRI), pp. 402–407. IEEE (2021)
25. Mao, M., Li, J., Humphrey, M.: Cloud auto-scaling with deadline and budget constraints. In: 2010 11th IEEE/ACM International Conference on Grid Computing, pp. 41–48. IEEE (2010)
26. Markets, Markets: Cloud computing market by service model, by deployment model, organization size, vertical and region - global forecast to 2027 (2022), https://www.marketsandmarkets.com/Market-Reports/cloud-computing-market-234.html
27. Minarolli, D., Mazrekaj, A., Freisleben, B.: Tackling uncertainty in long-term predictions for host overload and underload detection in cloud computing. J. Cloud Comput. 6(1), 1–18 (2017)
28. Mohammadi Bahram Abadi, R., Rahmani, A.M., Hossein Alizadeh, S.: Self-adaptive architecture for virtual machines consolidation based on probabilistic model evaluation of data centers in cloud computing. Cluster Comput. 21, 1711–1733 (2018)
29. Paparrizos, J., Gravano, L.: k-shape: Efficient and accurate clustering of time series. In: Proceedings of the 2015 ACM SIGMOD International Conference on Management of Data, pp. 1855–1870 (2015)

30. Paparrizos, J., Liu, C., Elmore, A.J., Franklin, M.J.: Debunking four long-standing misconceptions of time-series distance measures. In: Proceedings of the 2020 ACM SIGMOD International Conference on Management of Data, pp. 1887–1905 (2020)
31. Parsons, V.L.: Stratified sampling. Wiley StatsRef: Statistics Reference Online pp. 1–11 (2014)
32. Pearson, K.: LIII. on lines and planes of closest fit to systems of points in space. London Edinburgh Dublin Philos. Mag. J. Sci. **2**(11), 559–572 (1901)
33. Pereira, J., Silveira, M.: Unsupervised anomaly detection in energy time series data using variational recurrent autoencoders with attention. In: 2018 17th IEEE international conference on machine learning and applications (ICMLA), pp. 1275–1282. IEEE (2018)
34. Petitjean, F., Forestier, G., Webb, G.I., Nicholson, A.E., Chen, Y., Keogh, E.: Dynamic time warping averaging of time series allows faster and more accurate classification. In: 2014 IEEE International Conference on Data Mining, pp. 470–479. IEEE (2014)
35. Petitjean, F., Ketterlin, A., Gançarski, P.: A global averaging method for dynamic time warping, with applications to clustering. Pattern Recogn. **44**(3), 678–693 (2011)
36. Prasetyo, J., Setiawan, N.A., Adji, T.B.: Clustering based oil production rate forecasting using dynamic time warping with univariate time series data. In: 2021 International Conference on Advanced Mechatronics, Intelligent Manufacture and Industrial Automation (ICAMIMIA), pp. 204–208. IEEE (2021)
37. Rojat, T., Puget, R., Filliat, D., Del Ser, J., Gelin, R., Díaz-Rodríguez, N.: Explainable artificial intelligence (xai) on timeseries data: a survey. arXiv preprint arXiv:2104.00950 (2021)
38. Rossi, A., Visentin, A., Prestwich, S., Brown, K.N.: Bayesian uncertainty modelling for cloud workload prediction. In: 2022 IEEE 15th International Conference on Cloud Computing (CLOUD), pp. 19–29. IEEE (2022)
39. Rousseeuw, P.J.: Silhouettes: a graphical aid to the interpretation and validation of cluster analysis. J. Comput. Appl. Math. **20**, 53–65 (1987)
40. Salinas, D., Flunkert, V., Gasthaus, J., Januschowski, T.: DeepAR: probabilistic forecasting with autoregressive recurrent networks. Int. J. Forecast. **36**(3), 1181–1191 (2020)
41. Sarlin, P., Eklund, T.: Fuzzy clustering of the self-organizing map: some applications on financial time series. In: Laaksonen, J., Honkela, T. (eds.) WSOM 2011. LNCS, vol. 6731, pp. 40–50. Springer, Heidelberg (2011). https://doi.org/10.1007/978-3-642-21566-7_4
42. Song, B., Yu, Y., Zhou, Y., Wang, Z., Du, S.: Host load prediction with long short-term memory in cloud computing. J. Supercomput. **74**(12), 6554–6568 (2018)
43. Thorndike, R.L.: Who belongs in the family. In: Psychometrika. Citeseer (1953)
44. Varatharajan, R., Manogaran, G., Priyan, M.K., Sundarasekar, R.: Wearable sensor devices for early detection of Alzheimer disease using dynamic time warping algorithm. Clust. Comput. **21**, 681–690 (2018)
45. Visentin, A., Prestwich, S., Tarim, S.A.: Robust principal component analysis by reverse iterative linear programming. In: Frasconi, P., Landwehr, N., Manco, G., Vreeken, J. (eds.) ECML PKDD 2016. LNCS (LNAI), vol. 9852, pp. 593–605. Springer, Cham (2016). https://doi.org/10.1007/978-3-319-46227-1_37
46. Watson, J., Fitzallen, N., Fielding-Wells, J., Madden, S.: The practice of statistics. International Handbook of Research in Statistics Education, pp. 105–137 (2018)

47. Wibbeke, J., Teimourzadeh Baboli, P., Rohjans, S.: Optimal data reduction of training data in machine learning-based modelling: a multidimensional bin packing approach. Energies **15**(9), 3092 (2022)
48. Wilkes, J.: Google cluster-usage traces v3. Technical report, Google Inc., Mountain View, CA, USA (2020), posted at https://github.com/google/cluster-data/blob/master/ClusterData2019.md
49. Yu, Y., Jindal, V., Yen, I.L., Bastani, F.: Integrating clustering and learning for improved workload prediction in the cloud. In: 2016 IEEE 9th International Conference on Cloud Computing (CLOUD), pp. 876–879. IEEE (2016)
50. Zheng, Z., Wang, L., Yang, L., Zhang, Z.: Generative probabilistic wind speed forecasting: a variational recurrent autoencoder based method. IEEE Trans. Power Syst. **37**(2), 1386–1398 (2021)

Algorithmic Aspects of Distributed Hash Tables on Cloud, Fog, and Edge Computing Applications: A Survey

Aristeidis Karras[1]([📧]) [ID], Christos Karras[1] [ID], Nikolaos Schizas[1] [ID], Spyros Sioutas[1] [ID], and Christos Zaroliagis[1,2] [ID]

[1] Computer Engineering and Informatics Department, University of Patras, 26504 Patras, Greece
{akarras,c.karras,nschizas,sioutas,zaro}@ceid.upatras.gr
[2] Computer Technology Institute and Press "Diophantus", Patras University Campus, 26504 Patras, Greece

Abstract. In the current era, where data is expanding due to the unforeseen volume, velocity, and variety of data types produced by IoT devices, there is an imperative need to manage such data in remote IoT environments. However, these complexities have been inadequately addressed by conventional data management methods. In such scenarios, Distributed Hash Tables (DHTs) have emerged as an effective solution for efficient data storage and retrieval. Conversely, the dynamizature of IoT data presents its own set of challenges, such as decreased performance, inconsistent data, and increased overhead. To improve the performance of DHTs, we examine their algorithmic properties in cloud, fog, and edge computing environments, taking into account network designs, resource availability, latency requirements, and data proximity. This survey explores the adaptation of algorithmic elements in DHTs for optimal data administration in these cloud computing environments. Moreover, we examine advanced techniques such as effective hashing, adaptive routing, defect tolerance mechanisms, and load balancing. In addition, we address the challenges of managing vast and diverse volumes of IoT data, taking into account the unique features and constraints of cloud, fog, and edge environments. We also conduct contemporary research on security and privacy, focusing on algorithmic and architectural solutions for data integrity, confidentiality, and availability. This work enhances our comprehension of dynamic DHT algorithms and their potential for effective data management across multiple computing paradigms by investigating state-of-the-art research.

Keywords: DHTs · Cloud Computing · Fog Computing · Edge Computing · IoT Systems

1 Introduction

In the information era, where data is generated at an unprecedented scale, speed, and diversity due to the advent of the Internet of Things (IoT) devices, robust

I. Chatzigiannakis and I. Karydis (Eds.): ALGOCLOUD 2023, LNCS 14053, pp. 133–171, 2024.
https://doi.org/10.1007/978-3-031-49361-4_8

data management mechanisms are of paramount importance. Traditional data management techniques have had their limitations exposed due to these evolving complexities. Therefore, Distributed Hash Tables (DHTs) have been highlighted as a viable option for managing data in remote IoT contexts due to their effective, scalable data storage and retrieval capabilities. However, because of the dynamic and diverse nature of IoT data, these typical DHTs encounter their own difficulties, which can result in issues with decreased performance, inconsistent data, and higher overheads.

The demand to overcome these limitations and enhance the capabilities of DHTs is driving a new line of research into the algorithmic properties of DHTs in various computing environments, including cloud, fog, and edge computing. Due to variances in their network designs, resource availability, latency requirements, and closeness to data sources, each of these paradigms calls for certain algorithmic considerations and adaptations. This research provides an in-depth analysis of these algorithmic elements, evaluating how the methodology and underlying algorithms of DHTs can be tailored for optimal data management in the cloud, fog, and peripheral computing contexts. Focusing on the sophisticated algorithmic approaches inherent to DHTs, such as effective hashing, adaptive routing, fault tolerance mechanisms, and load balancing, we provide an analytical perspective on the operation of DHTs in these three distinct contexts. We focus on how these algorithmic choices operate while managing massive and varied data volumes produced by IoT systems, taking into consideration the unique properties and limitations of cloud, fog, and edge settings. Apart from that, we examine state-of-the-art methods in security and privacy research and difficulties linked to DHTs, highlighting algorithmic and architectural solutions that seek to guarantee data integrity, privacy, and availability. Additionaly, this work contributes to a deeper comprehension of the dynamic nature of DHTs algorithms and their potential for effective data management across many computing paradigms. We focus on underpinning the most recent findings in this field, offering insights into the potential advantages and the likely future advances that can arise.

The rest of this survey is organized as follows. Section 2 presents the background and related work in the field of Distributed Hash Tables (DHTs) as well as their algorithmic concepts. In Sect. 3, we present DHTs suitable for Cloud Computing while highlighting decentralized task management, privacy-preserving aggregation, and object storage. Section 4 presents DHTs in Fog and Edge Computing Environments along with data management and use cases, while Sect. 5 presents the Open Problems and Challenges. Ultimately, the survey concludes in Sect. 6 where the findings are presented as well as some possible Future Directions on DHTs.

2   Background and Related Work

The rapid growth in the volume, variety, and velocity of data has necessitated the development of innovative storage and management solutions to meet the demands of modern Big Data Systems. Traditional centralized data storage systems face limitations in scalability, performance, and fault tolerance as data volumes continue to expand. In response, Distributed Hash Tables (DHTs) have emerged as an essential technology, offering decentralized, scalable, and fault-tolerant mechanisms for distributed data storage and retrieval.

In this section, we overview the background and related work of various DHTs, highlighting their distinctive contributions, optimizations, and applications in the context of Big Data Systems and Big Data Management.

- **Pioneering DHTs:** Chord, Kademlia, and Pastry are considered pioneering DHTs, as they laid the groundwork for many subsequent designs. These early DHTs introduced key concepts such as consistent hashing, logarithmic routing tables, and baseSS routing, which remain relevant and influential in contemporary DHT implementations. By demonstrating the potential of decentralized data storage and retrieval, these DHTs helped shape the future of distributed systems.
- **Churn Resilience and Balanced Performance:** Some DHTs, like Bamboo and Kelips, have been designed to address specific challenges associated with distributed systems. Bamboo, for example, aims to provide efficient and robust routing under high churn rates which is a common issue in peer-to-peer networks. Conversely, Kelips focuses on achieving a balance between maintenance overhead and lookup performance by implementing a soft-state peer-to-peer membership protocol.
- **Latency Optimization and Locality-Awareness:** OneHop and SkipNet are DHTs that target latency optimization and locality awareness. OneHop prioritizes low-latency lookups by maintaining a larger amount of routing information, which results in increased maintenance overhead. SkipNet, on the other hand, employs the skip list data structure to enable efficient, locality-aware routing, leading to performance improvements in specific use cases.
- **High-Performance Object Location and Retrieval:** Coral is a DHT specifically designed for high-performance object location and retrieval, with a specialty similar to the BitTorrent protocol. By optimizing for a particular use case in the IoT context, Coral showcases the potential of DHTs for supporting efficient, distributed file-sharing systems.
- **Enterprise-Grade DHTs:** DHTs such as Apache Cassandra, Riak, and Voldemort have been tailored for enterprise use, underpinning large-scale distributed systems for organizations like LinkedIn and Amazon. These enterprise-grade DHTs often incorporate additional optimizations and features, such as tunable consistency levels, support for complex data types, and seamless integration with other Big Data technologies. This versatility renders them suitable for a broad range of industrial applications.

In summary, the variety of options of Distributed Hash Tables has played a crucial role in advancing Big Data Systems and Big Data Management in the IoT context. The ongoing adaptation and evolution of DHTs have paved the way for a new generation of distributed systems capable of managing the ever-increasing demands of a data-driven society.

2.1   Literature Review

Through our detailed research, we found a significant gap: there is not a single review that fully examines DHT-based strategies from various angles, including the structure and communication of systems, especially in multiple areas like blockchain, fog and cloud computing, IoT, and edge computing. This also extends into Online Social Networks (OSNs), Mobile Ad Hoc Networks (MANETs), and Vehicular Ad Hoc Networks (VANETs). In other words, there is a noticeable lack of deep-diving research that explores how DHT-based applications can be utilized in different technological fields, even with new insights emerging in specific domains. For example, interconnected clouds are explored in [82], fog computing in [35,84,91], and cloud computing in [4,21], each uncovering unique challenges and opportunities for integrating DHT approaches. In light of this, it is crucial to pull together these important, yet scattered, insights to better understand how DHT mechanisms can be applied and integrated into these fast-developing tech areas.

The sole extant study on DHT-based techniques in the blockchain area is [8], which provides a cursory evaluation of the application of DHT-based data storage capability. This work focuses on factors such as privacy, trustworthiness, integrity, data management and load balancing, all of which are thoroughly addressed in this survey. In the IoT context, existing DHT-based surveys primarily focus on features such as routing and lookup processes and mobility management [25]. The DHT-based approaches for scalability and service discovery, which are included in this survey, are, however, not covered in the talks in those surveys.

Neither of the previous studies, including those by [16,72,99] employ a DHT-oriented approach in their classification of Online Social Networks (OSNs). They only cover a brief analysis of DHTs as a potential contender for distributed routing and storage management among other OSN-based technologies. Aspects like spam prevention, service discovery, and data dependence management-all of which are thoroughly discussed in this survey-remain untouched as a result. The only current DHT-based survey in the realm of Mobile Ad Hoc Networks (MANETs), [2], concentrates on routing methods without diving deeper into elements covered by this study, such as data transfer, dynamic topology management, and traffic overhead relocation. Similar to how our survey covers service discovery, scalable routing, security, and privacy, the only DHT-based study [13] in the field of vehicular ad hoc networks (VANETs) to date only looks at the use of DHTs for distributed cluster management. Furthermore, these existing surveys lack a thorough investigation of the challenges, open problems, and research guidelines related to the utilization of DHTs in their respective domains.

In summary, this literature review highlights the absence of comprehensive surveys that encompass DHT-based approaches in various domains, including fog, blockchain, IoT, edge, OSNs, cloud computing, MANETs, and VANETs. It highlights the necessity of a survey that covers the utilization of DHTs in these domains and addresses aspects such as integrity, privacy, trustworthiness, data management, load balancing, scalability, service discovery, routing, security, and privacy.

2.2   Definition of a DHT

Distributed Hash Tables (DHTs) are an aspect of decentralized systems that map keys to values in a way that allows any participating node in the network to efficiently retrieve the value associated with a given key. Each network node and data item in a DHT is given a distinct key, which is commonly represented by an IP/port combination for nodes and by file names or other distinctive identifiers for data. Assuming that the keys are evenly distributed, this mapping is deterministic, guaranteeing that for every given input, the associated key will stay consistent.

DHTs are frequently used as the base for peer-to-peer (P2P) networks with overlays, where the structure of the DHT defines the underlying network architecture. This approach enables every network participant to easily find the node associated with a certain key. Furthermore, data may be stored in the network and accessed by utilizing the identity of the node linked with the key used to store the data.

Before we dive into the functionality of Distributed Hash Tables (DHTs) in the context described, let us briefly introduce the concepts of Voronoi cells, data points, and Delaunay triangulation to establish a foundation for the forthcoming discussion. In computational geometry, a Voronoi diagram partitions a plane into regions based on the distance to points in a specific subset of the plane. Imagine scattering seeds (data points) across a field. The region of land that is closest to a particular seed—where any point in that region is closer to that seed than to any other—forms a Voronoi cell. Essentially, each seed (data point) owns its own distinct Voronoi cell, comprising all points in a plane that are nearest to it relative to other seeds. This partitioning offers a structured, yet decentralized, method to efficiently locate and access data points in a distributed network. In harmony with this, Delaunay triangulation comes into play by connecting these data points in a way that no point is inside the circumcircle of any triangle in the triangulation, creating a network of neighbors that allows for efficient pathfinding and data retrieval strategies, seamlessly aligning with its application in DHTs.

A DHT can be conceptualized as an area populated by Voronoi cells and data points. Each node is responsible for preserving the data within its Voronoi cell, whose boundaries are determined by its closest neighbors. The Delaunay triangulation pertinent to the node in question includes Voronoi cell neighbors sharing a border with the node in question. From any node in the network, one can ascertain, in sublinear time, the node responsible for a particular key or a specific position in the DHT.

In essence, despite the variability in the specifics of different DHT protocols, the following features are indispensable to their design:

- **Distance Metric:** Central to any DHT is the concept of a distance metric. This requires establishing a mechanism to calculate the distance between two items. Once such a metric is defined, it allows us to articulate what it means to say that a certain node is responsible for the data in its vicinity.
- **Definition of Proximity:** Proximity or closeness is an essential concept in a DHT because it determines which node is responsible for which data, which nodes are its closest neighbours, and how a node should interact with them. Although the concepts of closeness and distance are interconnected, they are in fact distinct. To help clarify this point, we refer to the example of Chord [77], where the distance between two points a and b is defined as the shortest path around the circle in either direction.
- **Midpoint Definition:** This function determines the point in the DHT that is equally distant between any two specified locations.
- **Peer Management Strategy:** The backbone of a DHT's definition is its peer management strategy. Factors such as the size of the peer group, the data they contain, and the frequency at which their status is checked are all components of the peer management strategy. Most trade-off decisions are made at this stage of the DHT configuration process.

Generally, it is not necessary to devise a specific DHT routing scheme. In accordance with the universal routing concept, which is utilized by all DHTs, a message is sent to the closest known node to the destination. The exact routing scheme employed is determined by the protocol. Kademlia, for example, uses concurrent iterative queries for routing, whereas Chord permits both iterative and recursive routing. This illustrates the adaptability of DHT routing mechanisms.

2.3   Terminology

Due to the vast variety of DHTs, different authors have used different names to define congruent DHT components, as certain terminology may only make sense in particular contexts. Due to the fact that this work will discuss numerous DHTs with distinct terminology, we have developed a unified vocabulary:

key - A common hashing technique uses a 160-bit hash produced by a hash algorithm that correlates to a distinct[1] SHA-1[2].

ID - A key that connects to a certain node is the ID. A node's ID and the actual node cannot be distinguished from one another. In this work, nodes, and files are referred to by their IDs and keys, respectively.

---

[1] One-of-a-kind with a very high probability. Since it is extremely unlikely, formal DHT specifications frequently ignore the hash collision risk. Any of the collision resolution techniques, including chaining and linear probing, may be used to handle this for any file. The only canonical solution to a collision between two nodes, whether it is a node or a file, is to hope it doesn't happen.

[2] Many businesses are discontinuing SHA1 in 2017 because of the study on hash collisions [76] and the availability of hardware available to do SHA hash collisions.

Peer - Added to the network of active users. This section makes the assumption that each peer is made up of a unique set of hardware.

Peerlist - All of a node's peers that it is aware of. The *routing table* is the conventional name for this, however, various DHTs [67, 94] overload the terminology. A subset of the entire peer list is any table or list of peers.

Short-hops - The group of peers that, per the DHT's measurement, are "adjacent/nearest" to the node in the keyspace. These are the node's *predecessor(s)* and *successor(s)* in a 1-dimensional ring like Chord [77]. They may also be referred to as "*neighbours*". The part of the peer list that the node is not immediately next to is known as a long-hop, alternatively known as extended connections, shortcuts, or fingers.

Root Node - The node in charge of a certain key is identified as the Root Node.

Successor - The root node's alternate name. The neighbour who will take up a node's tasks if it leaves the network is known as its successor.

n **nodes** - It refers to how many network nodes exist.

Similarly, with slight variations, all DHTs carry out identical processes.

`lookup(key)` - This approach locates the root node of the `key`. The `lookup` function must be used in some fashion in almost all DHT operations.

`put(key, value)` - The root node of the `key` contains the `value`. Unless otherwise stated, `key` is taken to be the hash-key of `value`. The Tapestry is in opposition to this idea.

`get(key)` - Lookup-like, but returns the value stored by `key:put`. This is a minor distinction, as `lookup(key)` may be used to directly query the matching node. However, many systems utilize backup and caching techniques, which keep several copies of the object over the network. We can use `get` if it is a backup or if we do not emphasize which node provides the value mapped with `key`.

`delete(key, value)` - This does not require further explanation as DHTs typically do not focus on the key deletion and allow the application to make that choice. DHTs commonly make the assumption that the key-value pairs they store have a finite lifespan and are automatically deleted after that when they do address the problem.

Each node must have the ability to *join* and take care of itself locally.

`join()`. There are two steps to the join operation. Prior to joining, the connected node must create its peer list. It must initialize a peer list even if it is not required to have a complete peer list when it joins. The connecting node must secondly inform other nodes of its presence.

Maintenance. Typically, maintenance techniques fall into one of two categories: *lazy* or *active*. When doing lazy maintenance, peers are assumed to be in good health until they prove otherwise, at which time they are immediately replaced. Peers are periodically ping-ed and replaced in active maintenance if they can no longer be located. In fact, only neighbors receive proactive care, while everything else suffers slack upkeep.

The overlay peerlist, geometry, fault-tolerance and `lookup` function implementation in DHTs are all examined in this paper. Since the `leave()` procedure is quite straightforward and of little significance, we presume that nodes never depart the network gracefully and instead always fail unexpectedly.

2.4   Chord

Making a new ring-based DHT without being influenced by the Chord prototype, often known as Chord, is challenging [77]. It is highly renowned for its user-friendly routing, rules that make figuring out who owns a key very simple, and large number of variations. Chord has been awarded the 2011 SIGCOMM Test of Time Award for its prominence in Computer Science. Recent studies have revealed that Chord has not been implemented correctly for more than ten years and that many of the invariant qualities Chord claimed to have may occasionally fail [92].

List of Peers and Geometrical Distribution. All messages in Chord travel upstream and wrap around by bouncing from one node to the next with a larger ID. It is a 1-dimensional flexible ring. A unique m-bit key that corresponds to one of the $2m$ spots on a ring or ID is generated for each network participant and their associated data. Figure 1 depicts a Chord network example.

Fig. 1. 16 nodes in a Chord ring. The fingers are seen cutting through the ring (long hop connections).

All information whose keys are upstream from its predecessor's ID and downstream from its own ID is controlled by a network node. A node that controls a key is known as the root or successor of that key. Recursive upstream node queries are used to carry out the lookup and routing operations. In this strategy, searching for a key would take $\mathcal{O}(n)$ time if you just questioned your neighbors.

The *finger table*, a database containing m shortcuts to other peers, is present on each node to expedite lookups. The node that is the successor of the key

$n + 2^{i-1} \bmod 2^m$ is the i-th item in the finger table of a node n. The finger that is nearest to the key being looked for is queried by nodes during a lookup, but they do not pass the finger until they get to the root node. The search area for a key is roughly halved with each hop. With an average number of hops of $\frac{1}{2}O(\log_2(n))$, Chord now has a highly scalable lookup time of $\log_2(n)$ for any key [77]. The peer list also contains a list of s fault-tolerant neighbors in each direction in addition to finger tables. This increases the overall size of the peerlist to $log_2(2^m) + 2 \times s = m + 2 \times s$, assuming that each entry is unique.

Join Operations. Within the context of network integration, the act of joining the network entails a series of coordinated operations. This process initiates when a given node, referred to as n, initiates a request to node n', seeking assistance in locating its designated `successor`(n). This successor node is carefully chosen by node n based on relevant data, while the maintenance infrastructure promptly disseminates information to ensure that the existence of node n is acknowledged by other network nodes. During this transitional period, node n performs a crucial role in assuming certain responsibilities that were previously allocated to its predecessor's successor. Under this scenario, node n ensures the continuity and smooth functioning of the network, mitigating any potential disruption caused by the transition.

Robustness. In the spectrum of robust network architectures, the Chord protocol presents a noteworthy approach that ensures data resilience through a sophisticated backup mechanism. By using a strategy wherein nodes back up their data to their immediate predecessors, known as upstream nodes, Chord effectively fortifies the network against potential failures and disruptions. This mechanism becomes crucial due to the fundamental elements of Chord's key management system, wherein a node's closest successor assumes control over its keys upon departure or failure.

The employment of backup procedures to the immediate predecessors, or upstream nodes, serves as a vital safeguard for preserving data integrity within the Chord network. By distributing the responsibility of data storage among these preceding nodes, Chord significantly reduces the risk of material loss, particularly during scenarios where multiple nodes experience simultaneous failures. The presence of a successor list further diminishes the likelihood of data loss, as it allows for seamless reassignment of key control in the face of node departures or failures. It is worth noting that Chord's robustness is not achieved without an associated cost. In terms of message complexity, the backup mechanism necessitates $\mathcal{O}(\lg^2(n))$ messages. This factor indicates the computational overhead incurred by Chord's upkeep cycle, but it also demonstrates the protocol's meticulous attention to ensuring network resilience. By investing in this level of redundancy and backup mechanisms, Chord strives to uphold a high degree of robustness and data availability.

For a comprehensive understanding of Chord's maintenance cycle, including detailed insights into its backup mechanisms and resiliency features, interested readers can refer to the extensive documentation available in [77] which offers a comprehensive analysis of Chord's design principles, architectural nuances, and contributions to the field of robust network protocols.

Applications. An application of Chord DHT on IoT has been developed in [6]. The application focuses on leveraging the Chord protocol, which is a distributed lookup protocol for decentralized P2P systems, to enable efficient communication and coordination among LoRa wireless sensor nodes. LoRa technology is known for its low-power, long-range capabilities, making it suitable for wireless sensor networks.

2.5 Kademlia

Since a modified version of Kademlia (Mainline DHT) serves as the foundation of the BitTorrent protocol, it is possible that Kademlia [50] is the DHT that is most well-known and often utilized. In order to make nodes able to consume peer list changes with each query, Kademlia was created.

Peerlist and Geometry. Kademlia employs m-bit keys for files and nodes, similar to Chord. The binary tree-based architecture used by Kademlia, on the other hand, uses nodes as the tree's leaves. The XORing of the IDs of any two nodes in the tree yields the distance between them. In contrast to Chord, where distances are not symmetric, the XOR distance metric assumes that they are.

Kademlia nodes use a routing table with m lists, referred to as k-buckets, to keep information about the network. There are up to k nodes for each k-bucket that are between 2^i and 2^{i+1}, where $0 \leq i < m$. A network subtree that is external to the node is represented by each k-bucket. The least recently observed eviction approach, which avoids active nodes, is used to maintain each k-bucket. The sender's details are added to the tail of the relevant k-bucket each time the node gets a message. The information is relocated to the tail if it already exists. The node begins pinging the nodes in the list from the top down if the k-bucket is full. In order to make place for the new node at the tail, a node is deleted from the list as soon as it doesn't respond. If there are no further updates to the k-bucket for a while, the node does a `refresh` on it. A refresh in the k-bucket is a `lookup` of a random key.

Lookup. The `lookup(key)` transmits one message and returns the data for one node in the majority of DHTs. In Kademlia, both of these elements of `lookup` are different: each node that receives a `lookup(key)` returns the k nearest nodes to `key` that it is aware of. The `lookup` is performed simultaneously. The searching node initiates a `lookup(key)` process by sending parallel lookups to the α nodes from the corresponding k-bucket. These *alpha* nodes will each asynchronously provide the k closest nodes it is aware of that are closest to the given `key`. The node will keep sending lookups as they return their findings until no more nodes are identified. If the destination is a network-stored file, the `lookup` will also be successful if a node claims to have that file.

Joining. An initial contact is made by a joining node before it does a *lookup* on its own ID. New nodes are added to the joining node's peer list and made aware of by other nodes at each stage of the *lookup* method. Last but not least, the joining node does a `refresh` on each k-bucket that is farther away than the node it is aware of.

Fault-Tolerance. By repeatedly executing the `store` command, per file stored on the network is actively republished by nodes once every hour. Two optimizations are employed to prevent network flooding. If a node receives a `store` command on a file it is holding, the timer for that file is first reset, assuming that $k-1$ other nodes also received the command. This indicates that each hour, just one node republishes a file. Second, a republish does not include `lookup`. The `puts` operation of the file in the k closest nodes to the key during `store(data)` operation adds additional fault tolerance. Apart from the operations such as `lookup`, there is minimal active or routine maintenance involved.

2.6   CAN

The Content Addressable Network (CAN) [62] runs on a d-dimensional torus, having the entire coordinate space divided among members, in contrast to the other DHTs discussed in this article. The keys that are contained in the "zone" that a node owns are its responsibility. Every key gets hashed into one of the geometric space's points.

Peerlist and Geometry. The utilization of a peer list in the CAN (Content Addressable Network) protocol is characterized by its minimalistic nature, consisting solely of neighboring nodes. To establish an efficient routing scheme, CAN assigns a distinct geometric area within the coordinate space to each participating node. In addition, each node maintains a routing table that contains an extensive list of neighboring nodes in close proximity.

The size of the routing table in CAN is determined by the parameter $\mathcal{O}(d)$, which corresponds to the number of dimensions. This parameter influences the capacity of the routing table, dictating its ability to accommodate node entries. In a populated CAN network, characterized by the presence of at least $2d$ nodes, a lower bound constraint of $\Omega(2d)$ is imposed on the routing table size. This constraint becomes evident upon closer examination of each axis, as it guarantees that each axis is encompassed by at least one node at both ends. Crucially, when the network undergoes fragmentation due to a growing number of nodes joining, maintenance algorithms enable the routing table to dynamically expand and adapt, ensuring it can effectively accommodate the changing network topology.

Lookup. The lookup operation in CAN (Content Addressable Network) involves a structured routing process, in which each node collaborates with its neighbors. Every node maintains a routing table that establishes connections to adjacent nodes or those with which it shares a boundary area. According to the routing method, the lookup message is sent to the neighbor who is closest to the destination in each hop until it reaches the responsible node. This simplistic routing approach requires a minimal storage space of $2 \cdot d$ and achieves an average path length of $\frac{d}{4} \cdot n^{\frac{1}{d}}$ in a spatially uniform distribution across the network's n nodes. In CAN, the overall time required for a lookup operation is bounded by the expression $O(n^{\frac{1}{d}})$ hops, reflecting the scalability of the network.

Interestingly, during the creation of CAN, Kleinberg was concurrently investigating small-world networks, as mentioned in [40]. Kleinberg's research on lattice networks demonstrated analogous characteristics with the introduction of just a single shortcut. In contrast, CAN stands out as a network without any shortcuts. In the event of a lookup failure, a node resorts to selecting the next best available route. But it's crucial to remember that the greedy lookup strategy might not always work if it happens before a node can recover from churn-caused disturbances. Unsuitable candidates are found using an expanding ring search as a fallback method. This approach restarts the greedy forwarding mechanism and ensures the eventual completion of the lookup process.

Joining. The joining procedure involves splitting the geometric space among the nodes. In order to locate the node m now in charge of location P, a member of the node is contacted by node n with position P. The area of node m is divided so that each node is in control of half once node n informs node m of its intention to join. After the new zones are defined, n and m build the routing table for n from its previous neighbors and m. The tables of these nodes are then updated when they are notified of the most recent changes. As a consequence, only $O(d)$ nodes are impacted by the join operation. The original publication by CAN [62], provides further information on this splitting procedure.

Repairing. A node in a DHT alerts its neighbors that it is departing often has little impact on the network in CAN scenarios. A leaving node's (f) zone is simply moved to a neighboring zone of equal size, uniting the two zones. Minor issues arise when there isn't an equally-sized neighbor and this isn't practicable. Whenever this fragmentation happens, the zone belonging to f is assigned to the neighbor with the smallest area, which has to remain while it's been fixed.

Unexpected failures can also be handled very easily. Each node transmits a pulse to its neighbors that include both that of its neighbors and its own. A node starts a `takeover` countdown if it doesn't hear a pulse from f after a certain number of cycles and thinks that f has ended in failure. The node attempts to occupy f's space by sending a `takeover` message to all of f's neighbors after the timer expires. The volume of the node is included in this message. A node that gets a `takeover` message has two choices: it may either reply with a `takeover` message of its own or if its zone is smaller than the broadcaster's, it can cancel the countdown.

In CAN, when a node fails, the neighboring node with the smallest zone typically assumes control of the zone that belonged to the failed node. This rule produces rapid recoveries that only impact $O(d)$ nodes, but it necessitates the use of a zone reassignment method to eliminate the fragmentation brought on by takeovers. In conclusion, fragmentation must be repaired by a maintenance method even when a failing node is discovered very instantly and recovered rapidly. As mentioned earlier in the text, Ratnasamy et al. [62] also present the concept own using landmarks to choose coordinates, rather than a has function. The round-trip time (RTT) to each of the m landmarks is computed by each node. Which yields one of $m!$ permutations. The keyspace is partitioned into $m!$ regions, each corresponding to one of the orderings. A joining node now chooses a random location from the region corresponding to its landmark ordering.

Design Improvements. Ratnasamy et al. identified a number of improvements that could be made to CAN [62]. Some of these improvements have already been explored in Sect. 1. Adding more dimensions to the coordinate space is one way the system has been modified. Increasing d improves fault tolerance and reduces path length. One concept Ratnasamy et al. introduces is the idea of multiple coordinate spaces existing simultaneously, called *realities*. Each object in the DHT exists at a different set of coordinates for each reality simultaneously.

So a node might have coordinates (x_0, y_0, z_0) in one reality, while having coordinates (x_1, y_1, z_1) in another. Independent sets of neighbors for each reality yield different overall topologies and mappings of keys to nodes. Multiple realities increase the cost of maintenance and routing table sizes but provide greater fault tolerance and greater data availability. A final modification involves permitting multiple nodes to share the same zone, meaning that zones are not necessarily required to split during a join operation.

2.7 Pastry

Both Pastry and Tapestry [67,94], which share many similarities, employ a prefix-based routing mechanism first developed by Plaxton et al. (see [61]). In Tapestry and Pastry, every key is encoded as a base $2b$ number (usually in Pastry $b = 4$, producing a hexadecimal that is easily readable). The peer list that results most closely resembles an induced hypercube topology [11], with each node serving as a vertex. The use of a proximity metric is one noteworthy aspect of Pastry. This statistic indicates that IDs close to the node are used by the peer list.

Peerlist. Three elements make up Pastry's peer list: the routing table, a leaf set, and a neighborhood set. The routing table has $2^b - 1$ items per row and $\log_{2^b}(n)$ rows. The peers in the routing table whose first i digits match the sample node ID are found at the ith level. As a consequence, peers without a shared prefix with the node are found in row 0, followed by peers with a shared prefix in row 1, peers with a shared prefix in row 2, etc. There is one record for each of the $2^b - 1$ potential differences since each ID is a base $2b$ number. Using the system node 05AF as an example, which has a hexadecimal keyspace that spans from 0000 to FFFF and a $b = 4$ value, we can see how this works.

- A suitable peer for the first level 0 entry would be 1322.
- A suitable peer for the tenth[3] entry of level 1 would be 0AF2.
- A suitable peer for the ninth level one entry would be 09AA.
- For the second entrance of level 3, 05F2 would be a suitable peer.

The L nodes with the numerically closest IDs are stored in the leaf set, with half of it being utilized for lower IDs and the other half for bigger IDs. 2^b or 2^{b+1} is a common value for the constant L. The leaf set is utilized for routing when the destination key is close to the ID of the current node. The neighborhood set includes the L closest nodes, as measured by a certain proximity metric. However, this set is not typically used for routing purposes.

Lookup. The `lookup` procedure is a simple example of a recursive process. The `lookup(key)` is complete when the leaf set, which are the nodes closest to the current node, include the `key`. In this situation, the destination will be either the current node or the leaf set.

If the target node cannot be instantly identified, the node consults its routing database to ascertain which node it should connect to next. The length l shared prefix in the lth entry of the node's routing table is searched. The `lookup` is continued using the element from this row that matches at least one further digit of the prefix. The closest ID from the whole peer list is used to begin the `lookup` if this item is absent or has failed. Given that the search space is reduced by $\frac{1}{2^b}$ for each hop along the routing table, lookup is predicted to take $\lceil \log_{2^b} \rceil$.

Joining. In order to join the network, node J sends a `join` message to A, a node that is close by according to the proximity metric. The root of X receives the `join` message., which we'll refer to as *root*, much like a `lookup`. A copy of each node's peer list that got the `join` is sent to J. The routing table's ith row is created by copying the ith node contacted during the `join`, and the leaf set is created by copying the leaf set from the *root*. Because `join` requires that A and J be near to one other, from A's neighborhood set, the neighborhood setting is replicated. This indicates that the neighborhood specified for A would be nearby. Each node in the table receives a copy of the joining node's peer list after it has been created, allowing them to update their routing tables. A `join` has a constant coefficient of $3 * 2^b$ and a cost of $O(log_2^b n)$ messages.

---

[3] 0 is the 0th level.

Fault Tolerance. Pastry repairs its routing table and leaf set in a less thorough manner. If a leaf set node fails, the node contacts the leaf set node with the lowest or biggest ID, depending on whether the failed node's ID was smaller or bigger. The node replaces the rejected item and returns a copy of its leaf set. When a node fails and the node is present in the routing table, it contacts another node with an item in the same row to identify a replacement. In order to maintain track of its members, the neighborhood set is actively monitored. When a neighborhood set member becomes unresponsive, the node copies the neighborhood set of another entry and makes repairs from that selection.

Proximity Metric. Pastry's goal is to minimize the "distance" messages travel, where distance can be defined by some metric, typically the number of hops. The keyspace nodes closest to the node make up the leaf set. According to the distance measure, the nodes closest to the node make up the neighborhood set. Guarantees routing time is $< \log n$ in typical operation. Guarantees eventual delivery except when half of the leaf nodes fail simultaneously.

2.8 Tapestry

Tapestry [94] is based on the same prefix-based lookup [60] as Pastry [67] and the peer list and lookup operation share many similarities. Tapestry views itself more as a DOLR [14]. This essentially means that it is a distributed key-based lookup system like a DHT [30], but with some subtle differences at the abstract level which manifest as large % implementation changes. The essential difference here is that Tapestry has servers *publish* records/objects on the network, which direct lookups to the server. The assumption here seems to be that the servers, not the responsible node, serve the actual data. DHTs care or don't care on an application-to-application basis whether keys are associated with records or content.

Symphony and Small World Routing. Despite the fact that Chord [77] and Symphony [49] are both $1d$ ring-based DHTs, [40] uses small world network principles to build Symphony, which is a comparable DHT. The term "small world networks" originates from a phenomenon that psychologists observed in the late 1960s. In the experiments of [52], participants were assigned the task of delivering a letter to a specific recipient; in one experiment, the recipient was a stockbroker based in Boston, while in another, it was the wife of a divinity student in Cambridge. The participants were guided by instructions that allowed them to pass the letter only to someone they considered to have a stronger likelihood of personally knowing the intended recipient. For messages to reach their intended recipient in these communications, there were only an average of 5 hops between a theme and a participant.

This inspired research into building a network with links spread randomly yet with quick lookup times. Kleinberg's navigation technique [41] showed that nodes could deliver messages in $\mathcal{O}(\log^2 n)$ hops in a two-dimensional lattice network by using just their neighbors and a single randomly chosen[4] finger. This means that a $\mathcal{O}(1)$ sized routing table may do a $\mathcal{O}(\log^2 n)$ lookup.

Peerlist. Symphony employs a 1-dimensional ring as opposed to Kleinberg's 2-dimensional lattice[5], which is essentially a 1-dimensional lattice, like Chord. As opposed to employing a keyspace with values ranging from 0 to $2^n - 1$, Symphony distributes keys with m bits to the modular unit range $[0, 1)$. With the help of $\frac{hashkey}{2^m}$, this position was discovered. Although the design is somewhat arbitrary, it simplifies the process of making selections from a random distribution.

Similar to Chord, nodes are aware of both their immediate predecessor and successor. Similar to Chord, Nodes also maintain a list of $k \geq 1$ fingers, these fingers are chosen at random, unlike Chord. The probability distribution for these fingers is given by the equation $e^{ln(n)+(rand48()-1.0)}$, where **rand48()** is a C function that generates a random float double between "0.0" and "1.0" and "n" is the total number of nodes in the network. Since n is difficult to quantify in P2P networks because of their dynamic nature, each node approximates it based on how close or remote its neighbors are.

In Symphony, it is noteworthy that the links are bidirectional, which leads to each node having a total of $2k$ fingers. Essentially, when a node sends a finger to a peer, the peer responds by generating a finger in return.

Joining and Fault Tolerance. In Symphony, the fault tolerance and joining procedures are quite simple. In order to retrieve the parent node's ID after identifying it, to locate the parent node, a joining node requests help from a member. After integrating itself between its predecessor and successor, the connecting node creates its fingers at random. The usage of successor and predecessor lists handles failures of close neighbors. Failures for fingers are handled in a lazy manner, and when one is discovered, another randomly generated connection is used in its stead.

2.9   ZHT

One of the fundamental principles in DHT design is the recognition that churn - the continual process of nodes joining and leaving the network - is a critical factor necessitating ongoing maintenance. In light of this, nodes are designed to maintain only a minimal subset of the entire network for routing purposes. For the great majority of distributed systems, storing the complete network is not scalable owing to bandwidth restrictions and communication overhead brought on by the frequent joining and departing of nodes.

The bandwidth and memory requirements for every node to store a complete record of the routing table are insignificant in a system that does not account for churn. This would be the case with a high-performance computer cluster or data

---

[4] Randomly chosen from a specified distribution.
[5] Technically, this is a one-dimensional lattice.

center, where churn is often brought on by hardware failure rather than user attrition. Such a mechanism may be seen in ZHT [45] and Amazon's Dynamo [17]. A "zero-hop hash table," or ZHT, makes use of the predictable lifetime of nodes seen in High-End Computing systems. Nodes are added at the start of a job and deleted at its completion. ZHT can do a `lookup` in $O(1)$ time thanks to this attribute.

Peerlist. ZHT uses a 64-bit ring to operate, giving it a total of $N = 2^{64}$ addresses. ZHT strictly restricts the amount of physical nodes allowed in the network to n. Resulting in n divisions of $\frac{N}{n} = \frac{2^{64}}{n}$ keys. The partitions are distributed equally over the network.

There are i virtual nodes and k physical nodes in the network, and on each of them, ZHT is being used in at least one instance (virtual node). Each instance in the ring is in charge of a certain range of partitions. Since the network experiences minimal or no churn, each node maintains a current list of all other nodes. This list doesn't require frequent updates due to the network's stability. The cost of memory is remarkably low. The footprint of each instance is 10 MB, and each item in the membership table only requires 32 bytes per node. This indicates that there are 0–2 hops involved in routing.

Joining and Fault Tolerance. ZHT employs either a static or dynamic membership. In the case of static membership, once the network is bootstrapped, it does not allow any new nodes to join. In the case of ZHT, dynamic membership allows nodes to join at any moment. A random member is approached and asked for a copy of the peerlist in order to join. The most severely overloaded node can be identified by the joiner. To take over the partitions of that node, the joiner chooses a network address. As per Fault Tolerance, ZHT addresses only scheduled network exits or hardware failures. For data redundancy, nodes create backups with their neighboring nodes.

3   DHTs in Cloud Computing

DHTs are pivotal in orchestrating a symphony of seamless interactions within cloud computing environments, ensuring that resources are utilized efficiently and that data is accessible in a decentralized manner. Figure 2 encapsulates these concepts visually, providing an illustrative overview of the integral role and operational mechanics of DHTs in cloud computing environments.

The DHT-based solutions for cloud computing are summarized in Table 1. This table categorizes various proposed solutions according to certain key attributes, such as the type of solution (e.g., Infrastructure or Application), the Distributed Hash Table (DHT) strategy employed, the kind of nodes involved, the domain (i.e., Centralized, Decentralized, or Distributed), and the primary benefits associated with the solution. These strategies involve various DHT techniques, like Voldemort, Skip Graph, and Chord, and they cater to different layers

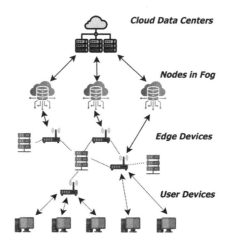

Fig. 2. An Overview of a DHT System in the Context of Cloud Computing.

and aspects of cloud computing, addressing challenges in storage, computation, task scheduling, and data distribution, among others. The varied domains and benefits indicate the versatility and applicability of DHT-based approaches in addressing the multifaceted challenges encountered in cloud computing environments.

Table 1. An overview of DHT-based Solutions for Cloud Computing

Solution	Type	DHT	Nodes	Domain	Benefits
Optimization of Storage Costs [97]	Infrastructure	Voldemort	Servers	Centralized	Cost Reduction
Optimization of Compute Costs [98]	Infrastructure	Voldemort	Virtual Machines	Centralized	Cost Reduction
Cluster Task Scheduling [88]	Application	Chord	Virtual Machines	Decentralized	Task Distribution
m-Cloud [53]	Application	General	Cloud Domains	Decentralized	Resource Integration
Game Object Storage [39]	Application	Chord	Game Objects	Distributed	Game Data Management
IPFS [7]	Application	Kademlia	Data Objects	Decentralized	Distributed File System
Time-sensitive Object Storage [89]	Application	General	Symmetric Keys	Decentralized	Temporal Data Storage
P2P Streaming [27]	Application	General	Video Chunks	Distributed	Media Distribution

3.1   Decentralized Task Management

A container encompasses a complete runtime atmosphere, encompassing an application alongside all its prerequisites and libraries essential for execution. The purpose of containerization is to facilitate software mobility across diverse computing environments through isolation. A container cloud, meanwhile, refers to a platform responsible for managing and scheduling the computational tasks within containers. Kubernetes stands as a prominent instance of such container clouds, widely employed within the industry.

Clustering the containers is how the container cloud orchestrates them. One master node oversees the administration of tasks across all of the nodes in each cluster, which controls how the cluster as a whole is run. However, depending only on a master node might be problematic since it presents a single point of failure and can lead to performance bottlenecks as the cluster gets bigger. This work presents a decentralized task management system based on a Distributed Hash Table (DHT) to address these scalability and reliability challenges [88].

The suggested approach replaces the whole cluster with a node-based decentralized DHT overlay. This overlay is used by nodes to find other nodes and their available resources. A node describes its state using a unique key and delivers its address as the associated value within the DHT to communicate its existence to others. The management protocol, which runs on each node, obtains from the DHT the status information of other cluster nodes. Utilizing this data, it makes informed task scheduling decisions, efficiently distributing jobs across the node itself or other nodes within the cluster.

3.2   Privacy Preserving Aggregation

A Distributed Hash Table (DHT) structure is used by the m-Cloud [53] system to aggregate sensor data while protecting user privacy. A federation of many cloud domains is used in this strategy. Cloud federation is a system concept where several administrative domains communicate information from their individual private clouds with one another [78]. A depiction of the cloud federation system model is presented in Fig. 3, where a larger federated cloud domain consists of four inner private cloud domains. The sensor data must be collected in parts by each cloud domain. To protect the privacy of specific sensor data, the data inside each cloud domain is aggregated before being shared with others.

A Distributed Hash Table (DHT) structure is used by the m-Cloud [53] system to aggregate sensor data while protecting user privacy. A federation of many cloud domains is used in this strategy. Cloud federation is a system concept where several administrative domains communicate information from their individual private clouds with one another [78]. In Fig. 3, a cloud federation system paradigm is shown, where a bigger federated cloud domain is made up of four inner private cloud domains. Some sensor data must be collected by each cloud domain. To protect the confidentiality of specific sensor data, the data inside each cloud domain is aggregated before being shared with others.

With m cloud domains, each sensor divides its data into chunks and shares the ith chunk with the ith cloud domain. The aggregated data bits inside each cloud domain are subjected to the calculation function, and the resulting computation is then forwarded to a single operator. In order to calculate the overall result, the operator then merges the separate cloud results. Each cloud domain is in charge of a certain set of keys and runs a DHT node while collaborating with other domains in a DHT overlay.

To assign sensor data chunks to the cloud nodes, the chunk's key is computed using its hash value, and the responsible DHT cloud node for that key is determined. It should be noted, however, that m-Cloud can only execute aggregated calculations on certain polynomials. All polynomial functions that can be calculated in this method are listed in the paper. $x + x^2 + x^3$ is an example of such a polynomial, with m-Cloud splitting and sharing the x term with one DHT node, x^2 with another, and so on.

Privacy Aspects of Distributed Hash Tables. Privacy-preserving aggregation (PPAgg) is crucial in safeguarding the individual data contributor's privacy while aggregating data from diverse sources, especially in contexts involving sensitive data such as Vehicular Ad Hoc Networks (VANETs), Federated Learning (FL), and Smart Grid Systems. In particular, PPAgg ensures secure aggregation of data and further maintains the confidentiality of each contributor during the process. Key application scenarios include:

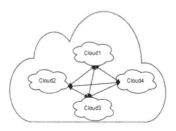

Fig. 3. A depiction of the cloud federation system model.

- VANETs: Utilizing PPAgg to securely aggregate traffic messages into an aggregated ciphertext and subsequently batch-unencrypt them, mitigating privacy, computational, and communication concerns [56,90].
- Federated Learning: Employing PPAgg to aggregate locally trained models into a global model, ensuring participant privacy throughout the aggregation process [36,37,47].
- Smart Grid Systems: Facilitating data privacy, confidentiality, authentication, and integrity during aggregation communication and function queries in fog computing-based smart grid systems [46,57].

– IoT: Enabling efficient aggregation of multidimensional data in IoT applications while preserving data contributor privacy [32,48,58].

Exploring the functionalities of Distributed Hash Tables (DHTs) in decentralized systems, particularly focusing on data storage and retrieval, necessitates a critical examination of the related privacy aspects. Although DHTs are not conventionally recognized as primary privacy-preserving solutions, they do offer scalable and fault-tolerant management of distributed data. However, this comes with inherent privacy challenges stemming from the systems' decentralized and distributed characteristics. Critical points include the potential for nodes to be manipulated and their vulnerability to assorted attacks.

Evaluating PPAgg and DHTs collectively, an essential inquiry emerges: is it plausible to effectively incorporate PPAgg with DHTs to mitigate some inherent privacy concerns? The objective would be to facilitate data aggregation which, in turn, guards individual contributions and ensures the protection of each data point from unauthorized access. Such scrutiny encompasses the implementation of privacy-preserving mechanisms within a DHT environment and the identification of challenges and opportunities therein. This balance between data aggregation and privacy preservation in decentralized networks is pivotal. Consequently, this investigation could lay the groundwork for ensuing research and modifications in the field, steering towards an augmented privacy framework in distributed systems.

Solutions for Privacy Preservation in DHTs. Distributed Hash Tables (DHTs), while widely recognized for their scalability and fault tolerance in managing distributed data, inherently present numerous privacy challenges due to their decentralized and distributed nature. Noteworthy here are the various initiatives aimed at securing both user and data privacy while maintaining the efficiency and functionality of DHTs.

– **Employing Oblivious Transfer for Query Privacy:** A strategy is introduced to protect the keys involved in DHT queries utilizing oblivious transfer (OT). The objective is to safeguard the queried key from intermediary peers involved in routing the queries to their respective destinations, without compromising spam resistance [5].
– **Adeona and Vanish:** These applications utilize DHTs to introduce innovative privacy-preserving solutions. Specifically, Adeona provides a solution for privacy-preserving laptop tracking, while Vanish aims to safeguard against retrospective assaults on cloud-archived data [23].
– **LaMRD:** LaMRD, a location-aware and privacy-preserving multi-layer resource discovery model for the Internet of Things (IoT), employs DHT technology to facilitate a peer-to-peer communication framework amongst fog nodes. This model ensures crucial security properties and reduced latency as compared to its centralized counterparts [34].
– **VPN0:** VPN0 utilizes a distributed architecture to address the privacy-trust issue inherent to a VPN's centralized authority. This system ensures a dVPN

node manages only pre-approved traffic, without revealing its whitelist or acknowledging the tunneled traffic through the employment of an attestation mechanism and a zero-knowledge proof, amongst other strategies [85].

- **Laribus:** Laribus, designed to detect local man-in-the-middle attacks against SSL/TLS, allows clients to validate the authenticity of a certificate without relying on a central notary service or the collaboration of website proprietors [51].

These studies underscore the feasibility and versatility of DHTs in maintaining data integrity and privacy, highlighting the potential pathways for further research and technological advancements in this domain.

3.3   Object Storage

The solution presented in Online Gaming [39] aims to create an adaptable infrastructure for large-scale peer-to-peer (P2P) online gaming platforms. All of the game's elements, including characters, are hosted on a game server, and players query the server to locate the items with which they interact. This is characteristic of traditional centralized methods. As the number of interacting users increases, the server's workload grows proportionally, making this centralized approach challenging to scale effectively.

To solve this issue, the suggested distributed system spreads user query load across a Distributed Hash Table (DHT) overlay made up of gaming servers. The DHT nodes in this arrangement reflect the game objects themselves. By using hash values as unique identifiers for game objects, these items are uniformly dispersed between game servers, guaranteeing balanced task allocation.

The Inter Planetary File System, frequently referred to as IPFS [7], is a peer-to-peer cloud storage platform. The technology is capable of distinguishing data objects throughout the whole network thanks to its special feature, content-addressing. IPFS does this by representing peers and data items in the Kademlia Distributed Hash Table (DHT).

In the case of small objects, typically around 1KB in size, they are directly stored on the DHT. The key-value pair for these objects consists of the object's hash value as the key and the object's content as the value. On the other hand, bigger items are held on peers, and the DHT is preserved with the reference to those peers. In this instance, the key is left unchanged, but the value is changed to the peer's address who owns the item.

Because IPFS objects are immutable, new versions of an item will always have a different hash value and different content. But in order to allow versioning, the new versions refer to their earlier iterations, resulting in a decentralized object graph. A graph with a single vertex is created by an item in its original form. As new versions of an object are created by making modifications directly to a vertex's children, each vertex serves as an object representation. It is possible to view and access all previous versions of an item by navigating through the object graph.

The accompanying object graph is completely decentralized and spread across several peers holding the object vertices of the network since each object is represented by a DHT node. Through its design, IPFS aims to be flexible enough for use in a wide range of scenarios, such as serving as a personal synchronization folder, a globally mounted file system, the base file system, or as a system for sharing encrypted data among distributed virtual machines.

A solution for time-sensitive access control in cloud storage for data objects is provided by time-sensitive object storage [89]. Under the concept of time-sensitive access control, sensitive data items are only available after a defined release time and are no longer accessible to new users after an expiry period.

To achieve this, the user encrypts their owned data objects using an asymmetric key scheme [38] and stores them on a cloud storage platform. The user additionally chunkifies the symmetric key and distributes it over a distinct DHT-based cloud storage made up of non-colluding nodes to provide time-based access control. This DHT-based cloud storage is distinct from the infrastructure in charge of maintaining customers' encrypted data objects and is solely used to store symmetric key chunks.

The user's symmetric key is encrypted and kept on each node of this DHT-based cloud storage system. These encrypted chunks that have expired are rejected by trustworthy DHT nodes. Even if the information is saved in the cloud, subsequent users won't be able to access it since the key will no longer be in the DHT nodes after the expiration time.

To distribute the symmetric keys of the data objects, a polynomial-based secret sharing algorithm [31] is utilized. The process divides the symmetric keys into parts and distributes them among the DHT nodes. Reconstructing a data object's symmetric key requires retrieving a data object's chunks from the DHT nodes and obtaining a secret timestamp that was supplied by a trustworthy timeserver at the time the relevant data item was published.

To achieve load balancing in Peer-to-Peer (P2P) video streaming systems, a two-tier DHT-based architecture is proposed [27]. Supernodes and user devices make up the first two levels of the architecture. The second tier, which consists of the users' devices, is composed of the supernodes, which are owned by the service provider and are managed by the same administrative domain.

This technique involves each supernode functioning as a service provider in the first tier maintaining a library of video files and streaming them as required to the user nodes in the second layer. The number of movies delivered concurrently on a supernode determines its load. The load is evenly distributed among the supernodes by establishing separate DHT overlays for each group of users watching the same video stream. The service provider's supernode, which initially broadcasts the content, is responsible for creating and managing the DHT overlay of users who are watching a particular stream.

Each stream is segmented into uniform-sized chunks, which are then distributed across the DHT overlay of devices belonging to users who are interested in the stream, aiding in load balancing. Instead of directly retrieving video segments from the content provider's supernode, users interact with their local

DHT overlay. By "local DHT", it is meant that the DHT overlay is specific to the video stream that the user is watching. This approach efficiently distributes the load of the supernode across the DHT overlays of all user devices.

3.4 DHTs for Enhanced Data Management in IoT Within Cloud Computing

Distributed Hash Tables (DHTs) offer a decentralized method for managing data and have become particularly important in the intersection of the Internet of Things (IoT) and cloud computing. Within the IoT domain, a peer-to-peer architecture utilizing DHTs ensures efficient management of elements like node IDs, capabilities, and sensor data [83]. This architecture extends its advantages to cloud services as well, where select peer nodes collaborate to share information, enhancing both scalability and fault-tolerance [96]. DHTs, with their structured approach, have also been adapted for larger cloud systems, exemplified by a cloud model that utilizes a hyperbolic tree structure for its DHT [81]. Further advancements in the field include the development of a digital twin management system for IoT devices using blockchain, highlighting the adaptability of DHT-based solutions [86].

Similarly, the DHT framework is being applied to improve traditional cloud structures, resulting in superior resource management and utilization [88]. The importance of distributing tasks evenly across various nodes in IoT-cloud interfaces has been addressed by introducing efficient load balancing methods, which employ algorithms designed for optimal distribution and resource management [1]. To ensure consistent data management in enterprise contexts, especially with the rise of industry 4.0 applications, DHTs have been incorporated into cloud storage systems. This approach facilitates a unified perspective on enterprise data, made possible by strategic mapping and rule-based systems [59]. These developments underline the essential role of DHTs in modern data management, especially within IoT, emphasizing the ongoing shift towards decentralized, efficient, and fault-resistant cloud computing solutions.

4   DHTs in Fog and Edge Computing

DHTs are turning into an increasingly significant technology in the context of fog and edge computing, considering that they provide an innovative method for developing and deploying applications in decentralized and distributed environments. As the need for real-time data processing and low-latency interactions grows, traditional cloud computing models confront scalability, reaction time, and bandwidth consumption limits. In contrast, fog and edge computing paradigms emphasize on the appropriate distribution of computing and storage resources among edge devices and end-users, which encourages the adoption of DHT-based applications in these environments.

DHTs, originally popularized in peer-to-peer systems, have found renewed significance in fog and edge computing due to their ability to facilitate efficient data storage, retrieval, and resource management in highly distributed networks. DHTs, as opposed to centralized alternatives that rely on a single powerful data center, spread processing and storage power across several nodes positioned closer to data sources and end-users. This decentralized architecture enhances the system's responsiveness and throughput while simultaneously reducing network congestion and bandwidth demands, thereby contributing to a more efficient and high-performing system.

Routers, base stations, and IoT devices serve as important data sources and processing units in fog and edge computing. DHT-based applications take advantage of these edge devices' processing power, allowing data to be processed and analyzed locally rather of having to go to a distant data center. DHT-based applications increase system performance by relocating computations and data storage closer to the edge, resulting in faster response times, lower latency, and better overall system performance.

Fog computing also introduces the idea of fog nodes, which function as processing hubs between edge devices and cloud data centers. The aggregation, filtering, and preprocessing of data from edge devices is crucial, and these fog nodes, which have more processing and storage capability, are crucial in this process. DHTs provide effective data interchange and job allocation between edge devices and fog nodes by facilitating smooth communication and collaboration between them.

Numerous benefits result from the use of DHT-based applications in fog and edge computing. DHTs offer dynamic scalability, fault tolerance, and load balancing in highly dispersed systems in addition to lowering network traffic and improving resource efficiency. Due to their decentralized architecture, DHTs offer the robust advantage of maintaining continuous data accessibility and responding smoothly to challenges such as node failures, network partitions, and dynamic modifications in network topology.

The uses of DHTs are becoming more varied and significant as fog and edge computing continue to spread across several industries. DHT-based applications are useful in a wide range of use cases, including smart cities, industrial IoT, healthcare systems, and autonomous cars. These applications provide cutting-edge solutions that make use of the close proximity of edge resources to improve effectiveness, dependability, and user experience. They also enable real-time analytics, collaborative data sharing, content distribution, distributed storage systems, and more.

In Table 2, we compare DHT-based applications in fog and edge computing, detailing solution type, DHT, nodes, identifiers, utilization, domain, and references.

Ultimately, applications and infrastructures built on Distributed Hash Table (DHT) technology play a crucial role in fog and edge computing, improving resource utilization, data processing, and application delivery in decentralized and distributed environments. In fog and edge computing systems, DHTs are essential for delivering low-latency interactions, effective resource management, and scalable applications because to their capacity to spread storage and processing power closer to the edge.

Table 2. Comparison among DHT-based Applications in Fog/Edge Computing.

Solution	Type	DHT	Nodes	Identifiers	DHT Utilization	Domain	References
Two-tier Storage	Inf	Chord	Storage Nodes	Content Hash	Object Storage	Decentralized	[74]
Two-tier Overlay	Inf	Chord	Super Peers	Peer IDs	Routing Overlay	Decentralized	[15]
Edge Gaming and AR	App	General	Game Nodes	Asset ID	Hybrid	Distributed	[63]
Access Control Management	App	Chord	Control Nodes	User IDs	Object Storage	Decentralized	[64]
Service Discovery	App	General	Service Nodes	Service Name	Routing Overlay	Decentralized	[70]
Content Distribution	App	Chord	Distribution Nodes	Content IP	Routing Overlay	Distributed	[54]
Cache-based Storage	Inf	Kademlia	Cache Nodes	Content Hash	Object Storage	Decentralized	[12]
Producer-Consumer Buffer	App	General	Buffer Nodes	Content Tag	Object Storage	Decentralized	[75]
Collaborative Computation	App	General	Compute Nodes	Result Hash	Object Storage	Distributed	[73]
Intrusion Detection	App	Kademlia	Monitor Nodes	Packet IP	Object Storage	Decentralized	[71]
Smart Energy Grids	App	General	Energy Nodes	Energy ID	Object Storage	Decentralized	[3,18,65]
Intelligent Transportation Systems	App	General	Vehicle Nodes	Vehicle ID	Routing Overlay	Decentralized	[20,43]
Distributed Healthcare Systems	App	General	Device Nodes	Patient ID	Hybrid[a]	Decentralized	[19,44,66,68]
Resource Discovery (Unreliable Environments)	App	General	Device Nodes	Device URI	Routing Overlay	Distributed	[79]
Resource Discovery (Mobile Environments)	App	General	Mobile Nodes	Resource Tag	Routing Overlay	Decentralized	[24,80]

[a] Combination of Routing Overlay and Object Storage.

4.1   Data Management with DHTs in Fog and Edge Computing

The role of managing substantial data in edge and fog computing environments is crucial, given the dispersed nature of these settings. By focusing on processing and managing data close to the data source, fog and edge computing reduce latency and enhance real-time data interactions [69]. They effectively navigate the limitations related to scalability, response time, and bandwidth, which are often observed in conventional cloud systems.

Distributed Hash Tables (DHTs), initially developed for peer-to-peer systems, are vital for managing diverse data flow and storage in fog and edge computing. DHTs facilitate decentralized processing and storage across nodes, which are often closer to data sources like Internet of Things (IoT) devices and sensors. Their scalability allows them to adjust their size dynamically, ensuring balanced load distribution and fault tolerance, even when the network experiences changes. DHTs support scalable object storage and resource discovery overlays, providing a resilient, scalable, and fault-tolerant data management platform [12,70,71,79].

Implementing DHTs in fog and edge computing offers several key advantages. Firstly, by managing data close to its source, DHTs enhance responsiveness and throughput, reducing latency and promptly serving data requests. Secondly, they alleviate network congestion and moderate bandwidth usage by intelligently routing data and storing it strategically within nearby nodes. Lastly, they bolster overall system performance by improving data interchange and effectively distributing computational tasks [69,95].

DHTs provide consistent data access and adapt to network changes, maintaining operational continuity in fog and edge computing environments. Furthermore, critical components such as routers and fog nodes are integrated into the DHT infrastructure, facilitating a comprehensive and collective approach to data management.

In the healthcare sector, the management of vast amounts of critical data from IoT devices highlights the need for proficient data management in fog computing [69]. A DHT-enabled, fault-tolerant data management scheme for healthcare IoT has been proposed, advocating a strategy to manage data efficiently and reliably, while ensuring low latency, minimal energy consumption, and cost-effectiveness. DHTs also provide a foundation for enhancing trust and security in data management across edge computing environments through blockchain technologies [95].

In conclusion, combining DHTs with fog and edge computing yields a resilient and scalable data management framework. As edge and fog computing become more integral to modern distributed systems, DHTs will increasingly guide the development of efficient and robust data management strategies in decentralized computing environments.

Utilizing DHTs for Data Management in IoT Within Fog and Edge Computing. Effective data management remains crucial in Internet of Things (IoT) systems, especially when operating within the complex environments shaped by fog and edge computing. Distributed Hash Tables (DHTs), with their fundamental capability to efficiently store and retrieve data across a network of nodes, become notably vital in ensuring smooth and scalable data management across a broad range of devices.

In this context, the utility of DHTs can be distilled into a few key points, showcasing their merit in addressing the unique challenges posed by IoT frameworks operating in fog and edge computing environments:

- **Consistent Data Availability:** DHTs ensure that data is always accessible, even if some nodes face downtime or failure, thus providing a steady data flow vital for the smooth operation of IoT systems.
- **Quick Data Access:** The structured nature of DHTs enables rapid and efficient data access, a necessity for maintaining the real-time responses that are fundamental in distributed IoT systems.
- **Flexible Scalability:** DHTs can easily adapt to varying loads, ensuring the data management layer continually meets the dynamic requirements of the network without sacrificing performance.
- **Even Load Distribution:** Through their inherent load-balancing capabilities, DHTs can evenly distribute loads across the network, preventing potential bottlenecks and ensuring smooth data and computational flow across the IoT network.
- **Data Security:** DHTs can be configured to bolster data security, ensuring that data interactions and transfers are both safe and reliable within the network.
- **Relevant Data Provision:** DHTs enable context-aware data management, ensuring that pertinent data is prioritized and made accessible as per the specific demands and operational contexts.
- **Efficient Network Management:** As IoT networks evolve, DHTs provide mechanisms to efficiently manage network topology, ensuring that changes in node statuses are addressed with minimal disruption to data consistency and access.

In summary, DHTs stand out as crucial enablers for robust and reliable data management and processing within IoT frameworks that are situated in fog and edge computing environments. They ensure not only reliable data availability, efficient data access, and scalable operations but also facilitate secure and context-aware data interactions and efficient network management, thereby enhancing the overall operational efficiency of IoT systems.

4.2   Use-Cases of DHT-Based Applications in Fog and Edge Computing

DHT-based applications in fog and edge computing exhibit remarkable versatility, finding utility across an expanding array of use cases within various domains. Beyond the previously mentioned examples, the following scenarios highlight the breadth of applications leveraging DHTs:

- Smart Energy Grids: DHTs enable efficient management and coordination of distributed energy resources in smart grids [3,18,65]. By utilizing DHT-based applications, energy producers, consumers, and grid operators can securely exchange information, optimize energy distribution, and enable demand response mechanisms. This empowers the grid with enhanced reliability, energy efficiency, and integration of renewable energy sources.
- Intelligent Transportation Systems: DHTs are essential to manage the enormous volumes of real-time data in these systems. In order to manage traffic flows effectively, cut down on travel times, and improve road safety, they enable dynamic routing, traffic prediction, and congestion management [20,43]. DHT-based systems can also facilitate cooperative communication between vehicles. Through this feature, vehicles can share information and collaborate in real-time, thereby enhancing situational awareness and potentially contributing to safer and more efficient roadways.
- Distributed Healthcare Systems: In distributed healthcare systems, DHTs provide a strong platform for organizing and securely sharing medical data as presented in [19,44,66,68]. Healthcare practitioners may securely access patient information, provide remote consultations, and enable dispersed care teams to make decisions together by utilizing DHT-based apps. The real-time monitoring and analysis of health data from wearable devices is also supported by DHTs, enabling prompt interventions and individualized medical treatment.
- Edge-based AI: DHTs are being used increasingly to implement edge-based artificial intelligence (AI) models. By using the computing capabilities of edge devices, DHT-based applications enable the deployment of AI models closer to the data source. As a result, real-time and context-aware AI inference at the edge is made possible, reducing the delay associated with relaying data to centralized cloud servers for processing. Applications span from object identification and video analytics in security systems to speech recognition and natural language processing in smart assistants.

– Edge Gaming and Augmented Reality: DHT-based applications support interactive gaming experiences and augmented reality (AR) applications at the network edge [63]. By distributing game assets, synchronization data, and AR overlays across edge devices, DHTs enable low-latency interactions, multiplayer capabilities, and seamless AR experiences. This enhances user engagement, reduces network dependency, and enables collaborative gaming and AR applications in various settings.

5   Open Problems and Challenges

– Typically, decisions regarding the performance of surveyed solutions are typically made based on the average value of the aggregated data. For example, when determining whether to be a regular peer or a super peer in the two-tier DHTs [15, 80]. However, it's important to note that the aggregated average value may not always be the optimal choice, particularly in situations where the standard deviation is significantly low or high. This can lead to decisions that are affected by noise. For instance, in the case of two-tier architectures, it could result in the majority of nodes being selected as peers or super peers. Exploring alternative methods of aggregating performance metrics, such as using the median, for edge and fog computing solutions is a future research direction that demands further study.

– One of the major issues with DHT-based systems is the expense of stabilizing lookup tables when nodes fail or move between online and offline states. According to various study citations [54, 79], DHT nodes (such as edge and fog servers) are configured with their DHT lookup tables by a central registry server, which regularly updates these tables based on the dynamic behavior of the nodes. However, it's crucial to research and includes [29], an efficient and decentralized DHT stabilizing technique, into the edge and fog computing ecosystems. This would aid in addressing the distributed lookup table stabilization's cost and scalability issues.

– Running distinct requests for each value inside the desired range is a standard way to handle range queries in DHT overlays. With this method, a range query with k values may be answered in a system with n DHT nodes with a message complexity of $\mathcal{O}(k \times log n)$. The range query may result in linear message complexity if k is greater than n. It is critical to create effective DHT-based approaches for answering range requests in order to improve system performance in edge and fog computing ecosystems. Further research should be conducted to explore and study these techniques, as they have the potential to significantly benefit system performance in scenarios involving edge and fog computing.

- Infrastructure-oriented resource optimization solutions, such as [97,98], often lean towards centralization by requiring almost the entire system behavior to be predefined. For example, they could rely on a specified time-based distribution of data items throughout the whole system. Furthermore, because they are not designed to respond to dynamic system changes such as abrupt changes in the distribution of data items, these solutions frequently have a static nature. There have been several attempts to advance toward completely decentralized, dynamic solutions, such as [29], which function based on the local perspective of individual nodes and react to system dynamics by predicting future behaviour based on current and previous states. A distributed system adds some mistakes when decisions are made entirely based on the local view of nodes. An intriguing research topic would be error margin minimization in decentralized and dynamic systems to calculate operational trade-off points. This investigation would help understand the limitations and trade-offs associated with decentralized decision-making in dynamic environments.
- Integrating DHTs in modern solutions such as autonomous vehicles, requires the use of technologies, such as the Cloud, which function as gateways or intermediaries between the DHT and other systems on the network. Cars for example can submit service requests through these gateways, which transmit signals on a regular basis to alert them of their presence. If the gateway vehicles are uniformly disseminated throughout the VANET (Vehicular Ad Hoc Network), the connection to the DHT is frequently strong. However, this may lead to conditions of congested channels. It is imperative to conduct research on the selection of entry-level vehicles in order to comprehend the trade-offs between performance and cost.
- Due to the dispersion of the VANET, numerous DHTs could exist outside of the vehicles, such as in the cloud or near edge layers. For service discovery, messages must be moved from one DHT to another on occasion. The service discovery messages can be sent and received without cutting the DHTs off altogether. The development of a suitable communication mechanism to keep DHTs connected at both the vehicle and cloud/edge levels is currently ongoing. Before DHT-assisted VANET applications can be effectively deployed, this issue has to be solved. Finding a reliable and efficient communication protocol that ensures seamless connectivity among the DHTs in different layers is crucial for the success of VANET applications [28].

6   Conclusions and Future Work

In conclusion, this comparative survey has explored six prominent DHT algorithms, namely Chord, Kademlia, CAN, Pastry, Symphony, and ZHT, which offer efficient and scalable solutions for creating peer-to-peer overlay networks.

These algorithms enable decentralized retrieval and storage of data and materials, eliminating the need for centralized network management. In contrast to first-generation peer-to-peer applications that rely on centralized indexes, these DHT algorithms facilitate content searching without centralized control. As the demand for P2P applications continues to grow, it becomes essential to develop systems capable of accommodating expansive network growth and dynamic network topologies. The innovative peer protocols discussed in this survey open up opportunities for applying peer-to-peer technologies beyond traditional file-sharing domains.

Future work should focus on advancing the capabilities of distributed hash tables and their integration with cloud and fog/edge computing paradigms. One promising avenue is to investigate techniques for efficient data storage and replication strategies in distributed hash tables operating within cloud and fog/edge environments. Additionally, future research directions can be directed towards developing robust and scalable algorithms for DHT stabilization, considering the dynamic nature of cloud and fog/edge networks. Furthermore, addressing the challenge of seamlessly connecting multiple DHTs across different layers, such as vehicles, cloud, and edge, remains an open problem. The practical deployment of DHT-assisted applications in VANETs and other distributed systems could be facilitated by the development of communication protocols that guarantee stable and efficient connections between DHTs in different environments. In the context of cloud and fog/edge computing, continued exploration and innovation in these areas have the potential to significantly improve the performance and capabilities of DHT-based systems.

Ultimately, the findings of our work are shown in Table 3, as presented in Appendix 6 where each DHT is presented along with key information. This table delineates key operational parameters and inner aspects of several DHT models, such as Chord and WiCHORD, among others, offering insights into their respective efficiencies and methodological variances concerning key management and node operations. Serving as a comprehensive reference, it thus facilitates an in-depth understanding and comparative assessment of the various DHT models, enabling astute decision-making in their application and deployment.

Appendix

In the following section, all DHT-based algorithms and protocols are summarized. The table contains the name of each DHT solution, the size of each routing table, the lookup and delete key operations, the join and leave operations, as well as some comments per each method. This table serves as a concluding remark for our survey, as it presents all information gathered in one easy-to-read place.

Table 3. A comparison and overview of several DHTs.

DHTs	Size of a routing table	Lookup, Insert, Delete Key	Join/Leave	Comments
Chord [77]	$\mathcal{O}(\log n)$, maximum $m+2s$	$\mathcal{O}(\log n)$, avg $(\frac{1}{2}\log n)$	$< \mathcal{O}(\log n)$ total messages	s is neighbors in 1 direction , m = keysize in bits
WiCHORD [6]	$\mathcal{O}(m)$	Lookup: $\mathcal{O}(\log n)$, Insert/Delete:-	$\mathcal{O}(\log n)$	m = keysize in bits. Suitable for Cloud and Edge applications in IoT
ZHT [45]	$\mathcal{O}(n)$	$\mathcal{O}(1)$	$\mathcal{O}(n)$	Expects a very low churn
CAN [62]	$\Omega(2d)$	$\mathcal{O}(n^{\frac{1}{d}})$, average $\frac{d}{4}\cdot n^{\frac{1}{d}}$	Affects $\mathcal{O}(d)$ nodes	d is the number of dimensions
Koorde [33]	$\mathcal{O}(\log_{2^{k+1}} n)$	$\mathcal{O}(\log_{2^{k+1}} n)$	$\mathcal{O}(\log_{2^{k+1}} n)$	Requires $\mathcal{O}(k\log n)$ state at each node, where k is the number of bits in a node identifier
Mainline DHT	$\mathcal{O}(\log n)$	$\mathcal{O}(\log n)$	$\mathcal{O}(\log n)$	Kademlia-based
Pastry [67]	$\mathcal{O}(\log_\beta n)$	$\mathcal{O}(\lceil \log_{2^\beta}\rceil)$	$\mathcal{O}(\log_\beta n)$	NodeIDs are base β numbers
Kademlia [50]	$\mathcal{O}(\log n)$, maximum $m\cdot k$	$(\lceil \log n \rceil) + c$	$\mathcal{O}(\log(n))$	This is without considering optimization
Riak [42]	$\mathcal{O}(\log n)$	$\mathcal{O}(\log n)$	$\mathcal{O}(\log n)$	Based on Amazon's Dynamo, uses consistent hashing
Symphony [49]	$2k+2$	average $\mathcal{O}(\frac{1}{k}\log^2 n)$	$\mathcal{O}(\frac{1}{k}\log^2 n)$ messages, constant < 1	$k \geq 1$, fingers are chosen at random
VHash	$\Omega(3d+1) + \mathcal{O}((3d+1)^2)$	$\mathcal{O}(\sqrt[d]{n})$ hops	$3d+1$	hops are based least latency, approximates regions
Apache Cassandra [10]	$\mathcal{O}(\log n)$	$\mathcal{O}(\log n)$	$\mathcal{O}(\log n)$	Uses consistent hashing, based on Chord
Voldemort [9]	$\mathcal{O}(\log n)$	$\mathcal{O}(\log n)$	$\mathcal{O}(\log n)$	Dynamo-like, used in LinkedIn and other services
MapChain [87]	$\mathcal{O}(\log n)$	$\mathcal{O}(\log n)$	$\mathcal{O}(\log n)$	Hybrid of Chord and Kademlia, high resilience
TomP2P [55]	$\mathcal{O}(\log n)$	$\mathcal{O}(\log n)$	$\mathcal{O}(\log n)$	Similar to Kademlia, uses consistent hashing
LPRS-Chord [93]	$\mathcal{O}(\log n)$	$\mathcal{O}(\log n)$	$\mathcal{O}(\log n)$	Latency-aware, efficient routing, based on Chord
CoralCDN [22]	$\mathcal{O}(\log n)$	$\mathcal{O}(\log n)$	$\mathcal{O}(\log n)$	Fast object location and retrieval, used with BitTorrent
Kelips [26]	$\mathcal{O}(\sqrt{n})$	$\mathcal{O}(1)$	$\mathcal{O}(1)$	Soft-state membership protocol, balances overhead and lookup performance
Bamboo	$\mathcal{O}(\log n)$	$\mathcal{O}(\log n)$	$\mathcal{O}(\log n)$	Efficient and robust routing under high churn rates
OneHop	$\mathcal{O}(n)$	$\mathcal{O}(1)$	$\mathcal{O}(n)$	Low-latency lookup, increased maintenance overhead
Plaxton-based DHTs, Pastry [67], Tapestry [94]	$\mathcal{O}(\log_\beta n)$	$\mathcal{O}(\log_\beta n)$	$\mathcal{O}(\log_\beta n)$	NodeIDs are base β numbers

References

1. Abed, M.M., Younis, M.F.: Developing load balancing for IoT-cloud computing based on advanced firefly and weighted round robin algorithms. Baghdad Sci. J. **16**(1), 130–139 (2019)
2. Abid, S.A., Othman, M., Shah, N.: A survey on DHT-based routing for large-scale mobile ad hoc networks. ACM Comput. Surv. (CSUR) **47**(2), 1–46 (2014)
3. Alladi, T., Chamola, V., Rodrigues, J.J.P.C., Kozlov, S.A.: Blockchain in smart grids: a review on different use cases. Sensors **19**(22) (2019). https://doi.org/10.3390/s19224862. https://www.mdpi.com/1424-8220/19/22/4862
4. Androutsellis-Theotokis, S., Spinellis, D.: A survey of peer-to-peer content distribution technologies. ACM Comput. Surv. (CSUR) **36**(4), 335–371 (2004)
5. Backes, M., Goldberg, I., Kate, A., Toft, T.: Adding query privacy to robust DHTs. In: Proceedings of the 7th ACM Symposium on Information, Computer and Communications Security, pp. 30–31 (2012)
6. Balatsouras, C.P., Karras, A., Karras, C., Tsolis, D., Sioutas, S.: WiCHORD: a chord protocol application on P2P LoRa wireless sensor networks. In: 2022 13th International Conference on Information, Intelligence, Systems & Applications (IISA), pp. 1–8 (2022). https://doi.org/10.1109/IISA56318.2022.9904339
7. Benet, J.: IPFS - content addressed, versioned, P2P file system. CoRR abs/1407.3561 (2014). arxiv.org/abs/1407.3561
8. Berdik, D., Otoum, S., Schmidt, N., Porter, D., Jararweh, Y.: A survey on blockchain for information systems management and security. Inf. Process. Manag. **58**(1), 102397 (2021)
9. Bonvin, N., Papaioannou, T.G., Aberer, K.: A self-organized, fault-tolerant and scalable replication scheme for cloud storage. In: Proceedings of the 1st ACM Symposium on Cloud Computing, SoCC 2010, pp. 205–216. Association for Computing Machinery, New York, NY, USA (2010). https://doi.org/10.1145/1807128.1807162
10. Cassandra, A.: Apache Cassandra. **13** (2014). http://www.planetcassandraorg/what-is-apache-cassandra
11. Condie, T., Kacholia, V., Sank, S., Hellerstein, J.M., Maniatis, P.: Induced churn as shelter from routing-table poisoning. In: NDSS (2006)
12. Confais, B., Lebre, A., Parrein, B.: An object store service for a fog/edge computing infrastructure based on IPFS and a scale-out NAS. In: 2017 IEEE 1st International Conference on Fog and Edge Computing (ICFEC), pp. 41–50. IEEE (2017)
13. Cooper, C., Franklin, D., Ros, M., Safaei, F., Abolhasan, M.: A comparative survey of VANET clustering techniques. IEEE Commun. Surv. Tutorials **19**(1), 657–681 (2016)
14. Dabek, F., Zhao, B., Druschel, P., Kubiatowicz, J., Stoica, I.: Towards a common API for structured peer-to-peer overlays. In: Kaashoek, M.F., Stoica, I. (eds.) IPTPS 2003. LNCS, vol. 2735, pp. 33–44. Springer, Heidelberg (2003). https://doi.org/10.1007/978-3-540-45172-3_3
15. D'Angelo, M., Caporuscio, M.: SA-Chord: a self-adaptive P2P overlay network. In: 2018 IEEE 3rd International Workshops on Foundations and Applications of Self* Systems (FAS* W), pp. 118–123. IEEE (2018)
16. De Salve, A., Mori, P., Ricci, L.: A survey on privacy in decentralized online social networks. Comput. Sci. Rev. **27**, 154–176 (2018)
17. DeCandia, G., et al.: Dynamo: Amazon's highly available key-value store. In: ACM SIGOPS Operating Systems Review, vol. 41, pp. 205–220. ACM (2007)

18. Demertzis, F.F., Karopoulos, G., Xenakis, C., Colarieti, A.: Self-organised key management for the smart grid. In: Papavassiliou, S., Ruehrup, S. (eds.) ADHOC-NOW 2015. LNCS, vol. 9143, pp. 303–316. Springer, Cham (2015). https://doi.org/10.1007/978-3-319-19662-6_21

19. Egala, B.S., Pradhan, A.K., Dey, P., Badarla, V., Mohanty, S.P.: Fortified-chain 2.0: intelligent blockchain for decentralized smart healthcare system. IEEE Internet Things J., 1 (2023). https://doi.org/10.1109/JIOT.2023.3247452

20. El-Salakawy, G., Abu El-Kheir, M.: Blockchain-based data management in vehicular networks. In: 2020 2nd Novel Intelligent and Leading Emerging Sciences Conference (NILES), pp. 146–151 (2020). https://doi.org/10.1109/NILES50944.2020.9257890

21. Fersi, G., Louati, W., Ben Jemaa, M.: Distributed hash table-based routing and data management in wireless sensor networks: a survey. Wireless Netw. **19**, 219–236 (2013)

22. Freedman, M.J., Freudenthal, E., Mazieres, D.: Democratizing content publication with coral. In: NSDI, vol. 4, p. 18 (2004)

23. Geambasu, R., Falkner, J., Gardner, P., Kohno, T., Krishnamurthy, A., Levy, H.M.: Experiences building security applications on DHTs. Technical report, UW-CSE-09-09-01 (2009)

24. Gedeon, J., Meurisch, C., Bhat, D., Stein, M., Wang, L., Mühlhäuser, M.: Router-based brokering for surrogate discovery in edge computing. In: 2017 IEEE 37th International Conference on Distributed Computing Systems Workshops (ICDCSW), pp. 145–150. IEEE (2017)

25. Ghaleb, S.M., Subramaniam, S., Zukarnain, Z.A., Muhammed, A.: Mobility management for IoT: a survey. EURASIP J. Wirel. Commun. Netw. **2016**, 1–25 (2016)

26. Gupta, I., Birman, K., Linga, P., Demers, A., van Renesse, R.: Kelips: building an efficient and stable P2P DHT through increased memory and background overhead. In: Kaashoek, M.F., Stoica, I. (eds.) IPTPS 2003. LNCS, vol. 2735, pp. 160–169. Springer, Heidelberg (2003). https://doi.org/10.1007/978-3-540-45172-3_15

27. Gupta, R.K., Hada, R., Sudhir, S.: 2-tiered cloud based content delivery network architecture: an efficient load balancing approach for video streaming. In: 2017 International Conference on Signal Processing and Communication (ICSPC), pp. 431–435 (2017). https://doi.org/10.1109/CSPC.2017.8305885

28. Hassanzadeh-Nazarabadi, Y., Boshrooyeh, S.T., Otoum, S., Ucar, S., Özkasap, Ö.: DHT-based communications survey: architectures and use cases. CoRR abs/2109.10787 (2021). arxiv.org/abs/2109.10787

29. Hassanzadeh-Nazarabadi, Y., Küpçü, A., Özkasap, Ö.: Interlaced: fully decentralized churn stabilization for skip graph-based DHTs. J. Parallel Distrib. Comput. **149**, 13–28 (2021)

30. Hildrum, K., Kubiatowicz, J.D., Rao, S., Zhao, B.Y.: Distributed object location in a dynamic network. Theory Comput. Syst. **37**(3), 405–440 (2004)

31. Ito, M., Saito, A., Nishizeki, T.: Secret sharing scheme realizing general access structure. Electron. Commun. Japan (Part III: Fundam. Electron. Sci.) **72**(9), 56–64 (1989)

32. Jastaniah, K., Zhang, N., Mustafa, M.A.: Efficient privacy-friendly and flexible IoT data aggregation with user-centric access control. arXiv preprint arXiv:2203.00465 (2022)

33. Kaashoek, M.F., Karger, D.R.: Koorde: a simple degree-optimal distributed hash table. In: Kaashoek, M.F., Stoica, I. (eds.) IPTPS 2003. LNCS, vol. 2735, pp. 98–107. Springer, Heidelberg (2003). https://doi.org/10.1007/978-3-540-45172-3_9

34. Kamel, M.B., Ligeti, P., Reich, C.: Lamred: location-aware and decentralized multi-layer resource discovery for IoT. Acta Cybernet. **25**(2), 319–349 (2021)

35. Karagiannis, V.: Compute node communication in the fog: survey and research challenges. In: Proceedings of the Workshop on Fog Computing and the IoT, pp. 36–40 (2019)

36. Karras, A., Karras, C., Giotopoulos, K.C., Tsolis, D., Oikonomou, K., Sioutas, S.: Peer to peer federated learning: towards decentralized machine learning on edge devices. In: 2022 7th South-East Europe Design Automation, Computer Engineering, Computer Networks and Social Media Conference (SEEDA-CECNSM), pp. 1–9 (2022). https://doi.org/10.1109/SEEDA-CECNSM57760.2022.9932980

37. Karras, A., Karras, C., Giotopoulos, K.C., Tsolis, D., Oikonomou, K., Sioutas, S.: Federated edge intelligence and edge caching mechanisms. Information **14**(7) (2023). https://doi.org/10.3390/info14070414. https://www.mdpi.com/2078-2489/14/7/414

38. Katz, J., Lindell, Y.: Introduction to Modern Cryptography. CRC Press (2020)

39. Kavalionak, H., Carlini, E., Ricci, L., Montresor, A., Coppola, M.: Integrating peer-to-peer and cloud computing for massively multiuser online games. Peer-to-Peer Network. Appl. **8**, 301–319 (2015)

40. Kleinberg, J.: The small-world phenomenon: an algorithmic perspective. In: Proceedings of the Thirty-Second Annual ACM Symposium on Theory of Computing, pp. 163–170. ACM (2000)

41. Kleinberg, J.M.: Navigation in a small world. Nature **406**(6798), 845 (2000)

42. Klophaus, R.: Riak core: building distributed applications without shared state. In: ACM SIGPLAN Commercial Users of Functional Programming, CUFP 2010. Association for Computing Machinery, New York, NY, USA (2010). https://doi.org/10.1145/1900160.1900176

43. Kuhn, E., Mordinyi, R., Goiss, H.D., Bessler, S., Tomic, S.: A P2P network of space containers for efficient management of spatial-temporal data in intelligent transportation scenarios. In: 2009 Eighth International Symposium on Parallel and Distributed Computing, pp. 218–225 (2009). https://doi.org/10.1109/ISPDC.2009.27

44. Kumar, R., Marchang, N., Tripathi, R.: Distributed off-chain storage of patient diagnostic reports in healthcare system using IPFS and blockchain. In: 2020 International Conference on COMmunication Systems & NETworkS (COMSNETS), pp. 1–5 (2020). https://doi.org/10.1109/COMSNETS48256.2020.9027313

45. Li, T., et al. ZHT: a light-weight reliable persistent dynamic scalable zero-hop distributed hash table. In: 2013 IEEE 27th International Symposium on Parallel & Distributed Processing (IPDPS), pp. 775–787. IEEE (2013)

46. Liu, J.N., Weng, J., Yang, A., Chen, Y., Lin, X.: Enabling efficient and privacy-preserving aggregation communication and function query for fog computing-based smart grid. IEEE Trans. Smart Grid **11**(1), 247–257 (2019)

47. Liu, Z., Guo, J., Yang, W., Fan, J., Lam, K.Y., Zhao, J.: Privacy-preserving aggregation in federated learning: a survey. IEEE Trans. Big Data (2022)

48. Loukil, F., Ghedira-Guegan, C., Boukadi, K., Benharkat, A.N.: Privacy-preserving IoT data aggregation based on blockchain and homomorphic encryption. Sensors **21**(7), 2452 (2021)

49. Manku, G.S., Bawa, M., Raghavan, P., et al.: Symphony: distributed hashing in a small world. In: USENIX Symposium on Internet Technologies and Systems, p. 10 (2003)

50. Maymounkov, P., Mazières, D.: Kademlia: a peer-to-peer information system based on the XOR metric. In: Druschel, P., Kaashoek, F., Rowstron, A. (eds.) IPTPS 2002. LNCS, vol. 2429, pp. 53–65. Springer, Heidelberg (2002). https://doi.org/10.1007/3-540-45748-8_5

51. Micheloni, A., Fuchs, K.P., Herrmann, D., Federrath, H.: Laribus: privacy-preserving detection of fake SSL certificates with a social P2P notary network. In: 2013 International Conference on Availability, Reliability and Security, pp. 1–10. IEEE (2013)

52. Milgram, S.: The small world problem. Psychol. Today **2**(1), 60–67 (1967)

53. Nakagawa, I., et al.: DHT extension of m-cloud - scalable and distributed privacy preserving statistical computation on public cloud. In: 2015 IEEE 39th Annual Computer Software and Applications Conference, vol. 3, pp. 682–683 (2015). https://doi.org/10.1109/COMPSAC.2015.94

54. Nakayama, T., Asaka, T.: Peer-to-peer bidirectional streaming using mobile edge computing. In: 2017 Fifth International Symposium on Computing and Networking (CANDAR), pp. 263–266. IEEE (2017)

55. Name, A.: TomP2P, a P2P-based key-value pair storage library (2012). https://tomp2p.net/. Accessed: insert-the-date-you-accessed-the-website

56. Napoli, A., et al.: Enabling router bypass and saving cost using point-to-multipoint transceivers for traffic aggregation. In: Optical Fiber Communication Conference, pp. W3F-5. Optica Publishing Group (2022)

57. Orda, L.D., Jensen, T.V., Gehrke, O., Bindner, H.W.: Efficient routing for overlay networks in a smart grid context. In: SMARTGREENS, pp. 131–136 (2019)

58. Peng, C., Luo, M., Wang, H., Khan, M.K., He, D.: An efficient privacy-preserving aggregation scheme for multidimensional data in IoT. IEEE Internet Things J. **9**(1), 589–600 (2021)

59. Petrasch, R., Hentschke, R.: Cloud storage hub: data management for IoT and industry 4.0 applications: towards a consistent enterprise information management system. In: 2016 Management and Innovation Technology International Conference (MITicon), pp. MIT-108–MIT-111 (2016). https://doi.org/10.1109/MITICON.2016.8025236

60. Plaxton, C.G., Rajaraman, R., Richa, A.W.: Accessing nearby copies of replicated objects in a distributed environment. In: Proceedings of the Ninth Annual ACM Symposium on Parallel Algorithms and Architectures, SPAA 1997, pp. 311–320. ACM, New York, NY, USA (1997). https://doi.org/10.1145/258492.258523

61. Plaxton, C.G., Rajaraman, R., Richa, A.W.: Accessing nearby copies of replicated objects in a distributed environment. Theory Comput. Syst. **32**(3), 241–280 (1999)

62. Ratnasamy, S., Francis, P., Handley, M., Karp, R., Shenker, S.: A scalable content-addressable network (2001)

63. Ren, P., Liu, L., Qiao, X., Chen, J.: Distributed edge system orchestration for web-based mobile augmented reality services. IEEE Trans. Serv. Comput. **16**(3), 1778–1792 (2023). https://doi.org/10.1109/TSC.2022.3190375

64. Riabi, I., Saidane, L.A., Ayed, H.K.B.: A proposal of a distributed access control over fog computing: the its use case. In: 2017 International Conference on Performance Evaluation and Modeling in Wired and Wireless Networks (PEMWN), pp. 1–7. IEEE (2017)

65. Rodrigues, A.S., Rizzetti, T.A., Canha, L.N., Milbradt, R.G., Appel, S.F., Duarte, Y.S.: Implementing a distributed firewall using a DHT network applied to smart grids. In: 2016 51st International Universities Power Engineering Conference (UPEC), pp. 1–5 (2016). https://doi.org/10.1109/UPEC.2016.8113985

66. Roehrs, A., da Costa, C.A., da Rosa Righi, R.: OmniPHR: a distributed architecture model to integrate personal health records. J. Biomed. Inform. **71**, 70–81 (2017)
67. Rowstron, A., Druschel, P.: Pastry: scalable, decentralized object location, and routing for large-scale peer-to-peer systems. In: Guerraoui, R. (ed.) Middleware 2001. LNCS, vol. 2218, pp. 329–350. Springer, Heidelberg (2001). https://doi.org/10.1007/3-540-45518-3_18
68. Saberi, M.A., Adda, M., Mcheick, H.: Break-glass conceptual model for distributed EHR management system based on blockchain, IPFS and ABAC. Procedia Comput. Sci. **198**, 185–192 (2022). https://doi.org/10.1016/j.procs.2021.12.227. https://www.sciencedirect.com/science/article/pii/S1877050921024662. 12th International Conference on Emerging Ubiquitous Systems and Pervasive Networks/11th International Conference on Current and Future Trends of Information and Communication Technologies in Healthcare
69. Saeed, W., Ahmad, Z., Jehangiri, A.I., Mohamed, N., Umar, A.I., Ahmad, J.: A fault tolerant data management scheme for healthcare internet of things in fog computing. KSII Trans. Internet Inf. Syst. (TIIS) **15**(1), 35–57 (2021)
70. Santos, J., Wauters, T., Volckaert, B., De Turck, F.: Towards dynamic fog resource provisioning for smart city applications. In: 2018 14th International Conference on Network and Service Management (CNSM), pp. 290–294. IEEE (2018)
71. Sharma, R., Chan, C.A., Leckie, C.: Evaluation of centralised vs distributed collaborative intrusion detection systems in multi-access edge computing. In: 2020 IFIP Networking Conference (Networking), pp. 343–351. IEEE (2020)
72. Siddula, M., Li, L., Li, Y.: An empirical study on the privacy preservation of online social networks. IEEE Access **6**, 19912–19922 (2018)
73. Simić, M., Stojkov, M., Sladić, G., Milosavljević, B.: Edge computing system for large-scale distributed sensing systems. In: ICIST, pp. 36–39 (2018)
74. Sonbol, K., Özkasap, Ö., Al-Oqily, I., Aloqaily, M.: EdgeKV: decentralized, scalable, and consistent storage for the edge. J. Parallel Distrib. Comput. **144**, 28–40 (2020)
75. Song, J., Gu, T., Ge, Y., Mohapatra, P.: Smart contract-based computing resources trading in edge computing. In: 2020 IEEE 31st Annual International Symposium on Personal, Indoor and Mobile Radio Communications, pp. 1–7. IEEE (2020)
76. Stevens, M.M.J., et al.: Attacks on hash functions and applications. Mathematical Institute, Faculty of Science, Leiden University (2012)
77. Stoica, I., Morris, R., Karger, D., Kaashoek, M.F., Balakrishnan, H.: Chord: a scalable peer-to-peer lookup service for internet applications. SIGCOMM Comput. Commun. Rev. **31**, 149–160 (2001). https://doi.org/10.1145/964723.383071
78. Tanenbaum, A.S., Steen, M.: Distributed systems [sl] (2007)
79. Tanganelli, G., Vallati, C., Mingozzi, E.: Edge-centric distributed discovery and access in the internet of things. IEEE Internet Things J. **5**(1), 425–438 (2017)
80. Tanganelli, G., Vallati, C., Mingozzi, E.: A fog-based distributed look-up service for intelligent transportation systems. In: 2017 IEEE 18th International Symposium on a World of Wireless, Mobile and Multimedia Networks (WoWMoM), pp. 1–6. IEEE (2017)
81. Tiendrebeogo, T.: A cloud computing system using virtual hyperbolic coordinates for services distribution. In: Zhang, Y., Peng, L., Youn, C.-H. (eds.) CloudComp 2015. LNICST, vol. 167, pp. 269–279. Springer, Cham (2016). https://doi.org/10.1007/978-3-319-38904-2_28

82. Toosi, A.N., Calheiros, R.N., Buyya, R.: Interconnected cloud computing environments: challenges, taxonomy, and survey. ACM Comput. Surv. (CSUR) **47**(1), 1–47 (2014)

83. Tracey, D., Sreenan, C.: Using a DHT in a peer to peer architecture for the internet of things. In: 2019 IEEE 5th World Forum on Internet of Things (WF-IoT), pp. 560–565 (2019). https://doi.org/10.1109/WF-IoT.2019.8767261

84. Varshney, P., Simmhan, Y.: Demystifying fog computing: characterizing architectures, applications and abstractions. In: 2017 IEEE 1st International Conference on Fog and Edge Computing (ICFEC), pp. 115–124. IEEE (2017)

85. Varvello, M., Azurmendi, I.Q., Nappa, A., Papadopoulos, P., Pestana, G., Livshits, B.: VPN0: a privacy-preserving decentralized virtual private network. arXiv preprint arXiv:1910.00159 (2019)

86. Wang, C., Cai, Z., Li, Y.: Sustainable blockchain-based digital twin management architecture for IoT devices. IEEE Internet Things J. **10**(8), 6535–6548 (2023). https://doi.org/10.1109/JIOT.2022.3153653

87. Wu, T., Yeoh, P.L., Jourjon, G., Thilakarathna, K.: MapChain: a DHT-based dual-blockchain data structure for large-scale IoT systems. In: 2021 IEEE 7th World Forum on Internet of Things (WF-IoT), pp. 177–182 (2021). https://doi.org/10.1109/WF-IoT51360.2021.9595910

88. Xie, X.L., Wang, Q., Wang, P.: Design of smart container cloud based on DHT. In: 2017 13th International Conference on Natural Computation, Fuzzy Systems and Knowledge Discovery (ICNC-FSKD), pp. 2971–2975 (2017). https://doi.org/10.1109/FSKD.2017.8393255

89. Xiong, J., Li, F., Ma, J., Liu, X., Yao, Z., Chen, P.S.: A full lifecycle privacy protection scheme for sensitive data in cloud computing. Peer-to-Peer Network. Appl. **8**, 1025–1037 (2015)

90. Yang, Y., Zhang, L., Zhao, Y., Choo, K.K.R., Zhang, Y.: Privacy-preserving aggregation-authentication scheme for safety warning system in fog-cloud based VANET. IEEE Trans. Inf. Forensics Secur. **17**, 317–331 (2022)

91. Yousefpour, A., et al.: All one needs to know about fog computing and related edge computing paradigms: a complete survey. J. Syst. Architect. **98**, 289–330 (2019)

92. Zave, P.: Using lightweight modeling to understand chord. ACM SIGCOMM Comput. Commun. Rev. **42**(2), 49–57 (2012)

93. Zhang, H., Goel, A., Govindan, R.: Incrementally improving lookup latency in distributed hash table systems. SIGMETRICS Perform. Eval. Rev. **31**(1), 114–125 (2003). https://doi.org/10.1145/885651.781042

94. Zhao, B.Y., Huang, L., Stribling, J., Rhea, S.C., Joseph, A.D., Kubiatowicz, J.D.: Tapestry: a resilient global-scale overlay for service deployment. IEEE J. Sel. Areas Commun. **22**(1), 41–53 (2004)

95. Zhaofeng, M., Xiaochang, W., Jain, D.K., Khan, H., Hongmin, G., Zhen, W.: A blockchain-based trusted data management scheme in edge computing. IEEE Trans. Industr. Inf. **16**(3), 2013–2021 (2020). https://doi.org/10.1109/TII.2019.2933482

96. Zhelev, R., Georgiev, V.: A DHT-based scalable and fault-tolerant cloud information service. UBICOMM **2011**, 67 (2011)

97. Zhou, J., Fan, J., Jia, J.: A cost-efficient resource provisioning algorithm for DHT-based cloud storage systems. Concurrency Comput. Pract. Exp. **28**(18), 4485–4506 (2016)

98. Zhou, J., He, W.: A novel resource provisioning model for DHT-based cloud storage systems. In: Hsu, C.-H., Shi, X., Salapura, V. (eds.) NPC 2014. LNCS, vol. 8707, pp. 257–268. Springer, Heidelberg (2014). https://doi.org/10.1007/978-3-662-44917-2_22
99. Zuo, X., Iamnitchi, A.: A survey of socially aware peer-to-peer systems. ACM Comput. Surv. (CSUR) **49**(1), 1–28 (2016)

i-Deliver P&D Engine: A Decentralized Middleware for a Delivery-as-a-Service System

Spyros Kontogiannis[1,2] ⓘ, Andreas Paraskevopoulos[2] ⓘ, Meletis Pogkas[1,2],
and Christos Zaroliagis[1,2(✉)] ⓘ

[1] Department of Computer Engineering & Informatics, University of Patras, Patras, Greece
spyridon.kontogiannis@upatras.gr, {pogkas,zaro}@ceid.upatras.gr
[2] Computer Technology Institute and Press "Diophantus" (CTI), Patras, Greece
paraskevop@ceid.upatras.gr

Abstract. We present the *i-Deliver pickup-and-delivery (P&D) core algorithmic engine*, a decentralized middleware which takes over the delivery logistics in an ecosystem of providers, consumers, couriers, and brokers who match orders for goods (e.g., food, parcels, shopping orders, etc.) between providers and consumers by appropriately (and automatically) allocating them to couriers in such a way that a global performance criterion (e.g., the total travel-time of couriers) is optimized. The middleware consists of two fundamental modules: (i) an *order allocation* module that assigns P&D orders to couriers in such a way that all spatiotemporal constraints for the orders, as well as constraints related to the couriers' working conditions (e.g., working shifts) are respected; (ii) a *courier guidance* module that aids each courier by providing timely-service alerts and routing instructions, while servicing the orders assigned to them. We present the details for the P&D *order allocation problem* to be solved, via an appropriate MILP formulation. We then discuss both an offline algorithm whose goal is to solve this MILP in its entirety, and an online algorithm that handles the orders in real-time. The online solver (which can also be seen as a heuristic for solving the offline problem) is very suitable for servicing real-time orders, as demonstrated by the evidence provided by our thorough experimentation with real-world data.

Keywords: pickup-and-delivery VRP with spatiotemporal constraints ·
decentralized systems · MILP formulation · route planning and navigation engine

1 Introduction

The efficient and effective delivery of ordered goods is a prime application of the transportation and logistics sectors. The application becomes very demanding when dealing with real-time orders and timely service of orders for critical goods (e.g., food orders, urgent parcels, etc.). Our work focuses on the i-Deliver platform (i-Deliver, 2022) which materializes an ecosystem of providers, consumers, couriers, and brokers who match

© The Author(s), under exclusive license to Springer Nature Switzerland AG 2024
I. Chatzigiannakis and I. Karydis (Eds.): ALGOCLOUD 2023, LNCS 14053, pp. 172–183, 2024.
https://doi.org/10.1007/978-3-031-49361-4_9

orders for goods between providers and consumers and then appropriately (and automatically) allocate the orders to couriers. Couriers (or workers), with their own vehicles, are considered to be *active* during their working shifts, starting from one or several depots. Orders, on the other hand, specify origins for pick-ups and destinations for drop-offs of goods under certain spatiotemporal constraints. The goal is to serve as many orders as possible, in such a way that the overall service cost is minimized but also that all the spatiotemporal constraints of both the couriers and the orders are absolutely respected.

The i-Deliver platform is a decentralized middleware representing a P&D broker that provides *Delivery-as-a-Service* (DaaS) functionalities and integrates crowdsourcing techniques with the P&D core algorithmic engine. The couriers exploit crowdsourcing techniques to provide the necessary information to the i-Deliver platform for auditing in real-time the service of each active order. The P&D core algorithmic engine proposes subtours (i.e., order-servicing routes) for the couriers – represented as sequences of consecutive pickup and delivery locations for the orders assigned to them within their working shifts. This should be done in such a way that: (i) a maximum number of orders is served by the i-Deliver system; (ii) all spatiotemporal constraints, for both the orders and the couriers, are respected by the subtours; and (iii) the operational cost for having the orders served is minimized. Also, as the orders may be revealed to the management system in real-time, the P&D core algorithmic engine should be able to adapt the current subtours of the couriers in such a way that each new order is also served by some courier, if possible. The P&D core algorithmic engine has to decide both the allocation (what?) and the explicit way (how?) for serving each order that is accepted by the i-Deliver system. Moreover, at runtime it audits the evolution (when?) of order-servicing process per courier, by providing real-time guidance via navigation recommendations and timely alerts.

In this paper, we present the *i-Deliver pickup-and-delivery (P&D) algorithmic engine*, comprising two main modules: the *P&D order allocation* module and the *courier guidance* module. In Sect. 2 we present the details for the P&D *order allocation* module. We start with the description of the combinatorial problem to be solved, a variant of the one-to-one Vehicle-Routing Problem with pickups, deliveries and time windows per order, and working-shifts and capacity constraints for the workers. We also provide an appropriate MILP formulation for the problem. We then discuss a computationally intensive offline algorithm whose goal is to solve this MILP in its entirety, as well as a much more efficient online algorithm that handles the orders in real-time. Section 3 provides an overview of the *courier guidance* module. Section 4 presents a thorough experimentation of both algorithms on real-world data concerning food orders in an urban area of Greece. It is demonstrated that the online solver, which can also be seen as a heuristic for solving the offline problem, is very suitable for servicing real-time orders.

2 P&D Order Allocation Module

The main combinatorial problem of our P&D algorithmic engine is a variant of the one-to-one Vehicle Routing Problem (**VRP**), e.g., see (Parragh, 2008) (Toth, 2014), with point-to-point delivery requests (orders) from pickup points towards delivery points and with time windows, to be served by workers with their vehicles having specific capacity constraints and with certain working shifts. This variant is denoted by $\mathbf{VRP}_{\text{PD:TW:VC:WS}}$. Moreover, we consider two different scenarios: the *offline scenario*, denoted as $\mathbf{VRP}_{\text{PD:TW:VC:WS}}^{\textit{offline}}$ which considers the entire sequences of orders and workers to be provided as input; and the online scenario, denoted as $\mathbf{VRP}_{\text{PD:TW:VC:WS}}^{\textit{online}}$, according to which all workers are a priori known but the sequence of orders appears to the system sequentially, and the scheduler has to make rapid acceptance-and-allocation or rejection decisions upon their appearance.

An instance of $\mathbf{VRP}_{\text{PD:TW:VC:WS}}$ consists of a set R of *orders* (the pickup-and-delivery requests to be served), a set W of *workers* (the active couriers), the corresponding set H of their *working shifts*, and a set C of spatiotemporal constraints and parameters that regulate the context in which the service of each order is feasible and acceptable. The output consists of a set P of subtours, one per active worker, which are sequences of consecutive pickup/delivery points for the orders assigned to them. Each subtour is then translated into an actual route within an underlying road network with *time-dependent* traversal-times at each road segment. The goal is to select subtours that maximize the number of accepted orders for service, and also minimize the aggregate cost to service all the accepted orders. Each subtour is associated with a specific worker $w \in W$ and it is required to be feasible with respect to all the relevant spatiotemporal constraints for the orders assigned to w, in such a way that it does not violate any temporal restrictions of C (concerning earliest-pickup and latest-delivery deadlines for the orders) or H (concerning the working shifts and the capacities of the involved vehicles). The cost of each solution is assessed through a customizable objective function. As previously mentioned, the primary *objective* is to serve as many orders as possible, without violating any of the spatiotemporal constraints related to them. Given that, as a secondary optimization criterion we consider the minimization of the operational cost to serve all the requests, represented as either the aggregate distance, or total travel duration of the involved workers. Another optimization criterion is to provide balanced amounts of work to the workers.

The rest of this section describes the problem, its formal modeling as a mixed integer linear program (MILP), and two solution approaches.

2.1 MILP Formulation of $\mathbf{VRP}_{\text{PD:TW:VC:WS}}$

An instance of $\mathbf{VRP}_{\text{PD:TW:VC:WS}}$ consists of a collection of orders, $r_1, \cdots, r_{|R|} \in R$ and a set of workers, $w_1, \cdots, w_{|W|} \in W$. Each request is represented as a tuple $r_i = (t_i, q_i, l_i, p_i, d_i, t_{p_i}^{\geq}, t_{d_i}^{\leq})$, where t_i is its *release-time* of the order (i.e., when it is revealed to the system), q_i is its *load capacity* requirement, l_i is the *required vehicle type*, p_i is the *pickup point*, d_i is the *delivery point*, $t_{p_i}^{\geq}$ is the *earliest-pickup time*, and $t_{d_i}^{\leq}$ is the *latest-delivery time*. Analogously, a worker is represented as a tuple $w_j = (b_j, f_j, t_{b_j}, t_{f_j}, Q_j, y_j)$, where b_j is the *starting point* of j's shift, f_j is the ending point of the shift, t_{b_j} is the *start-time* of the shift, t_{f_j} is *end-time* of the shift, Q_j is the *maximum vehicle capacity*, and y_j is j's vehicle type. A set C contains some spatiotemporal feasibility constraints: i) each order is served by a single worker, who will first pick up the good from its pickup point and will then deliver it to its delivery point, using a vehicle type that is eligible for the good, and respecting the corresponding deadlines for servicing the order; ii) each good has load capacity requirements for its storage in the worker's vehicle; iii) all workers use specific vehicles with given maximum capacities for storage and cannot be assigned any goods that exceed the capacity of their vehicles, at any time.

For the needs of the *i-Deliver P&D Engine*, which is responsible for the provision of solutions to instances of **VRP**$_{\text{PD:TW:VC:WS}}$, the instance is first represented by a "*pickup-and-delivery*" (PD) graph. Based on this graph, a mixed integer linear program (MILP) is constructed to guarantee that all the spatiotemporal constraints are respected by any feasible solution, while optimizing the selected objective function. The representation of the **VRP**$_{\text{PD:TW:VC:WS}}$ instance as a PD graph, $G = (V, E)$, involves the encoding of the entire set of *service points* (i.e., pickup or delivery points) as the vertex set V, and all potential courier movement events as the edge set E. Each service point is accompanied by its actual coordinates in the underlying road map. When a worker traverses an edge, s/he is "charged" according to two cost metrics: i) the *distance* from the tail to the head of the edge, independently of the used vehicle; and ii) the *traversal-time* to move from the tail to the head of the edge (based on historical traffic data), which depends on the type of vehicle (motorbike, car, truck) and the departure-time of the worker from the tail of the edge. The dataset regarding the actual road network is provided by the OpenStreetMap[1] service. The travel-time metric is provided by the OpenStreetMap service and the traffic prediction service of the i-Deliver platform.

For the construction of the PD graph G, a preprocessing is initially carried out in the underlying road network. Initially, the required geographical points (i.e., starting/ending points of shifts, pickup/delivery points of orders) are identified in the road network. This procedure involves finding the nearest points on road segments of the road network. The search is efficiently implemented using an R-tree (Guttman, 1984), utilizing the indexing and classification of the coordinates in geographic partitions (in the form of rectangular blocks). Consequently, we conduct sequential shortest-path tree computations to provide a set of (one-to-many) optimal routes among these points of interest, minimizing either the distances or travel-times from each vertex of G. We use executions of Dijkstra's algorithm (Dijkstra, 1959) for the (static) distance metric, and state-of-art travel-time oracles (Kontogiannis, Papastavrou, Paraskevopoulos, Wagner, & Zaroliagis, 2017) for the (time-dependent) travel-time metric.

The resulting paths in the road network, represented in a condensed manner as edges of G, are equipped with two distinct cost values (minimum travel time and distance). Eventually, the construction of the PD graph (Fig. 1) is carried out in such a way that: (a) each vertex in the graph represents a distinct geographical point on the road network, at which a time-dependent event make occur, concerning a worker (e.g., arrival or departure), an order (e.g., pick-up or delivery), or a working shift (e.g., start or end); and (b) each edge in the graph represents transitions and successive visits between two vertices.

---

[1] https://www.openstreetmap.org.

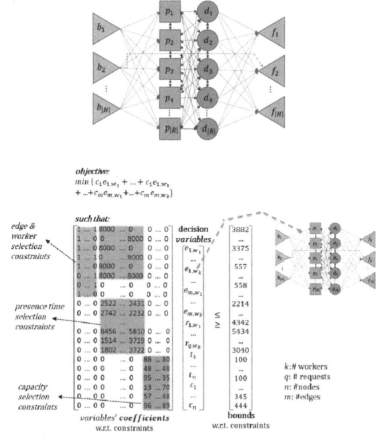

Fig. 1. Representation of a **VRP**$_{PD:TW:VC:WS}$ instance: PD graph (top) and MILP (bottom). (Color figure online)

It is worth mentioning at this point that, for any pair of vertices in G, we create two parallel edges between them, one representing the minimum distance (with a possibly suboptimal travel-time) and one representing the (time-dependent) minimum travel-time (with a possibly suboptimal distance) between them. The vertices of G are grouped into *type-b* nodes representing the **beginning** of a worker's shift, the *type-p* nodes representing **pickups** of goods that have been ordered, the type-d nodes representing **deliveries** of goods to the consumers, and the type-f nodes representing the **end** of a worker's shift: $V_B = \{b_i:$ worker's shift-start from $H\}$, $V_P = \{ p_j :$ pickup order from $R\}$, $V_D = \{d_j:$ delivery order from $R\}$, $V_F = \{f_i:$ worker's shift-end from $H\}$. Overall, $V = V_B \bigcup V_P \bigcup V_D \bigcup V_F$. The following edges of G are then considered: $E = \{ (b_i, p_j):$ edges from any worker start-shift to any pickup point$\} \bigcup \{ (p_x/d_x, p_y/d_y):$ edges from any pickup/delivery point to any other pickup/delivery point$\} - \{ (d_j, p_j):$ useless edges from a delivery point to the pickup point of the same order from $R\}^2$) $\bigcup$ { (d_j, f_i): edges from any delivery point to any worker's shift-end}.

The existence of two parallel edges between two vertices u and v, one for each of the two optimization criteria (distance or travel-time), allows for the determination of the two extreme *Pareto-optimal* (u, v)-routes in the underlying road network, per different vehicle type: for each vehicle type h, the first (u, v)-route, $\pi^l_{h, u \to v}$, is length-optimal, while the second (u, v)-route, $\pi^t_{h, u \to v}$, is travel-time-optimal. When solving the **VRP**$_{PD:TW:VC:WS}$ instance at hand, for each of these two parallel edges, at most one may be selected as part of the solution, depending on the optimization criterion that we consider and considering all the feasibility constraints, since at most one worker may serve an order.

The inclusion of two Pareto-optimal routes per pair $(u, v) \in V \times V$ and different vehicle types is important for the case where the secondary objective is the minimization of the total travel-distance. In such a case, it is necessary to take both routes $\pi^l_{h, u \to v}$ and $\pi^t_{h, u \to v}$ into account, because our primary objective is to construct a feasible solution with the *maximum number* of satisfied orders, that respects all spatiotemporal constraints. When all the distance-minimal routes are not sufficient to provide such a feasible solution (that respects all the spatiotemporal constraints), as an alternative we allow the exploitation of a minimal number of travel-time-optimal routes so as to overcome this infeasibility and provide at least a feasible solution with the maximum number of served orders, exploiting only an absolutely necessary number of travel-time-optimal routes. For instance, in the example of Fig. 2, a worker with a motorbike arrives at u at 8:00. The arrival at node v via the path $\pi^l_{h, u \to v}$ is at 8:45, but the latest-delivery-time deadline is until 8:30. On the other hand, via the path $\pi^t_{h, u \to v}$ the worker arrives at v at 8:27, i.e., before the deadline, traveling for a slightly longer distance. Therefore, the only option for this worker to move from u to v in G, is via the route $\pi^t_{h, u \to v}$.

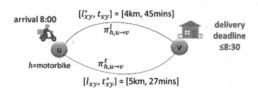

Fig. 2. Finding a feasible solution to minimize distance while respecting the time constraints.

It is mentioned at this point that this approach does not necessarily lead to a distance-optimal solution, since an optimal solution (with respect to the full Pareto-optimal set) might also exploit paths in the road network which are suboptimal in both cost metrics. Nevertheless, given that only distance-optimal or travel-time-optimal movements of the couriers are allowed between consecutive service points, this approach certainly has a fairly good ratio of solution quality to computational cost.

---

[2] They cannot be part of a feasible solution.

The representation of the **VRP**$_{\text{PD:TW:VC:WS}}$ instance as a mixed integer linear program - MILP (see Fig. 1) consists of a set of linear inequalities that determine: i) the set of feasible solutions based on the constraints of the instance; and ii) the objective cost function that determines the optimal one(s). The coefficients of the linear inequalities are described by a matrix A and a vector b of constants, in the form $Ax \leq b$. The rows correspond to spatiotemporal constraints, and the columns correspond to continuous or discrete (decision) variables. The decision variables determine which edges of G are used in the solution, as part of the collection of paths that serve the orders, or indicator variables for assigning orders to workers. The continuous variables determine actual pickup and delivery times, as well as the vehicles actual capacities while serving orders. The precise formulation of MILP is as follows:

Decision variables:

Range	Variables
$\forall e \in E$	$x_{\langle e \rangle}$: the edge e is selected (1) or not (0) as part of the solution
$\forall r \in R, \forall w \in W$	$x_{\langle r,w \rangle}$: the request r is assigned (1) or not (0) to worker w
$\forall v \in V$	$a_{\langle v \rangle}$: the presence time (continuous) at node v by some worker
$\forall v \in V$	$q_{\langle v \rangle}$: the vehicle load capacity (integer) at node v by some worker

Constants:

Range	Values
$\forall e = (u, v) \in E$	$c_{\langle e \rangle}$: the cost (= length $l_{\langle e \rangle}$ or travel-time $t_{\langle e \rangle}$) of edge e $l_{\langle e \rangle}$: length of edge e $t_{\langle e \rangle}$: travel-time of edge e $q_{\langle e \rangle}$: the delivery load capacity of edge e • if $v \in V_P$, then $q_{\langle e \rangle} = q_{\langle r \rangle}$, where r corresponds to v • if $v \in V_D$, then $q_{\langle e \rangle} = -q_{\langle r \rangle}$, where r corresponds to v • if $v \in V_B \cup V_F$, then $q_{\langle e \rangle} = 0$
$\forall v \in V$	Worker's shift time windows: $\forall v = b_i \in V_B \vee f_i \in V_F$ $t_{s\langle v \rangle} = t_{b_i}, t_{\rceil \langle v \rangle} = t_{f_i}$ Orders' permitted service time windows: $\forall v = p_i \in V_P \vee d_i \in V_D$ $t_{s\langle v \rangle} = t_{\overline{p_i}}^{\geq}, t_{\rceil \langle v \rangle} = t_{\overline{d_i}}^{\leq}$
$\forall r \in R$	$M_{\langle r \rangle}$: a constant coefficient as the gain (if positive) or the penalty (if negative) for serving order r
$\forall w \in W$	$Q_{\langle w \rangle}$: the maximum capacity of vehicle of w

Objective:

$min \sum_{e \in E} c_{\langle e \rangle} x_{\langle e \rangle} - \sum_{r \in R} \sum_{w \in W} M_{\langle r \rangle} x_{\langle r,w \rangle}$

Constraints:

(continued)

(*continued*)

---

(1) Each worker path must contain up to one shift-starting edge:

$\sum_{e \in \{(b,p) \in E | p \in V_P\}} x_{\langle e \rangle} \leq 1, \forall b \in V_B$

(2) Any (pickup and delivery) order must be served by no more than two workers:

$\sum_{w \in W} x_{\langle r,w \rangle} \leq 1, \forall r \in R$

(3) Any pickup order must be served only by its assigned worker:

$\sum_{e \in \{(v,p) \in E | v \in V, W(e)=w, R(p)=r\}} x_{\langle e \rangle} = x_{\langle r,w \rangle}, \forall r \in R, w \in W$

$\sum_{e \in \{(p,v) \in E | v \in V, W(e)=w, R(p)=r\}} x_{\langle e \rangle} = x_{\langle r,w \rangle}, \forall r \in R, w \in W$

(4) Any delivery order must be served by its assigned worker:

$\sum_{e \in \{(v,d) \in E | v \in V, W(e)=w, R(d)=r\}} x_{\langle e \rangle} = x_{\langle r,w \rangle}, \forall r \in R, w \in W$

$\sum_{e \in \{(d,v) \in E | v \in V, W(e)=w, R(d)=r\}} x_{\langle e \rangle} = x_{\langle r,w \rangle}, \forall r \in R, w \in W$

(5) The departure/arrival time along the path gets increased:

$a_{\langle v \rangle} \geq (a_{\langle u \rangle} + t_{\langle e \rangle}) x_{\langle e \rangle}, \forall e = (u, v) \in E$

(6) For any request, its pickup precedes of its delivery:

$a_{\langle v \rangle} \geq a_{\langle u \rangle}, \forall v \in V_D, u \in V_P \wedge R(v) = R(u)$

(7) The defined shift or delivery time window must be abided:

$t_{s\langle v \rangle} \leq a_{\langle v \rangle} \leq t_{\eta \langle v \rangle}, \forall v \in V$

(8) Along the path, the capacity gets increased for pickups and decreased for deliveries:

$q_{\langle v \rangle} \geq (q_{\langle u \rangle} + q_{\langle e \rangle}) x_{\langle e \rangle}, \forall e = (u, v) \in E$

(9) The maximum worker vehicle capacity is not allowed to be exceeded:

$q_{\langle v \rangle} x_{\langle r,w \rangle} \leq Q_{\langle w \rangle}, \forall v \in V_P, w \in W$, where $r = R(v)$

Observe that assigning for each $r \in R$ a high value into $M_{\langle r \rangle}$ (based on an upper bound to the worst possible path travel time cost from any origin towards any order), we may enforce the *order allocation* module to accept as many orders as possible (ideally all of them), alongside the minimum total travel cost. The constraints (5), (8) and (9) can easily be linearized by using the "big M" method.

2.2 Algorithms for VRP$_{PD:TW:VC:WS}$

The aim of the *i-Deliver P&D Engine* is twofold: (i) to allocate the accepted orders for service among the active workers; and (ii) to determine a set of non-overlapping subtours in G, one per worker, corresponding to (possibly overlapping) routes in the underlying road network, which specify the exact way that the workers serve the orders assigned to them, so that there is no violation of any of the spatiotemporal constraints of the instance, and also minimizing (exactly or approximately) the cost of the provided solution, as determined by the objective function. The process of constructing a feasible solution is done in two modes: a) the *offline mode*, in which all the orders and working shifts are known in advance; and b) the *online mode*, where the orders are revealed in real time to the solver, which must then adapt the current solution appropriately.

The *offline scheduler* solves the entire mixed integer linear program constructed for the instance at hand, using the "Brunch and Bound" method (Land & Doig, 1960), as a basis for searching for and pruning solutions.

The *online (re)scheduler* is used along with the PD graph, to support the dynamic operations for fitting new orders that are revealed in real-time to an existing schedule.

In the online mode, the rescheduling algorithm must confront a constantly changing state, as new orders may be released and some of the already allocated orders will be completely served by some worker. The focus of the *i-Deliver P&D Engine* is to provide, as fast as possible, immediate decisions on how to adjust the allocation of the still-pending orders among the available workers, in a very efficient manner. The proposed *plain-insertion algorithm* adopts and extends an idea in (Tong, Zeng, Zhou, Chen, & Xu, 2022): upon the release of a new order, it actually tries the unilateral extension of each worker's scheduled path, so as to add this order to their schedule in a locally-optimal but also feasible manner, and then simply allocates this new order to the workers that can fit it in their schedule with the minimum additional overhead to the objective value. The experimental evaluation has shown that the use of the constraint-based "plain insertion" algorithm is quite efficient not only for the online mode, but also as a heuristic method for the offline mode as well (handling the orders one by one, in an arbitrary sequence).

3 P&D Courier Guidance Module

This section provides the details of a mobile app that interacts with the i-Deliver Routing and Navigation Engine (which is not presented in this work) in order to provide guidance to workers for delivering the goods to customers. We begin by going through the app's functionalities for shift creation, modification, and overview, as well as for real-time navigation and routing. The mobile app, along with the routing and navigation backend services, jointly constitute the courier guidance module of the *i-Deliver P&D Engine*. Our main goals while designing the app were ease of use, efficiency, and above all consistency. We have also taken into account that the courier, while using the courier guidance app, might work on busy roads with heavy traffic, so the time needed to look at the screen should be minimized, providing just essential information for the timely delivery of the goods.

The app separates all the shifts into three categories, namely *completed*, *active*, and *due*. When a new shift is created, it is considered due, until its starting time. After that and until its finishing time, it is considered active. Any other shift is considered completed. When the couriers log in to the guidance app, the "main app screen" appears which provides a list of all their essential shifts, sorted by ascending starting times. All the due shifts are shown as well as the last completed shift. The due shifts are colored magenta while the completed shift gets a gray color. When the first due shift in the list changes its status to active, it gets a green color.

After tapping on the active shift, the worker is greeted with the "navigation screen". At the same time all the information about the shift is sent, in JSON format, to the guidance app by the *i-Deliver P&D Engine*. Afterwards, the pickup, delivery, and road points that comprise the shift's subtour are parsed, and the whole shift gets separated into segments. Each segment has two endpoints and a series of contiguous road points in between. An endpoint can either be a pickup or a delivery point.

The "navigation screen" provides three features for guiding the worker to all pickup and delivery points on time. The first feature is *route coloring*. The app visualizes one segment at a time with a lucid color. As the worker moves along a segment, the color might change based on how many minutes the courier is behind schedule. If the worker is up to two minutes late, the segment gets a blue color. Otherwise, if the worker is up to five minutes late, the segment gets a yellow color. Eventually, a red color is used when the worker is even more behind schedule. The second feature is *course change*. When the worker is near an imminent turn, a warning message is shown at the top of the screen that shows when and which way to turn. The third feature is *rerouting*, which is activated whenever the worker deviates from the predetermined route segment.

4   Experimental Evaluation of Algorithms for $VRP_{PD:TW:VC:WS}$

We evaluated our algorithms using collected historical data of actual orders for two consecutive working days (Monday, 6/3/2023 - Tuesday, 7/3/2023) in a city in N. Greece (Ptolemaida). Our experiment evaluates the real-time performance of the pickup and delivery vehicle rescheduling engine of the *i-Deliver P&D Engine*. The real-time, user-determined, and real-time GPS-recorded delivery routes from the i-Deliver platform's database were used as the baseline for comparison and as a point of reference. The experiment is performed in relation to the set of workers and the pickup-delivery orders that appeared during the 3-h time windows 1:[06:00 - 9:00], 2:[09:00 - 12:00], ..., and 6:[21:00 - 23:59]. Respectively, the pairs of workers and orders to be serviced are 1:(8, 110), 2:(10, 98), 3:(18, 165), 4:(10, 166), 5:(11, 168), 6:(7, 25). The experimental evaluation was conducted over three different scenarios:

- *Raw*: only the primary constraints are considered. In this case, the idle parameters are as follows: for each order $r_i = (t_i, c_i, l_i, p_i, d_i, t_{p_i}^{\geq}, t_{d_i}^{\leq}) \in R$, $c_i = 0$, $t_{p_i}^{\geq} = t_i$ and $t_{d_i}^{\leq} = \infty$; and for each worker $w_j = (b_j, f_j, t_{b_j}, t_{f_j}, C_j, y_j) \in W$, $C_j = \infty$.
- Constraint L1: A capacity limitation is applied. Specifically, for each $r_i \in R$ the pickup capacity is set to $c_i = 1$ unit, and for each $w_j \in W$ the maximum vehicle load capacity of all workers is set to $C_j = 3$ units.
- Constraint L2: In addition to the above limitations (L1), a maximum delivery pickup duration time of 40 min on each order and a workload balancer are applied. The former implies that for each $r_i \in R$ $t_{d_i}^{\leq} = t_{p_i}^{\geq} + 40\text{min}$. The latter implies that workers who have travelled less than 1.5 times the average distance travelled by all the workers so far are being prioritized towards being assigned a newly released order so that a more balanced schedule for the active schedulers is produced.

Our results (cf. Fig. 3) show that the *plain-insertion* (re)scheduling online solver of the *i-Deliver P&D Engine* computes a solution that achieves a significant improvement percentage in the overall cost, both in terms of both travel-distance and travel-time metrics, compared to the solution constructed (in real-time also) by a human operator, as they were stored in the i-Deliver database. With respect to the travel-time, the improvement is much more notable in rush hours (e.g., around noon), where the number of orders increases too much, to a degree that is not easily manageable by a human operator. Naturally, the incorporation of additional constraints into the scenarios negatively affects the cost minimization, as the number of acceptable solutions decreases to meet the constraints. In the first row of the charts' tables, the results are based on the user-based assignments, interposing optimal paths between the sequence of pickup/delivery

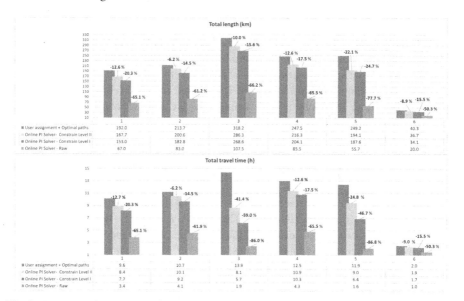

Fig. 3. Percentage improvement in total length and travel time depending on the constraint settings of the problem.

points. In this case, the optimal paths are free from any real-time-originated detour, in contrast to the plain insertion solver, where possible detours from rerouting and order reassignment are counted. The detours from rescheduling lead to an average increase in total length of around 6.1% and in total travel time of around 5.5%. The *plain-insertion online scheduler* updates the delivery routes for each new request within (on average) 43ms, even in midrange server endpoints.

5   Conclusions

We presented the *i-Deliver pickup-and-delivery (P&D) algorithmic engine*, a decentralized middleware which handles the delivery logistics in an ecosystem of providers, consumers, couriers, and brokers who match orders for goods between providers and consumers by appropriately (and automatically) allocating them to couriers in such a way that a global performance criterion is optimized. We described its two main modules, the P&D order allocation module, and the courier guidance module. We presented a MILP formulation of the P&D order allocation problem, along with an offline algorithm (that solves the MILP) and an online algorithm that handles the orders in real-time. Experimenting with real-world data demonstrates the suitability of the online solver for handling orders in real-time.

Acknowledgments. This work was co-financed by the European Regional Development Fund of EU and Greek national funds through the Operational Program Competitiveness, Entrepreneurship, and Innovation (call RESEARCH-CREATE-INNOVATE) under contract no. T2EDK-03472 (project "i-Deliver").

References

Dijkstra, E.: A note on two problems in connexion with graphs. Numer. Math. **1**, 269–271 (1959)

Guttman, A.: R-Trees: a dynamic index structure for spatial searching. ACM SIGMOD Rec. **14**(2), 47–57 (1984). https://doi.org/10.1145/971697.602266

i-Deliver: Delivering platform for delivering goods as a service (2022). https://i-deliver.gr

Kontogiannis, S., Papastavrou, G., Paraskevopoulos, A., Wagner, D., Zaroliagis, C.: Improved oracles for time-dependent road networks. In: 17th Workshop on Algorithmic Approaches for Transportation Modelling, Optimization, and Systems (ATMOS), vol. 4, pp. 1–17 (2017). http://drops.dagstuhl.de/opus/volltexte/2017/7895

Land, A.H., Doig, A.G.: An automatic method of solving discrete programming problems. Econometrica **28**(3), 497–520 (1960). https://doi.org/10.2307/1910129

Parragh, S.N.: A survey on pickup and delivery problems. J. für Betriebswirtschaft **58**(1), 21–51 (2008)

Tong, Y., Zeng, Y., Zhou, Z., Chen, L., Xu, K.: Unified route planning for shared mobility: an insertion-based framework. ACM Trans. Database Syst. (TODS) **47**(1), 1–48 (2022)

Toth, P.: Vehicle Routing (2nd edition). Society for Industrial and Applied Mathematics (SIAM) (2014)

Intent-Based Allocation of Cloud Computing Resources Using Q-Learning

Panagiotis Kokkinos[1,2], Andreas Varvarigos[3], Dimitrios Konidaris[1(✉)], and Konstantinos Tserpes[3]

[1] Department of Digital Systems, University of Peloponnese, Sparta, Greece
dimkonidaris@gmail.com
[2] Institute of Communication and Computer Systems (ICCS),
National Technical University of Athens, Athens, Greece
[3] Department of Informatics and Telematics,
Harokopio University of Athens, Athens, Greece

Abstract. In cloud computing, resource allocation is a critical operation that is usually performed in an infrastructure-aware manner. In practice, however, users often are not able to specify accurately their requirements, while an infrastructure's specific characteristics are not always known. In our work, we assume that users provide their workload requirements in an infrastructure-agnostic manner, by describing their intentions regarding the way the workload should be served, e.g., with high capacity, with low cost etc. Towards this end, we propose the use of a Q-learning based Reinforcement Learning (RL) methodology that translates the users' intentions to efficient resource allocations in a cloud infrastructure. The proposed mechanism is able to improve continuously the allocation of resources based on the user satisfaction and the infrastructure's efficiency. Simulation results showcase the applicability of this approach, investigating various aspects of it.

Keywords: Resource allocation · Intents · Q-learning · Cloud computing

1 Introduction

Cloud computing handles the processing and storage workload of numerous services and applications, with various requirements in terms of the allocated resources, the security, the availability and the cost. Lately, edge computing has also emerged, offering computation and storage capacity at the edge of network, where data is being produced, so as to decrease the applications' experienced latency and limit the load that is carried to the higher layers of the infrastructure. Edge resources in combination with the cloud ones, formulate the so called edge-cloud continuum [1], so as to combine the benefits of both infrastructures. In this continuum, the available resources increase moving from the edge to the cloud, along however with the applications' latency. Tasks and data are assigned

I. Chatzigiannakis and I. Karydis (Eds.): ALGOCLOUD 2023, LNCS 14053, pp. 184–196, 2024.
https://doi.org/10.1007/978-3-031-49361-4_10

respectively: temporary storage and low-latency required computations on the edge, while permanent storage and complex computations at the cloud.

Evidently, resource allocation is a critical operation regarding the efficient use of the infrastructures. The majority of the formulated resource allocation problems and respective mechanisms assume a model where workload requirements are provided with certainty e.g., from a user, while orchestration mechanisms that assign the workloads have a clear view of the resources' characteristics and status. In practice, however, these assumptions are not always valid. Users often have a subjective notion of their needs (e.g., what one considers of low or high cost) and an abstract view of the available infrastructures. As a result, they are not able to specify in a certain, numeric manner, their requirements or match them to an infrastructure's actual characteristics. Also, orchestration mechanisms can not always monitor efficiently the resources due to their high number and the dynamicity of their status. In addition, since not all resources belong to the same providers, it is reasonable that some providers are not willing to share the same level of details regarding their resources.

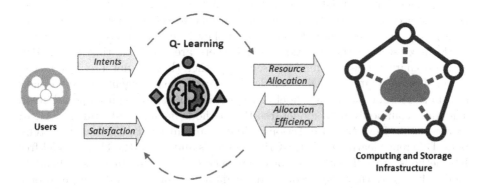

Fig. 1. Intent-driven resource allocation.

Recently, intent-based operations have been presented by various actors (providers, standardization organizations, academia) [2,3] as a way for applications and users to express their requirements regarding the use of Information and Communication Technology infrastructures, e.g., computing, networking etc. Overall the goal is to focus on what one needs from an infrastructure, instead of how to achieve it.

In this context, our work considers the use of intent-based resource-allocation for cloud computing infrastructures (Fig. 1). The idea is that application requirements are provided in an infrastructure agnostic manner, assuming that application owners cannot provide the numeric requirements of their workload. The main contribution of our work is a Q-learning based Reinforcement Learning (RL) methodology that translates the users'/applications' intentions to efficient resource allocations. The proposed mechanism improves continuously the allocation of resources based on the user satisfaction and the allocation status provided by the infrastructure, which are combined to the required by the RL mechanism, reward. The simulation results performed, showcase the validity of our approach.

The remainder of this paper is organized as follows. In Sect. 2, we report on previous work. In Sect. 3, we present the system model and the infrastructure-agnostic operations. In Sect. 4, we describe our Reinforcement learning methodology for intent-drive resource allocation. Simulation experiments are presented in Sect. 5. Finally, our work is concluded in Sect. 6.

2   Previous Work

The importance of resource management in edge and cloud computing has been acknowledge by several works, proposing various methodologies [4].

Reinforcement Learning (RL) is a type of machine learning method that has recently gained a lot of attention from the research community. This is based on one or more agents that learn the environment of interest by interacting with it [5]. The RL agent gives recommendations and receives rewards from the environment. The ultimate goal of the agent is to maximize the total reward. If the reward is positive, the agent will continue to try its effort. If the reward is negative, the agent should change its policy in order to have a good value in the next step of the iteration. In RL there are problems that use models and are characterized as model-based and other that do not use a model of the environment and are called model-free. In the latter, agents learn to make decisions without having a model of the environment, through trial-and error. The most commonly used model-free RL methods include: Q-learning, SARSA (State-Action-Reward-State-Action), Monte Carlo methods, TD-learning (Temporal Difference learning), Actor-Critic methods and Deep RL. These model-free RL methods are well-suited for problems where the environment is difficult to model, however, they may require more data for training and computational resources to learn an optimal state-to-action policy, compared to model-based RL methods.

RL methods have been employed in various problems, like zero-sum games [6], stock market forecasting [7], decision-making for autonomous driving [8]. Resource allocations is also an area where it it been extensively used lately: For optimal wireless resource allocation in order to avoid interference by hidden nodes in CSMA/CA method [9], in 5G services using deep Q-learning [10–12], in hybrid networks that contain access points, radio frequency and multiple visible light communications [13], in satellite-terrestrial networks [14] and in optical networks [15]. RL methods have also been used for resource allocation in edge and cloud computing. [11] proposes a joint task assignment and resource allocation approach in a multi-user WiFi-based mobile edge computing architecture. [16] proposed a Q-learning scheme to efficiently allocate edge-cloud resources for Internet of Things (IoT) applications. In [17] a computation offloading methodology for deep neural networks in edge-cloud environments is formulated. [18] use a Deep Reinforcement Learning-based approach to balance, in an edge computing environment, workload from mobile devices, so as to decrease service time and reduce failed task rate. In [19] a model-free Deep Reinforcement Learning approach is also introduced, in order to orchestrate the resources at the network edge and minimize the operational cost at runtime.

Intent-driven operations have the goal to overcome the complexity of utilizing complex infrastructures, decoupling the users' intentions regarding "what" should be done, from the actual resource orchestration, which specifies "how" it is done. Intent-driven operations have initially focused on networks [20–22] but recently their application in cloud and edge computing is also investigated [23–26]. Authors in [23] define rules that enable users to express service-layer requirements. The Label Management Service in [24] helps cloud administrators to model their policy requirements. In [25] a learning-based intent-aware task offloading framework for air-ground integrated vehicular edge computing is developed. [26] proposes a framework to translate cloud performance-related intents into specific cloud computation resource requirements. [27] proposes a strategy that matches multi-attribute tasks to cloud resources. In [28] it is used an intent-based network system to automate the deployment of virtual network functions in a cloud-based infrastructure.

Our work differentiates from the state of the art, by utilizing a Q-learning RL methodology to translate users' intentions to resource allocations in a cloud infrastructure. In this process, the provided rewards are based both on the users' feedback and the infrastructure's status.

3   System Model and Infrastructure-Agnostic Operations

3.1   Infrastructure

In our work, we assume a computing infrastructure composed of N interconnected resources (edge and cloud) with different characteristics in terms of:

- capacity $C = \{c_1, c_2, ..., c_N\}$. This can be expressed as the number of (virtual) CPUs in case of a computing resource or the number of GB in case of a storage resource.
- Cost of use $U = \{u_1, u_2, ..., u_N\}$. This can be formulated with different ways either as a fixed price or as cost per quantity per time unit (e.g. GB per hour used).
- security $E = \{e_1, e_2, ..., e_N\}$. This may depend on particular security features that the respective resource employs.

Other parameters of interest can also be considered.

We also assume that these characteristics are discrete and selected from a set of possible values. This is reasonable to assume based on the cloud computing paradigm of virtualized instances. In particular, all public cloud providers, offer various types of instances, which comprise of varying combinations of (virtual) CPU, memory, storage and networking capacity and are optimized for different workloads, e.g. compute or memory intensive [29]. In this context, the considered infrastructure's virtualized resources have capacity, cost and security capabilities with discrete values from the following sets:

– N_c levels of capacity: $S_C = \{TC_1, TC_2, \ldots, TC_{N_c}\}$, and $c_i \in S_C$ where $1 \leq i \leq N$
– N_u levels of cost: $S_U = \{TU_1, TU_2, \ldots, TU_{N_u}\}$ and $u_i \in S_U$ where $1 \leq i \leq N$
– N_e levels of security: $S_E = \{TE_1, TE_2, \ldots, TE_{N_e}\}$, and $e_i \in S_E$ where $1 \leq i \leq N$.

3.2 Workload

The user/application requests for computing workload or storage space are submitted to an orchestration entity that manages the infrastructure. The request is described by the static characteristics of the workload to be submitted e.g., the requested computing capacity (e.g., in terms of virtual CPUs) or the size of the data that need to be stored (e.g., 2 GB). It also includes infrastructure-agnostic parameters, for example regarding the preferable cost, security and performance, in the form of intents. This intent can take various forms and shapes, e.g., by characterizing the need to execute a workload "fast" or to store data with "high" security or with "low" cost. In our work, we formulate this with a small number of what we call "intent levels" for the different types of parameters of interest:

– $\hat{N}_c$ levels of capacity: $\hat{S}_C = \{\hat{TC}_1, \hat{TC}_2, \ldots, \hat{TC}_{\hat{N}_c}\}$, where $\hat{N}_c << N_c$
– $\hat{N}_u$ levels of cost: $\hat{S}_U = \{\hat{TU}_1, \hat{TU}_2, \ldots, \hat{TU}_{\hat{N}_u}\}$, where $\hat{N}_u << N_u$
– $\hat{N}_e$ levels of security: $\hat{S}_E = \{\hat{TE}_1, \hat{TE}_2, \ldots, \hat{TE}_{\hat{N}_e}\}$, where $\hat{N}_e << N_e$

So, the j submitted workload of user k, w_{jk}, can be described with the tuple $\{\hat{TC}_{jk}, \hat{TU}_{jk}, \hat{TE}_{jk}\}$, where $\hat{TC}_{jk} \in \hat{S}_C$, $\hat{TU}_{jk} \in \hat{S}_U$ and $\hat{TE}_{jk} \in \hat{S}_E$. The way these infrastructure-agnostic intent levels match to the different infrastructure-related resource levels (Sect. 3.1) is the key for the intent-based operations that we research on the present work.

3.3 Example of Infrastructure-Agnostic Operation

Based on the above, we describe the following example of an infrastructure agnostic storage workload request R to be served by the infrastructure. This request's static parameters, include the size of the data to be stored, e.g., measured in GB. Also, the request is accompanied with intents specifying that this should be served with "low" cost, "high" security: $R = \{\hat{u}, \hat{e}\} = \{$ "low", "high"$\}$. Assuming that we have $\hat{S}_U = 1, 2, 3$ and $\hat{S}_E = 1, 2, 3$ "intent levels" for cost and security and the intention "low" matches to the value 1, while the "high" to value 3, then these intents can also be expressed numerically with the tuple $R = \{\hat{u}, \hat{e}\} = 1, 3$.

The goal of the methodology that we present next, is to efficiently translate the intents provided, to specific decisions regarding the way the tasks will be served, so as to match as closely as possible to the users' or applications' intentions. For example, let assume that our infrastructure has $N_u = 10$ different cost levels for a storage resource, in terms of euros per GB per month stored, e.g., $S_u = \{10, 20, 30, 40, 50, 60, 70, 80, 90, 100\}$. So, when a user has an intent for cost $\hat{e} = 1$, this means that the methodology has to match this ("intent level") to an actual cost value ("resource level") from the set S_u. In general, we may expect that $\hat{e} = 1$ ("intent level") of cost, matches to 10, 20, 30 or even 40 euros per GB per month ("resource level"). In practice, however, this "intent level" is user specific and can match to any of the available "resource levels" or even to none of them.

4   Q-Learning Based Intent Translation

In our work, we are using Q-learning, model-free Reinforcement Learning (RL), approach to translate the infrastructure-agnostic intent of a user regarding submitted workload, to infrastructure-aware parameters.

4.1   State, Action Spaces and Reward

The basic design principles used in our RL-based method and need to be defined, include the state space S, the action space A, and the reward r. The RL process is executed in time steps t.

The **state of the system environment** $s \in S$ at time t, describes the current status of the cloud infrastructure in terms of the availability of the resources. For simplicity, we assume that a single task/workload utilizes fully a resource from the N available ones. As a result, the environment can be represented through a tuple that shows the availability of the resources: $s = \{o_1, \ldots, o_N\}$, where $o_i = \in \{-1, 1\}$ indicates whether the respective resource i is utilized or not.

The **action space** A contains all possible actions that can be taken, defining the transfer rules between states. As the agent explores the environment, it experiments with different actions so as to learn which ones are the most effective in achieving the goals set. In our work, we assume that at each step t we can either assign a new task of a user to an available resource or migrate an existing task to another resource that is available. As a result, $A_t = \{r_1, \ldots, r_N\}$, where N are all the available resources. In practice, though, not all transitions/actions from one state to another are possible, since we assume that at a single step only one new task can be served or one existing task can migrate to different resource. For example, in an infrastructure with $N = 4$ resources, from the state $s_1 = \{-1, -1, 1, 1\}$, indicating that the 3rd and the 4th resources are utilized, an action is possible to the state $s_2 = \{1, -1, -1, 1\}$, indicating that a task migrates from the 3rd resource to the 1st one, while no action is possible to the state $s_3 = \{1, 1, -1, -1\}$, since this requires multiple task migrations.

After the agent takes an action at state s at time t, it will receive a **reward** r, which can be used to evaluate the action performed. In order to design the reward function, it is necessary to determine the objectives based on which a positive or a negative reward will be provided.

One important novelty of our work, is that rewards depend not only on the infrastructure (the typical environment in most related works) but also on the user that submits the task. On the user side, the reward relates to the level of satisfaction for serving the submitted task according to (or close to) the user's intention. On the infrastructure-side, we focus on the efficiency with which the infrastructure is actually utilized. These objectives are to some extent interrelated, since failing to serve a task due to poor utilization of the available resources, results in users that are unsatisfied from the provided services.

In practice, the user satisfaction can be provided from the user through an immediate feedback mechanism (e.g., using a User Interface [2]), after the infrastructure serves a task request, while the infrastructure's utilization can be monitored through a respective system. e.g., Prometheus.

In our work, we consider the following reward function: $R_t = a \cdot sf + b \cdot ul$, where sf is the satisfaction level based on the action performed at time slot t and ul the utilization of the resources at time slot t. The a and b weights, balance between the user feedback and resource utilization objectives. Also, we quantitatively calculate the satisfaction level as the difference between the user's intents and the resources' parameter (cost, security etc.) levels, where these tasks have been assigned to. For example, lets assume that a user has submitted two tasks with cost intent levels equal to $\hat{TU}_1 = 1$ and $\hat{TU}_3 = 3$ that actually correspond to cost $u = 15$ and $u' = 45$ respectively (based on the user's actual intention). If these tasks are assigned to resources with cost levels $TU_4 = 10$ and $TU_7 = 30$ then we calculate the satisfaction level as equal to:

$$sf = \frac{1}{1 + |TU_4 - u| + |TU_7 - u'|} = \frac{1}{1 + |(10 - 15) + (30 - 45)|} = \frac{1}{21}.$$

In practice of course, a user submitted satisfaction level will be somewhat subjective and will deviate from this "optimal" calculated value.

4.2   Q-Learning Methodology

Q-learning as any machine learning mechanisms has two phases: the training and the inference. During the training phase the agent iteratively interacts with the infrastructure and (in our work) with the user and learns the optimal action-value function that maps states and actions so as to maximize the expected cumulative reward. Through this process the agent explores the infrastructure characteristics and the user's intentions. The Q-learning algorithm updates the estimate of the action-value function for each state-action pair visited by the agent, using the well-known Bellman equation:

$$Q(s, a) = Q(s, a) + \alpha \cdot [r + \gamma \cdot max(Q(s', a')) - Q(s, a)],$$

where $Q(s, a)$ is the estimated value of taking action a in state s, α is the learning rate that determines how much weight to give to new information, r is the immediate reward received for taking action a in state s, γ is the discount factor between 0 and 1, which determines the importance of future rewards relative to immediate rewards, $max(Q(s', a'))$ is the estimated value of the best action a' in the next state s'. These so-called Q-values for all possible state-action pairs are stored in a table, namely the Q-Table. Different selection strategies are possible for the agent in every state, for example select randomly an action, select the action that it has executed the least number of times or select the action with the largest Q-value. In many formulation of the Q-learning process an ϵ probability parameter is defined that sets a trade-off between exploitation that is choosing the optimal action for the next step, based on the Q-Table and exploration that is choosing a random action. In all cases, the reward after an action is taken, leads to the update of the respective state-action Q-value $Q(s,a)$ and the update of the Q-Table.

The cumulative reward at each time step t is defined as:

$$G_t = R_{t+1} + \gamma \cdot R_{t+2} + \gamma^2 \cdot R_{t+3} + \cdots ,$$

where R_{t+1} is the immediate reward received by the agent at time step $t+1$ for taking action a_t in state s_t and γ is again the discount factor. The agent aims to find the optimal policy that maximizes the expected value of G_t over all possible sequences of actions and states, that is the expected cumulative reward. In the inference phase, the trained agent simply exploits the learned action-value function and serves new demands based on the current state and user satisfaction level, using the action with the highest expected reward.

5   Evaluation

We performed a number of simulation experiments to evaluate the manner with which the Q-learning methodology succeeds in identifying a user's intentions in the submitted infrastructure-agnostic requests. Our experiments focus on the training phase of the Q-learning mechanism.

We consider a cloud environment consisting of storage resources, with $N_c = 10$ resource levels of capacity: $S_c = \{10, 20, \cdots, 100\}$ GB and with various combinations of the available characteristics in terms cost and security levels. We also assume that storage capacity is a deterministic parameter of the submitted tasks, while capacity and security are expressed through respective intents. In the experiment performed we employ various scenarios for translating intents to resource levels that correspond to different user intentions. It is clear that there is not necessarily a linear match between the intent and the resource levels. This means for example that an intent level $\hat{TU}_1$ is not necessarily equal to TU_1, but depends on the user preferences. In what follows, for simplicity we assume a single user that submits storage task requests in an infrastructure-agnostic manner through intents.

Initially, in the experiments performed we assumed resources that have different cost resource levels: $3, 5, 7$, while the generated task requests had 2 intent levels. We run the training process for over 10000 timesteps. The Bellman's Equations parameters had the following values $\alpha = 0.5, \gamma = 0.9$, while $\epsilon = 0.5$. Figure 2 illustrates the average reward over time for the first 1k timesteps. We observe that in all scenarios the average reward increases over the first 100 timesteps and then stabilizes, increasing just slightly till 10k timesteps (not illustrated in this figure). This is of course reasonable considering the learning processes and the fact that we selected $\epsilon = 0.5$, meaning that on average half of the selected actions are random, that is not based on the calculated Q-values. What is important to notice, is the effect of the number of cost resource levels in the learning process. Higher number of cost resource levels results in a smaller on average reward and vice versa lower number of resource levels results in larger average reward. This is due to the fact that a small number of resource levels means that there is a close relation between resource and intent levels, making easier their matching.

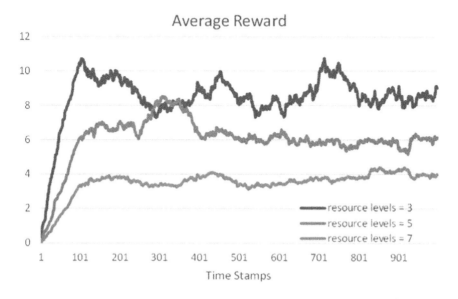

Fig. 2. The average reward over time for different cost resource levels.

Figure 3 illustrates the average reward over time for different ϵ values $\{0.1, 0.2, \ldots, 0.9\}$ over 10k timesteps. In this way, ϵ controls the rate with which the agent explores the environment and identifies an optimal policy. The figure shows that the reward is the highest for $\epsilon = 0.2$, making it the optimal value for the specific problem and the goals set. Another approach is to use a variable epsilon strategy, where the value of epsilon changes over time, being high at first to enable more exploration and decrease at some point in order to exploit that calculated Q-values.

Next, we considered the effect of multiple intent parameters (cost, security and other) in the training process (Fig. 4). By increasing the number of different intents provided by a user for a single task request, this leads in a smaller average reward and slower increase of its value over time. This due to the fact that it is more difficult to match an increasing number of intents to the actual parameters' resource levels.

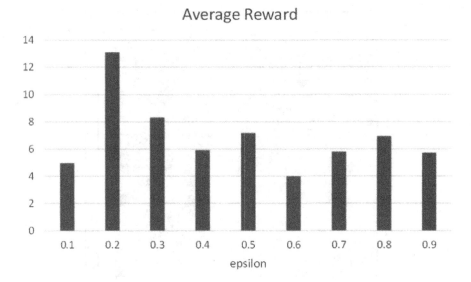

Fig. 3. The average reward over time for different ϵ values.

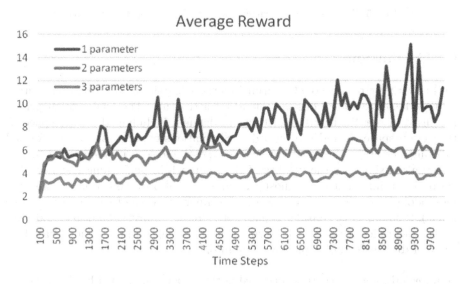

Fig. 4. The average reward over time for different number of intent parameters

Finally, we also created a heatmap of the Q-Table (Fig. 5) for $\epsilon = 0.5$, 50000 timesteps and a single intent parameter. This was created out of curiosity mainly, in order to identify any properties of the Q-Table. One thing that we can observe is a kind of symmetry of the Q-Table. This is mainly due to the way the Q-Table is created in terms of step-pairs and the fact that we consider as valid actions those in which only a single task is migrated to a new resource.

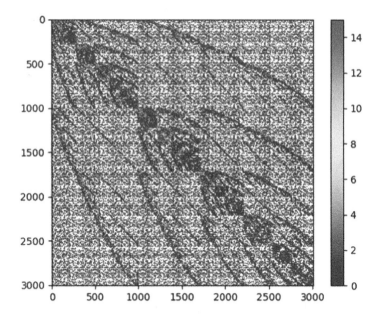

Fig. 5. The Q-Table's heatmap for ϵ=0.5 and 50000 timesteps

6   Conclusions

In this work, we presented a Q-learning methodology for translating users' intentions in resource allocations in a cloud infrastructure. The basic design principles used in our RL-based algorithm are defined, including the state space S, the action space A, and the reward r. Simulations experiments are performed focusing on storage tasks that have capacity, cost and security requirements. The experiments showcase the validity of the approach in performing resource allocation in an infrastructure-agnostic manner. We also discussed on the way the methodology is affected by the number of different types of resources (resource levels), the number of considered parameters (cost, security and other) and evaluated the trade-off between performing in each step optimal actions based on the Q-Table, instead of exploring random ones.

Acknowledgment. The work presented in this paper is supported by the European Union's Horizon 2020 research and innovation program under grant agreement No. 101017168 in the context of the SERRANO project.

References

1. Kretsis, A., et al.: SERRANO: transparent application deployment in a secure, accelerated and cognitive cloud continuum. In: 2021 IEEE International Mediterranean Conference on Communications and Networking (MeditCom). Athens, Greece, pp. 55–60. IEEE (2021)

2. Kokkinos, P., Margaris, D., Spiliotopoulos, D.: A quality of experience illustrator user interface for cloud provider recommendations. In: Stephanidis, C., Antona, M., Ntoa, S. (eds) HCI International 2022 Posters. HCII 2022. Communications in Computer and Information Science, vol. 1580. Springer, Cham (2022). https://doi.org/10.1007/978-3-031-06417-3_42

3. Clemm, A., Ciavaglia, L., Granville, L.Z., Tantsura, J.: Intent-based networking-concepts and definitions. IRTF draft work-in-progress.: "Intent-based networking-concepts and definitions". IRTF draft work-in-progress (2020)

4. Hong, C.H., Varghese, B.: Resource management in fog/edge computing: a survey on architectures, infrastructure, and algorithms. ACM Comput. Surv. (CSUR) **52**(5), 1–37 (2019)

5. Sutton, R.S., Barto, A.G.: Reinforcement Learning: An Introduction, 2nd edn. The MIT Press Cambridge, Massachusetts, USA (2018)

6. Al-Tamimi, A., Lewis, F.L., Abu-Khalaf, M.: Model-free Q-learning designs for discrete-time zero-sum games with application to H-infinity control. In: European Control Conference (ECC). Kos, Greece, vol. 2007, pp. 1668–1675 (2007)

7. Carta, S.M., Ferreira, A., Podda, A.S., Recupero, D.R., Sanna, A.: Multi-DQN: an ensemble of deep Q-learning agents for stock market forecasting. Expert Syst. Appl. **164**, 113820 (2021)

8. Gao, Z., Sun, T., Xiao, H.: Decision-making method for vehicle longitudinal automatic driving based on reinforcement Q-learning. Int. J. Adv. Rob. Syst. **16**(3), 1729881419853185 (2019)

9. Aihara, N., Adachi, K., Takyu, O., Ohta, M., Fujii, T.: Q-Learning Aided Resource Allocation and Environment Recognition in LoRaWAN With CSMA/CA. IEEE Access **7**, 152126–152137 (2019). https://doi.org/10.1109/ACCESS.2019.2948111

10. Rezwan, S., Choi, W.: Priority-based joint resource allocation with deep Q-Learning for heterogeneous NOMA systems. IEEE Access **9**, 41468–41481 (2021). https://doi.org/10.1109/ACCESS.2021.3065314

11. Dab, B., Aitsaadi, N., Langar, R.: Q-learning algorithm for joint computation offloading and resource allocation in edge cloud. In: IFIP/IEEE Symposium on Integrated Network and Service Management (IM). Arlington, VA, USA, pp. 45–52 (2019)

12. Ning, Z., Wang, X., Rodrigues, J.J.P.C., Xia, F.: Joint computation offloading power allocation and channel assignment for 5G-enabled traffic management systems. IEEE Trans. Ind. Informat. **15**(5), 3058–3067 (2019)

13. J. Kong, J., Wu, Z.-Y., Ismail, M., Serpedin, E., Qaraqe, K. A.: Q-Learning based two-timescale power allocation for multi-homing hybrid RF/VLC networks. In: IEEE Wireless Communications Letters, vol. 9, no. 4, pp. 443–447 (2020). https://doi.org/10.1109/LWC.2019.2958121

14. Qiu, C., Yao, H., Yu, F.R., Xu, F., Zhao, C.: Deep Q-Learning aided networking, caching, and computing resources allocation in software-defined satellite-terrestrial networks. IEEE Trans. Veh. Technol. **68**(6), 5871–5883 (2019). https://doi.org/10.1109/TVT.2019.2907682

15. Valkanis, A., Beletsioti, G.A., Nicopolitidis, P., Papadimitriou, G., Varvarigos, E.: Reinforcement learning in traffic prediction of core optical networks using learning automata. In: IEEE International Conference on Communications, Computing, Cybersecurity, and Informatics (CCCI), pp. 1–6 (2020)

16. AlQerm, I., Pan, J.: Enhanced online Q-learning scheme for resource allocation with maximum utility and fairness in Edge-IoT networks. IEEE Trans. Netw. Sci. Eng. **7**(4), 3074–3086 (2020). https://doi.org/10.1109/TNSE.2020.3015689

17. Eshratifar, A.E., Pedram, M.: Energy and performance efficient computation offloading for deep neural networks in a mobile cloud computing environment. In: Proceedings on Great Lakes Symposium VLSI (GLSVLSI). Chicago, IL, USA, pp. 111–116 (2018). https://doi.org/10.1145/3194554.3194565

18. Zheng, T., Wan, J., Zhang, J., Jiang, C.: Deep reinforcement learning-based workload scheduling for edge computing. J. Cloud Comput. 11(1), 3 (2022)

19. Zeng, D., Gu, L., Pan, S., Cai., J., Guo, S.: Resource management at the network edge: a deep reinforcement learning approach. IEEE Network 33(3), 26–33 (2019). https://doi.org/10.1109/MNET.2019.1800386

20. Pang, L., Yang, C., Chen, D., Song, Y., Guizani, M.: A survey on intent-driven networks. IEEE Access 8, 22862–22873 (2020)

21. Abbas, K., Afaq, M., Ahmed Khan, T., Rafiq, A., Song, W.C.: Slicing the core network and radio access network domains through intent-based networking for 5G networks. Electronics 9(10), 1710 (2020)

22. Mehmood, K., Kralevska, K., Palma, D.: Intent-driven autonomous network and service management in future networks: a structured literature review (2021)

23. Chao, W., Horiuchi, S.: Intent-based cloud service management. In: 2018 21st Conference on Innovation in Clouds, Internet and Networks and Workshops (ICIN), pp. 1–5. IEEE (2018)

24. Kang, J.M., Lee, J., Nagendra, V., Banerjee, S.: LMS: label management service for intent-driven cloud management. In: 2017 IFIP/IEEE Symposium on Integrated Network and Service Management (IM), pp. 177–185. IEEE (2017)

25. Liao, H., et al.: Learning-based intent-aware task offloading for air-ground integrated vehicular edge computing. IEEE Trans. Intell. Transp. Syst. 22(8), 5127–5139 (2020)

26. Wu, C., Horiuchi, S., Murase, K., Kikushima, H., Tayama, K.: Intent-driven cloud resource design framework to meet cloud performance requirements and its application to a cloud-sensor system. J. Cloud Comput. 10(1), 1–22 (2021)

27. He, L., Qian, Z.: Intent-based resource matching strategy in cloud. Inf. Sci. 538, 1–18 (2020)

28. Leivadeas, A., Falkner, M.: VNF placement problem: a multi-tenant intent-based networking approach. In: 2021 24th Conference on Innovation in Clouds, Internet and Networks and Workshops (ICIN), pp. 143–150. IEEE (2021)

29. Amazon instance types (2019). http://aws.amazon.com/ec2/instance-types/

A Double-Decision Reinforcement Learning Based Algorithm for Online Scheduling in Edge and Fog Computing

Ahmed Fayez Moustafa Tayel⬡, Gabriele Proietti Mattia$^{(\boxtimes)}$⬡, and Roberto Beraldi⬡

Department of Computer, Control and Management Engineering "Antonio Ruberti", Sapienza University of Rome, Rome, Italy
tayel.1972085@studenti.uniroma1.it,
{proiettimattia,beraldi}@diag.uniroma1.it

Abstract. Fog and Edge Computing are two paradigms specifically suitable for real-time and time-critical applications, which are usually distributed among a set of nodes that constitutes the core idea of both Fog and Edge Computing. Since nodes are heterogeneous and subject to different traffic patterns, distributed scheduling algorithms are in charge of making each request meet the specified deadline. In this paper, we exploit the approach of Reinforcement Learning based decision-making for designing a cooperative and decentralized task online scheduling approach which is composed of two RL-based decisions. One for selecting the node to which to offload the traffic and one for accepting or not the incoming offloading request. The experiments that we conducted on a cluster of Raspberry Pi 4 show that introducing a second RL decision increases the rate of tasks executed within the deadline of 4% as it introduces more flexibility during the decision-making process, consequently enabling better scheduling decisions.

Keywords: Fog Computing · Online Scheduling · Distributed Scheduling · Reinforcement Learning

1 Introduction

Fog Computing is a paradigm that links edge devices to cloud computing data centers by offering processing, storage, and networking resources [14]. It might be viewed as an addition to cloud computing rather than as a substitute, and its main objective is to support services and applications that are not supported by cloud computing [6], such as those which need predictable and low latency, geographically distributed, require quick responses from mobile devices, and require large-scale distributed control systems. The three primary layers of an IoT environment (Edge Processing, Fog Computing, and Cloud Computing) can be considered a hierarchical arrangement of network resources, computing, and storage.

ⓒ The Author(s), under exclusive license to Springer Nature Switzerland AG 2024
I. Chatzigiannakis and I. Karydis (Eds.): ALGOCLOUD 2023, LNCS 14053, pp. 197–210, 2024.
https://doi.org/10.1007/978-3-031-49361-4_11

Recently Fog Computing applications drastically increased due to the unique solution it provides with time-critical applications [12], as over the past few years, cloud computing and native cloud services were used for deploying applications due to the fast deployment methods, and the provided scalability options by the cloud providers, in addition to the ready maintained packages for configuring the infrastructure according to every application-specific needs. One of the important flaws to be considered in this approach is that the application is deployed in one of the cloud provider's centers which are placed evenly all over the globe to serve applications from anywhere in the world, and it does not behave very well with the time-critical applications due to network (and geographic) latency. Use cases like real-time face detection applications, machine learning-based applications, or general applications which are time critical [5,7,10] and need some computational effort would not get much use of the basic cloud services, this is when fog computing comes into action. Fog computing would be an optimal solution for applications and use cases which are time critical, need some computational power to be executed successfully and most importantly could be executed in a distributed fashion by dividing and delegating the tasks to other geographically nearby servers [2,9,23] to execute the function in the shortest time possible, this has multiple benefits, the work could be split among different servers which speed up the execution process, also the tasks allocations process [21] could be scheduled in an optimized way to serve the overall execution of the task with respect to multiple things, the servers geographical locations, the complexity of the tasks, and the servers capability in terms of memory and computational power. Many scheduling algorithms were used to solve this problem, and most focused on using Reinforcement Learning approaches [15] which, in this particular context, allows for adapting the scheduling policy in a very dynamic context that can regard Edge or Fog Computing, where nodes can unpredictably go down or saturate due to high traffic.

This work focuses on designing an improved approach [16] for a cooperative, decentralized, and online scheduling of tasks among a set of nodes using Reinforcement Learning. We suppose that clients request tasks to be executed on the nodes, and each task has defined a specific deadline that makes the task usable by the clients. Each node can be seen as a worker and a scheduler that takes decisions according to the RL model. The model is used to make two kinds of decisions. Figure 1 shows our double-step decision model during the cooperation. Firstly, when (1) Node A (which we call the "originator node") receives a task to be executed by the client, the node decides whether to execute, reject or forward it to another neighbor node, suppose Node B (which we call the "delegated node"). When the task is forwarded, even node Node B decides whether to execute it locally or reject it. Both decisions are made with an online learning RL model, and we suppose a task cannot be forwarded more than once since every forwarding step adds network delay to tasks that already have a deadline.

The rest of the paper is organized as follows. In Sect. 2, we present some related work, then in Sect. 3, we show the model of the system, in Sect. 4, we present the double-step RL-based algorithm for online scheduling and in Sect. 5

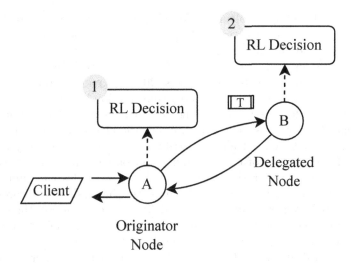

Fig. 1. The proposed double-decision scheme for cooperative and decentralized scheduling. Node A receives a task to be executed and decides whether to forward it to another node; when the task is forwarded, even Node B makes the decision whether to accept or reject it.

we show the experimental results of the proposed approach. Finally, we draw the conclusions in Sect. 6.

2   Related Work

Dynamic scheduling solutions address scheduling issues the most when the scheduler lacks precise knowledge of the jobs. Starting from the classic Job-shop scheduling problem [3], lots of techniques and algorithms were introduced to solve this problem.

Various sets of heuristic algorithms are used for the job scheduling process, popular algorithms include the genetic algorithm, ant colony optimization, bee life [18] and symbiotic organization used to optimize the scheduling process [13]. However these categories belong to static scheduling techniques which need all the details about the task to be known beforehand, and this is in general not optimal for online and real-time scheduling. In some studies multi-agent-based models were introduced to evaluate task scheduling based on a priority rule, the work introduced by Hosseinioun et al. [8] has the objective of minimizing energy consumption, as it's a major factor when working in a fog environment, and the approach was pivoted around dynamic voltage and frequency scaling (DVFS) methodology [4] which does not care much about the tasks' deadline as much as the energy consumption. Wang and Chen [22] also contributed to optimizing resource allocation but without experimenting with the model in a real-world application. There was also a significant contribution to using neural networks with the task scheduling problem [11] [1]. Witanto et al. [24] proposed neural network based on adaptive selection of VM consolidation algorithms which selects the most adequate algorithm based on a specified priority, also CNNs started getting involved in task scheduling but with very limited use cases compared to other popular neural networks models [20]. The main characteristic of NN approaches is that it optimizes for energy consumption but it lacks speed due to the high inference latency when dealing with task deadline-critical applications.

The main focus of this work is to improve the algorithm introduced in [16], which implemented a decentralized distributed system for efficient job scheduling. It used the concept of task deadlines and online scheduling to determine which node in the cluster should execute the task. Nodes communicate in a peer-to-peer fashion and the node which executes that task gets rewarded based on whether the task is executed by the predefined deadline or not, then the client is able to train the node based on the knowledge of the node's state when the task was sent, the scheduling action taken by the node, and the reward gained based on the task deadline. Consequently, based on this reinforcement learning approach, the environment is not modeled, and the state of each node is determined online in a real deployment.

3   System Model

The system model is formulated using a Markov decision process, which does not require the knowledge of any previous states, but only the current one is meaningful. For learning the policy, since we use a model-free approach in which we do not know the probabilities $p(s', r|s, a)$, we rely on a time differential approach. Therefore the agent needs to interact directly with the environment, obtain the reward and train the model. This basic RL framework comprises the environment, the agent, and the reward, which we will now see in detail.

3.1   Environment

The system is composed of a set $\mathcal{N}$ of nodes with the same capabilities (same computing power and memory), the nodes are aware of each other's existence, the nodes are communicating only in a peer-to-peer fashion, no consensus or broadcast communication algorithms are used, all the nodes have the same configuration settings of tasks concurrent execution and queuing. Also, all the computing nodes have predefined functions to execute different types of tasks. The main purpose of this distributed system is to collaborate to execute as many tasks as possible within the deadline by executing these tasks locally or delegating them to other peers to achieve optimal performance in aggregate.

3.2   Agent

Each node is seen as an independent agent responsible for making a decision based on the current state of the node, and this is a powerful capability of the system as the nodes have independent agents, so they communicate in a peer-to-peer fashion. The node's state is calculated when a new task arrives, and a scheduling decision must be taken. Equation 1 shows the state of node i when the k-th task arrives at the node at time t. The state S_{ik}^t is a triple composed by the type of the task k (we suppose $v_i^k \in \Upsilon$), the load of node i at time t which is l_i^t (where $l_i^t \in \mathbb{N}$ and $0 \leq l_i^t \leq K$) and the node to which the client sent the task at first ($n_{if}^k \in \mathcal{N}$), the originator node.

$$S_{ik}^t = \{v_i^k,\ l_i^t,\ n_{if}^k\} \tag{1}$$

The node's actions also depend on its role in the execution flow. Since we allow only one hop, if a node i receives the task k from a client (and therefore $n_{if}^k \neq i$) it can reject the request (action Re), execute it locally (action Ex), forward the request to a random node (action Fw), or to delegate the request to another peer, otherwise, if the same node i receives the task k from another peer node (suppose $j \neq i$ and n_{if}^k) then it only can execute the task locally or reject it. Equation 2 shows the formalization of the set of the actions that node i can execute on task k at time t.

$$A_{ik}^t = \begin{cases} \{Ex, Re, Fw\} \cup \mathcal{N} & \text{if } n_{if}^k \neq i \\ \{Ex, Re\} & \text{otherwise} \end{cases} \tag{2}$$

3.3   Reward

As shown in Table 1, the reward is calculated by evaluating if the task is executed within the deadline, and it's calculated on the client side to consider the network latency. This is how the node's location and network capabilities are considered in the learning process, and time is calculated on the client side, from sending the request until the response is returned. As the execution flow might involve one or two nodes based on the action of the node which receives the request from the client whether to forward the task or not, in this case, both nodes get the same reward (which is equal to one) also depending on whether the task is executed within the deadline or not. This approach makes sense as in the case of having two nodes in the task execution flow, both nodes act as a team, and they should collaborate to execute the task within the deadline, and therefore they'll get the same reward. Also, this is the best abstraction from a client's point of view as it should not know how the execution flow works and the client should only care about the task execution time. We do not choose to use a more articulated reward, since once the task is over the deadline we suppose to become useless to the client as it would be in a real-time image processing application.

4   Reinforcement Learning Based Scheduling

Recalling the RL-based scheduler in [16], when the node's action is to forward the task to another node, the node receiving the task always executes the task

Table 1. Summary of reward assignment. The reward is positive when the task is completed within the deadline and when forwarded, the reward is assigned to both nodes.

Originator Node Action	Task Result	Reward on Node	
		Originator	Delegated
Rejected	-	0	-
Executed Locally	Within-Deadline	1	-
	Over-Deadline	0	-
Forwarded	Within-Deadline	1	1
	Over-Deadline	0	0

locally unless it is fully utilized so, in this case, the task is not executed. The proposed approach introduces an extra learning step to be done on the delegated node side so that instead of having only one option, which is to execute the task locally, it can now choose if it executes the task locally or rejects it. This approach enhanced the system as the delegated node could be trained in such a way that if the task is achievable within the deadline so the node executes the task, and the system works the same as before, and if the task would not be executed within the deadline so the node would reject it, and a node rejecting a task gets the same reward as executing a task which does not meet the deadline but in this case rejecting the task is better as this would save more time for the cluster to execute other tasks which would meet the deadline, and hence improve the overall system efficiency, which is maximizing the number of successfully executed tasks in a time unit. Therefore, the node's state and actions selections are based on the node's role in the task execution flow as described in Eqs. 1 and 2.

The reinforcement learning algorithm used for training the agent uses Sarsa properly adapted for continuous learning. The average reward is used as a baseline for directing the policy in such approaches. Therefore, given a node i which receives a task k and its current state S_{ik}^t, the optimal policy π selects an action A_{ik}^t, a reward r is obtained, and the long-term reward is maximized [19].

Given the state description in Eq. 1, the set of states is finite and can be stored in a Q table. Therefore, the Q-table is used as a function approximator mechanism. The average-reward concept is used in Differential Semi-Gradient Sarsa Algorithm, and the table is updated according to Eq. 3.

$$Q(S_t, A_t) \leftarrow Q(S_t, A_t) + \alpha \Delta_t \tag{3}$$

Where $Q(S_t, A_t)$ is the Q value of the state S_t and an action A_t, and it gets updated by using Δ_t defined in Eq. 4 multiplied by a hyper-parameter α as follows:

$$\Delta_t = [R_{t+1} - \bar{R}_{t+1} + Q(S_{t+1}, A_{t+1}) - Q(S_t, A_t)] \tag{4}$$

Here, R_{t+1} is the immediate reward, and $\bar{R}$ is the average reward which is updated according to the following Eq. 5, given β as another hyper-parameter of the algorithm.

$$\bar{R}_{t+1} = \bar{R}_t + \beta\Delta_t \tag{5}$$

In the proposed double decision scheduler, the execution flow starts when the client sends a request to execute a task to a node in the cluster and records the task's start timestamp, then the node executes Algorithm 1, which calculates the current node state according to the node's current load and the type of the task, it also stamp the request with a generated request number, which is enumerated in an ascending order, then the node sends the state to the learner for inference, it receives an action which could be one of the following:

- deliberately rejecting the request;
- executing the task locally;
- picking random node, and if this node is less loaded than the current node, the random node executes the task. Otherwise, the task is executed locally by the current node;
- the task is forwarded to a random node in the nodes' list, including the current node itself.

If the action is to send the request to another node, then the other node (or, as we call it, the delegated node) does the following:

- calculates the current state with respect to the following:
  - node's current load;
  - the type of the task;
  - the sender node id;
- It stamps the request with a generated request number, which is enumerated in an ascending order;
- It sends the state to the learner for inference;
- It receives an action that could be either deliberately rejecting the request or executing the task locally;
- If the latter is the case, then it executes the task;
- it sends back its state, which action is executed, and the task execution result if the chosen action was to execute the task;

Finally, the peer node returns the response to the client with all the learning information.

As mentioned before, each node could act as an originator node (receiving the request from the client) or a delegated node (receiving the request from another peer) based on its role in the execution flow, so the algorithm should be compact to accommodate for both roles, and this is done by using the *requestIsExternal* Boolean, if it's true so the node acts as a delegated node, otherwise, it acts as the originator node.

Algorithm 1. Double Learner Scheduler

Require: Node, Task, A, qTable, requestIsExternal, SenderNodeId
   if requestIsExternal **then** (Get State for Delegated Node)
      $s \leftarrow$ aggregate(Node.getLoad(), Task.getType(), SenderNodeId)
   else
      $s \leftarrow$ aggregate(Node.getLoad(), Task.getType())
   end if
   $a \leftarrow$ max(qTable.getActionsList(s)) with prob. 1-e otherwise random(A)
   if $a == 0$ **then**
      Node.reject(Task)
   else if $a == 1$ **or** requestIsExternal **then**
      Node.execute(Task)
   else if $a == 2$ **then** (Probe and Forward)
      RandomNode $\leftarrow$ pickRandom(Node.getNeighbors())
      if RandomNode.getLoad() $<$ Node.getLoad() **then**
         forwardTo(RandomNode, Task)
      else
         Node.execute(Task)
      end if
   else
      Node $\leftarrow$ pickNode(a)
      forwardTo(Node, Task)
   end if

5   Experimental Results

The proposed algorithm has been implemented into the P2PFaas framework [17]. In particular, the modules that have been improved are the learner service which implements the RL model and is also responsible for training the model and the decision-making process, and the scheduler service, which implements the actual scheduler algorithm. In this architecture, the client is not only responsible for sending task requests to the cluster but also for parsing the learning entries from the node's returned state and action, calculating the reward, and training the nodes. The client sends the learning parameters to every node in batches that contain, in order: the request's id, state, action, and reward. The node's learner service receives the batch, sorts it based on the request's id, and starts the learning process using the current average reward method.

Two studies have been performed comparing a single decision scheduler (where the decision is made only in the originator node) and our proposed double decision scheduler regarding performance. The first study was done by applying static loads (requests/second) but not balanced over the nodes (heterogeneous loads), and the second experiment is done using data extracted from the open data for New York City as done in the previous work as well [16]. The performance metric will always be the same: the number of completed tasks within the deadline per second, also called "within-deadline rate".

The cluster consists of 11 Raspberry Pis 4 Model B, five of which are 8 GB of RAM, and the rest are 4 GB of RAM. For each Raspberry, we installed a face recognition FaaS (Function-as-a-Service) triggered upon the HTTP call with an image as payload. The experiment is done using a script that generates 11 concurrent flows of requests to all the nodes in the cluster at different rates (requests per second), and it uses two payloads as in Table 2.

Table 2. Benchmark payload images used in the tests

	Image A	Image B
Resolution	320 × 210	180 × 118
Size (kB)	28.3	23.8
Processing Time (ms)	188.25	74.95

To calculate the reward, the client has to set a deadline for the nodes executing the tasks, calculates the node's task execution time, and compare these values, and consequently, the reward is assigned as described in Sect. 3.3. The assigned deadlines setting are the Processing Time of the image multiplied by a factor of 1.1, and it sends requests for Image A and Image B with a ratio of 1:1. The benchmark time is set to 1800 s, and the nodes are loaded heterogeneously, so every node is experiencing fixed traffic but loaded differently from the other nodes, and this traffic is distributed with the following values (in requests per second): 4, 6, 8, 12, 13, 14, 15, 16, 17, 18, 19. The "Dynamic Study" traffic is extracted from open data of New York City data set, which estimates the average taxi traffic across several locations in the city. The traffic data covers only six nodes, so it is repeated for the other five nodes. As the traffic is normalized, it is scaled by a range from 0 to 20, so, for example, when the traffic data at a point in time is 0.9, the actual load on the node is 0.9 * 20 = 18.

5.1 The Within-Deadline Rate Comparison

In Figs. 2 and 3, the comparison shows that the double decision scheduler (called "Double Learner" in charts) is at least as good as the single decision scheduler (called "Single Learner" in charts) on average for both the static and the dynamic traffic.

In Fig. 2, the single decision scheduler was better than the double decision one at the first 200 s for most of the nodes before the double decision taking over for the rest of the experiment. This behavior is expected as the double decision needs some time for delegated node's learner to take effect, starting from time 200 s and upwards. The double decision scheduler within-deadline rate was noticeably higher than the single decision for some nodes, the double decision within-deadline rate is better than the single decision by 3% on average, and it has a within-deadline rate of 90% on average. For the dynamic study shown in Fig. 3, the results are the same as the static load study as the double decision scheduler reacts the same for dynamic loads as the static loads, the double decision is constantly performing over the single decision, for nodes 1, 2, and 9, the performance is almost the same, but for the whole system on average, the double decision rate was better by 4.1%.

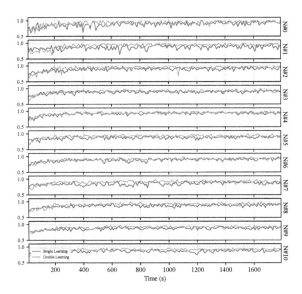

Fig. 2. The within-deadline rate for the single decision vs double decision when applied static loads in Raspberry Pis cluster, the double decision was better than the single decision by 3% on average

However, it is also noticeable that when the loads increase, the double decision degrades to the performance of the single decision, as nodes 8, 9, and 10 performances were lower than nodes 5, 6, and 7 by 0.3%, and this is because the double decision takes more time to execute the task in the general case, as it involves extra inference step on the delegated node side. This latency takes effect when the traffic increases and the double decision degrades.

5.2 Delegated Node Performance

A separate monitor has been applied to the decision behavior of all nodes but only acting in the second node role during the task execution process. It was necessary to be sure that the delegated node's decision was getting better over time and it is choosing a decision that maximized the number of successfully executed tasks per second. Figure 4 describes the node's execution in the "delegated node role" and how it behaves over time.

It shows that the learning process starts low at first and then it saturates by the time, and the average within-deadline rate for nodes with lower loads for

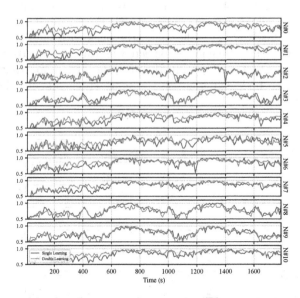

Fig. 3. The within-deadline rate for the single decision vs. double decision when applied dynamic loads in Raspberry Pis cluster, the double decision was better than the single decision by 4.1% on average

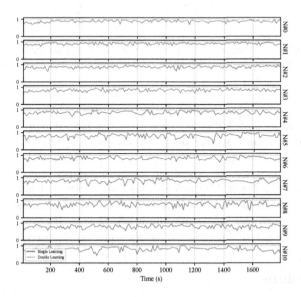

Fig. 4. The within-deadline rate for nodes Raspberry Pis cluster with respect to static loads when they act as delegated nodes as double learning is activated

example, nodes from 0 to 4 is 81% which is by a small amount better than the ones with nodes from 5 to 10 with 80%, so that the within-deadline rate for the nodes with lower loads is 1% higher than the ones with high loads (from node 5 to node 10), and this behavior is expected as the more loads applied to the node, the less it achieves task within the deadline. It is important to note that the more loads the node experiences, the more stochastic the delegated node performance will be.

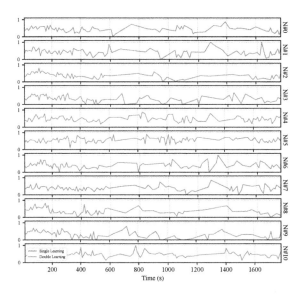

Fig. 5. The within-deadline rate for nodes in Raspberry Pis cluster with respect to dynamic loads when they act as delegated nodes as double learning is activated

It is shown in Fig. 4 for the nodes which experience high loads (from node 5 to node 10), and it is also shown in Fig. 5 as the more the loads are dynamic, the more spikes and oscillations the delegated node experiences. The reason for the within-deadline rate instability shown in Fig. 5 is that the delegated node is always trying to follow the dynamic loads by adapting it is policy. This is normal, as shown in Fig. 3. Figure 5 also shows that the delegated node within-deadline rate is resilient to load changes for most of the nodes, as the node is always trying not to fall below minimum effectiveness because of the varying loads, keeping the average rate for all nodes equals to 1.06 requests/seconds.

6   Conclusions

This paper proposes a double-decision online distributed scheduler using reinforcement learning and improves an online learner scheduler [16] with a second decision if the node's action is to delegate the task to another node so that now the second node learns to choose the correct action between accepting or rejecting the task based on its state and the originator node. The delegated node learns to reject a task if it would not be executed within the deadline and therefore saving time for executing other tasks which potentially can be completed within the deadline. By performing different experiments implementing the approach in a cluster of 11 Raspberry Pi we show that our approach increases the in-deadline rate showing an improvement over the single decision scheduler performances. However, different aspects could have a more detailed analysis. For example, it could be further studied the energy aspect of the nodes which may make a decision also based on the power consumption.

References

1. Ali, A.M., Tirel, L.: Action masked deep reinforcement learning for controlling industrial assembly lines. In: 2023 IEEE World AI IoT Congress (AIIoT), pp. 0797–0803 (2023). https://doi.org/10.1109/AIIoT58121.2023.10174426
2. AlOrbani, A., Bauer, M.: Load balancing and resource allocation in smart cities using reinforcement learning. In: 2021 IEEE International Smart Cities Conference (ISC2), pp. 1–7. IEEE (2021)
3. Aydin, M.E., Öztemel, E.: Dynamic job-shop scheduling using reinforcement learning agents. Robot. Auton. Syst. **33**(2–3), 169–178 (2000)
4. Bansal, S., Kumar, P., Singh, K.: Duplication-based scheduling algorithm for interconnection-constrained distributed memory machines. In: Sahni, S., Prasanna, V.K., Shukla, U. (eds.) HiPC 2002. LNCS, vol. 2552, pp. 52–62. Springer, Heidelberg (2002). https://doi.org/10.1007/3-540-36265-7_6
5. Barthélemy, J., Verstaevel, N., Forehead, H., Perez, P.: Edge-computing video analytics for real-time traffic monitoring in a smart city. Sensors **19**(9), 2048 (2019)
6. Bonomi, F., Milito, R., Natarajan, P., Zhu, J.: Fog computing: a platform for internet of things and analytics. In: Bessis, N., Dobre, C. (eds.) Big Data and Internet of Things: A Roadmap for Smart Environments. SCI, vol. 546, pp. 169–186. Springer, Cham (2014). https://doi.org/10.1007/978-3-319-05029-4_7
7. Broucke, S.V., Deligiannis, N.: Visualization of real-time heterogeneous smart city data using virtual reality. In: 2019 IEEE International Smart Cities Conference (ISC2), pp. 685–690. IEEE (2019)
8. Hosseinioun, P., Kheirabadi, M., Tabbakh, S.R.K., Ghaemi, R.: A new energy-aware tasks scheduling approach in fog computing using hybrid meta-heuristic algorithm. J. Parallel Distrib. Comput. **143**, 88–96 (2020)
9. Houidi, O., et al.: Constrained deep reinforcement learning for smart load balancing. In: 2022 IEEE 19th Annual Consumer Communications and Networking Conference (CCNC), pp. 207–215. IEEE (2022)
10. Hu, F., Deng, Y., Saad, W., Bennis, M., Aghvami, A.H.: Cellular-connected wireless virtual reality: requirements, challenges, and solutions. IEEE Commun. Mag. **58**(5), 105–111 (2020)
11. Iftikhar, S., et al.: HunterPlus: AI based energy-efficient task scheduling for cloud-fog computing environments. Internet Things **21**, 100667 (2023)
12. Iorga, M., Feldman, L., Barton, R., Martin, M.J., Goren, N.S., Mahmoudi, C.: Fog computing conceptual model (2018)
13. Kaur, N., Bansal, S., Bansal, R.K.: Survey on energy efficient scheduling techniques on cloud computing. Multiagent Grid Syst. **17**(4), 351–366 (2021)

14. Liu, Y., Fieldsend, J.E., Min, G.: A framework of fog computing: architecture, challenges, and optimization. IEEE Access **5**, 25445–25454 (2017)
15. Orhean, A.I., Pop, F., Raicu, I.: New scheduling approach using reinforcement learning for heterogeneous distributed systems. J. Parallel Distrib. Comput. **117**, 292–302 (2018)
16. Proietti Mattia, G., Beraldi, R.: On real-time scheduling in fog computing: a reinforcement learning algorithm with application to smart cities. In: 2022 IEEE International Conference on Pervasive Computing and Communications Workshops and other Affiliated Events (PerCom Workshops), pp. 187–193 (2022). https://doi.org/10.1109/PerComWorkshops53856.2022.9767498
17. Proietti Mattia, G., Beraldi, R.: P2PFaaS: a framework for FaaS peer-to-peer scheduling and load balancing in Fog and Edge computing. SoftwareX **21**, 101290 (2023)
18. Sehgal, N., Bansal, S., Bansal, R.: Task scheduling in fog computing environment: an overview. Int. J. Eng. Technol. Manag. Sci. **7**(1), 47–54 (2023)
19. Sutton, R.S., Barto, A.G.: Reinforcement Learning: An Introduction. MIT Press, Cambridge (2018)
20. Talaat, F.M., Ali, H.A., Saraya, M.S., Saleh, A.I.: Effective scheduling algorithm for load balancing in fog environment using CNN and MPSO. Knowl. Inf. Syst. **64**(3), 773–797 (2022)
21. Wang, J., Zhao, L., Liu, J., Kato, N.: Smart resource allocation for mobile edge computing: a deep reinforcement learning approach. IEEE Trans. Emerg. Top. Comput. **9**(3), 1529–1541 (2019)
22. Wang, Q., Chen, S.: Latency-minimum offloading decision and resource allocation for fog-enabled internet of things networks. Trans. Emerg. Telecommun. Technol. **31**(12), e3880 (2020)
23. Wang, S., Guo, Y., Zhang, N., Yang, P., Zhou, A., Shen, X.: Delay-aware microservice coordination in mobile edge computing: a reinforcement learning approach. IEEE Trans. Mob. Comput. **20**(3), 939–951 (2019)
24. Witanto, J.N., Lim, H., Atiquzzaman, M.: Adaptive selection of dynamic VM consolidation algorithm using neural network for cloud resource management. Futur. Gener. Comput. Syst. **87**, 35–42 (2018)

Decentralized Algorithms for Efficient Energy Management over Cloud-Edge Infrastructures

Aristeidis Karras[1]([✉]) [ID], Christos Karras[1] [ID], Ioanna Giannoukou[2] [ID],
Konstantinos C. Giotopoulos[2] [ID], Dimitrios Tsolis[3] [ID], Ioannis Karydis[4] [ID],
and Spyros Sioutas[1] [ID]

[1] Computer Engineering and Informatics Department, University of Patras,
26504 Patras, Greece
{akarras,c.karras,sioutas}@ceid.upatras.gr
[2] Department of Management Science and Technology, University of Patras,
26334 Patras, Greece
{igian,kgiotop}@upatras.gr
[3] Department of History and Archaeology, University of Patras, 26504 Patras, Greece
dtsolis@upatras.gr
[4] Department of Informatics, Ionian University, 49100 Corfu, Greece
karydis@ionio.gr

Abstract. This paper presents an innovative approach to overcoming
the limitations of traditional cloud-centric architectures in the evolving Internet of Things (IoT) landscape. We introduce a set of novel
decentralized algorithms boosting Mobile Edge Computing (MEC),
a paradigm shift towards placing computational resources near data
sources, thus boosting real-time processing and energy efficiency. Our
approach addresses the challenges of managing distributed Cloud-edge
infrastructures in high-mobility environments, such as drone networks.
Utilizing the Random Waypoint Model to anticipate device trajectories,
our algorithms ensure effective resource allocation, enhanced load balancing, and improved Quality of Service (QoS). An in-depth complexity
analysis further improves the scalability and performance of our method,
demonstrating their ability to optimize energy efficiency and minimize
latency, offering optimized offloading strategies in dynamic IoT environments.

Keywords: Decentralized Computing · Cloud Computing · Edge
Computing · IoT Systems · Energy Management · High-mobility
Environments

1 Introduction

The rapid proliferation of Internet of Things (IoT) technology in recent years,
alongside the increasing demand for high-performance, low-latency applications,

© The Author(s), under exclusive license to Springer Nature Switzerland AG 2024
I. Chatzigiannakis and I. Karydis (Eds.): ALGOCLOUD 2023, LNCS 14053, pp. 211–230, 2024.
https://doi.org/10.1007/978-3-031-49361-4_12

has placed a significant role on existing cloud-centric infrastructures. IoT devices, commonly referred to as edge devices due to their proximity to data sources, frequently generate massive volumes of data that need to be processed in real-time. However, the limitive nature of centralized cloud architectures can introduce latency that undermines the real-time processing capabilities and energy efficiency of such systems. Some emerging paradigms, such as the Mobile Edge Computing (MEC), are designed to overcome these constraints by placing computation and storage resources closer to data sources, thereby enabling prompt data processing while conserving energy sources.

This progression towards the network edge indicates a transformative change in infrastructure management, where tasks are no longer exclusively offloaded to a central Cloud. Instead, computational workloads can be distributed across the edge of a network, ensuring the proximity of MEC servers to data sources for swift, efficient computation. By bringing computation closer to end-devices, MEC minimizes transmission delays and reduces the volume of data that must traverse the network, leading to enhanced quality of service (QoS) and improved energy efficiency.

Apart from the potential benefits, the effective management of these distributed, Cloud-edge infrastructures presents a complex set of challenges. In a dynamic environment characterized by high device mobility, such as drones, finding the optimal offloading strategy becomes a challenging problem. Existing offloading methods that assume static device positions may prove inadequate in this new context. The added complexity of drone mobility necessitates algorithms that can efficiently determine the most suitable MEC server for task execution. The challenges are further compounded by the multitude of available MEC servers, which could lead to suboptimal offloading decisions if tasks are blindly assigned to directly linked servers.

The objective of this paper is to delve into these complexities and propose a novel set of decentralized algorithms that optimize energy management across cloud-edge infrastructures with mobile edge devices, like drones, and also to assess mobility and task allocation. Our proposed algorithms anticipate device mobility, utilizing the Random Waypoint Model to predict device trajectories and appropriately allocate resources. With the consideration of unique delay restrictions for each task, our approach aims to strike a balance between efficient energy use and minimal latency, thereby improving QoS.

This paper is organized as follows: Sect. 2 discusses the relevant literature. Section 3.2 presents the architecture of our model and formulates the problem. The proposed algorithms are elaborated in Sect. 3.3. Section 4 assesses the performance of these algorithms and discusses the results. Finally, Sect. 5 concludes the paper and explores potential future research directions.

2   Background and Related Work

In the dynamic and swiftly-evolving field of cloud computing, and its increasingly significant extensions-edge, fog, and decentralized architectures-several innovative improvements are changing the topic of resource management and performance optimization across a combination of applications. Essential to this transformation, tools, and algorithms such as CloudSim, a toolkit developed by Calheiros et al. [2], and the novel bio-inspired hybrid algorithm (NBIHA) proposed by Rafique et al. [17]. These novel ideas aim to increase resource provisioning and improve energy efficiency and execution times within these different computing environments, thereby establishing new benchmarks for enhancing operational efficiency and performance.

Smart grid systems are also significantly affected by the ground-breaking impact of these cutting-edge developments. Chekired et al.'s decentralized Cloud-SDN architecture, which employs a dynamic pricing model [4], and Zahoor et al.'s cloud-fog-based smart grid model are establishing the way for this technological breakthrough [23,24]. The model proposed by Zahoor effectively combines the ideas of ant colony optimization and artificial bee colony optimization. These revolutionary improvements not only enhance efficient energy management and utilization but additionally optimize resource utilization, even in the most high-demanding cases, demonstrating effectiveness and flexibility in the current energy environment.

Alongside the recent advances in smart grid systems, there is a simultaneous growth of innovation that incorporates the power of cloud computing with the broad Internet of Things (IoT) network. Han et al.'s efficient deep learning framework for intelligent energy management effectively incorporates this synergy [8]. This framework improves smart grid models, such as those presented by [4] and [23,24], by facilitating the demand for energy and response processes efficiently. Pantazoglou et al. have proposed a decentralized, energy-efficient workload management system for enterprise clouds to complement this technological integration [16]. Each node operates independently, simulating the autonomous behavior of ant and bee colonies in Zahoor's model, consequently enhancing the autonomy and efficiency of the system as an entire unit.

Regarding the progress made in combining cloud computing and IoT networks, major improvements are also being made in the fields of edge networks and vehicular edge computing. Liu et al. are on the leading edge with their multi-factor energy-aware resource management system [14], while Wang et al. have developed a cloud-edge collaborative strategy for computation offloading [21]. Alongside addressing increased traffic flow demands and expansive distribution distances, these cutting-edge methodologies enhance vehicular edge computing performance to levels never before achieved.

Machine learning and deep reinforcement learning approaches have become powerful factors in the direction of enhanced energy efficiency and optimized resource utilization. This is demonstrated by Tian et al.'s decentralized collaborative power management system [20]. By applying the power of multi-device knowledge sharing, their system leads to significant energy savings. Alongside this, Jayanetti et al. have utilized deep reinforcement learning to create an innovative scheduling framework, deftly managing complex workflow scheduling problems in edge-cloud environments [9].

As a result of the progress made essential through machine learning and deep reinforcement learning, Rey-Jouanchicot et al. [18] and Blanco et al. [6] emphasize on the essential role that IoT device availability and robust consensus models have. These components prove to be critical in determining computational capacity and managing resources in applications such as smart buildings or cities. Xiong et al.'s study on blockchain network management provides a major new dimension to the optimization of system performance by delving into this complex and data-rich environment [22]. Ultimately, these innovations represent the rapid development and great possibilities offered by cloud, edge, and fog computing, significantly enhancing the performance of a wide spectrum of applications.

2.1   Decentralized Energy Management

The complexities of energy management in cloud-edge infrastructures arise due to the dynamic nature of resources, especially when compared to traditional cloud settings [13]. Edge computing, a decentralized paradigm, capitalizes on resources at the network's edge to facilitate local data processing, making it closer to user-end devices such as smartphones or wearables. Recently, edge, there has been a marked increase in the application of machine learning (ML) at this network edge. This trend mainly seeks to enhance computational services, especially focusing on reduced latency, energy conservation, and resource optimization [1].

In the exploration of energy-efficient resource allocation, adapting distributed machine learning (ML) algorithms for execution at the edge is crucial. This strategic adaptation promotes synergy with cloud systems, aiming to achieve reduced latency, enhanced energy efficiency, safeguarded user privacy, and improved system scalability [15]. Recent technological advancements encompass a deep reinforcement learning-based mechanism, specifically designed for cloud-edge collaborative offloading, addressing the dynamic requirements of industrial networks [5]. Additionally, for advanced energy management in smart grids, a privacy-focused average consensus algorithm has been introduced, seamlessly integrating the benefits of both cloud and edge computing [7].

In summary, achieving energy efficiency in cloud-edge infrastructures primarily requires adapting machine learning algorithms for edge environments, utilizing distributed learning techniques, and designing privacy-centric methodologies to ensure secure and effective resource allocation.

2.2   Mobile Edge Computing vs Traditional Cloud-Centric Architectures

Mobile Edge Computing (MEC) is a paradigm shift towards placing computational resources near data sources, thus boosting real-time processing and energy efficiency. MEC is a distributed computing architecture that extends cloud computing capabilities to the edge of the network, closer to the end-users and data sources. This tension towards the network edge indicates a transformative change in infrastructure management, where tasks are no longer exclusively offloaded to a central Cloud. Instead, computational workloads can be distributed across the edge of a network, ensuring the proximity of MEC servers to data sources for swift, efficient computation. By making the computation closer to end devices, MEC minimizes transmission delays and reduces the volume of data that must traverse the network, leading to enhanced quality of service (QoS) and improved energy efficiency. In contrast, traditional cloud-centric architectures rely on centralized data centers to process and store data, which can result in higher latency and increased network traffic.

2.3 Energy-Efficient Resource Allocation in Cloud-Edge Infrastructures

The escalating demand for computing capabilities coupled with increasing energy consumption of data centers has emphasized the significance of energy-efficient resource allocation in cloud-edge infrastructures [3,19]. Integrating renewable energy into data centers offers the potential to reduce their energy use and carbon footprints [12]. However, the natural variability of renewable sources often results in under-utilization. To counter this, research has focused on two primary strategies: energy storage and opportunistic scheduling [12].

In the context of mini data centers, combined optimization of virtual machines (VMs) and energy resources has shown to reduce grid electricity usage by 22%, as compared to solely focusing on VM allocation [19]. This reduction further extends to 28.5% when considering less energy-efficient servers [19]. In distributed cloud-edge systems, the challenge of joint workload distribution and computational resource adjustment has been approached using the Dynamic Voltage and Frequency Scaling (DVFS) method. By dynamically adjusting VM computation frequencies based on demand, this method offers energy conservation benefits [25].

Regarding UAV-enabled secure edge-cloud computing systems, strategies for efficient resource allocation and computation offloading have been identified as key to reducing energy consumption [11]. This problem is approached by segmenting it into resource allocation, task distribution, and computation offloading. Systematic solutions for each segment have been proposed to ensure energy-efficient resource allocation and offloading [11].

In conclusion, achieving energy efficiency in cloud-edge infrastructures demands a comprehensive approach. This includes the integration of renewable energy, strategic scheduling, optimized VM and energy allocation, and advanced computation offloading methods. These collective efforts can lead to considerable reductions in energy consumption and carbon output, addressing the growing need for computational resources.

2.4 Comparison Analysis of Algorithms

In recent years, the necessity for optimized resource allocation in computing systems has yielded several algorithms, with OptiMEC leading the initial charge.

Introduced in our foundational work [10], OptiMEC sought to efficiently allocate resources by minimizing energy consumption. Building upon the groundwork laid by OptiMEC, this paper presents advancements in the form of three novel methods: EffiMEC, E-OptiMEC, and a dedicated Load-Balancing approach.

EffiMEC shifts its primary focus to maximizing efficiency, while E-OptiMEC combines elements from both OptiMEC and EffiMEC, targeting energy-efficient solutions with an emphasis on drones. Lastly, our Load-Balancing method introduces a dynamic way of distributing workloads, thereby reducing latency and further promoting energy efficiency.

Table 1 below provides a comparative analysis of these methods, shedding light on their objectives, focal points, and underlying mechanisms.

Table 1. Comparative Analysis of Algorithms

Feature	Aspect	Algorithm			
		OptiMEC	EffiMEC	E-OptiMEC	Load-Balancing
Objective	Minimize Energy	✓	-	✓	-
	Maximize Efficiency	-	✓	-	-
Focus	Mobility	User	Drone	Drone	UAV
	Load Distribution	-	-	-	✓
Input	Task	Task, User Mob., Deadl	Task, Server Effic	Task, Drone Mob., Deadl	Task, UAV Mob., Deadl
Output	Type	Workload Distrib	Server Selection	Drone-based Distrib	Balancing Plan
Mechanism	Action	Min. Energy for Tasks	Max. Efficiency	Identify Low Energy Servers	Balance Workload and Latency

Comparative Overview

- **OptiMEC** [10]: Focused on scenarios involving mobile users, OptiMEC diligently minimizes energy use, accounting for user mobility and task deadlines through its predictive architecture.
- **EffiMEC**: Developed as an alternative for UAVs, EffiMEC transitions from a sole focus on energy to prioritize computational efficiency, adjusting structural considerations to suit drone operations.
- **E-OptiMEC**: A drone-adapted variant, E-OptiMEC, maintains an energy optimization focus, adjusted for drone-specific contexts.
- **Load-Balancing**: The Load-Balancing method is a comprehensive strategy accentuating real-time task distribution while ensuring adherence to energy constraints and task deadlines.

Structural and Architectural Variances with OptiMEC

- Energy versus Efficiency: While OptiMEC seeks to optimize energy consumption, EffiMEC targets optimal computational efficiency.
- Mobility Consideration: OptiMEC's architecture is devised for mobile user scenarios, a stark contrast to E-OptiMEC and Load-Balancing, both of which cater to UAV operations.
- Task Management Mechanisms: Load-Balancing introduces a more refined task management framework, contrasting with the more general approach in OptiMEC.

Design Distinctions. The choice between EffiMEC, E-OptiMEC, or the Load-Balancing algorithm should align with specific operational priorities and contexts:

- EffiMEC is optimal in environments where computational efficiency takes precedence over energy conservation.
- E-OptiMEC and Load-Balancing are best suited for scenarios that demand a comprehensive strategy, especially when contending with dynamic task necessities and constrained energy supplies.
- OptiMEC remains the preferred choice for environments primarily driven by the objective of energy conservation, particularly in mobile user scenarios.

Final Analysis of Proposed Algorithms: EffiMEC and E-OptiMEC. The algorithms introduced in this paper, EffiMEC and E-OptiMEC, have been compared with two alternative methods: Random Allocation and Load-Balancing. Both methods are explained in depth in our previous work [10]. Analytical results demonstrate that EffiMEC emerges as the most efficient, registering the least average energy consumption, with E-OptiMEC showcasing a comparable performance.

In its operational mechanics, the E-OptiMEC heuristic assigns each task to a MEC server, ensuring the task deadline is achieved while optimizing energy consumption. At every time interval, for each drone, the heuristic evaluates accessible MEC servers, gravitating towards the one that minimizes total energy expended during task execution. The end product of this algorithm is a server assignment aimed at attenuating the transmission energy indispensable for task distribution. When contrasted with the Random-Allocation method, OptiMEC's energy efficiency surpasses it by 10.42%.

Load-Balancing serves as a standard reference for this analysis. The data affirms that both EffiMEC and E-OptiMEC display superior performance over Load-Balancing.

3   Methodology

3.1   Problem Formulation

A Mobile Edge Network (MEN) is structured with multiple Base Stations (BS). Each BS is fortified with a MEC server, tailored for energy-efficient operations as per algorithms like OptiMEC and EffiMEC which are further analyzed below. These servers are adept at receiving, processing, and relaying computational tasks offloaded by users within their signal domains. Notably, BSs are interlinked via a Central Base Station (CBS), ensuring efficient load-balancing and task distribution.

Mobile users (MUs) or Mobile Devices (MDs), in their quest for reduced latency and energy conservation, as emphasized by the E-OptiMEC framework, can offload tasks to MEC servers. Given the inherent mobility, users and devices might transition beyond the range of an initial BS. As illustrated in Fig. 1, after MU1 offloads task T1 to BS1, it moves out of its range. Here, leveraging the adaptive strategies of algorithms, the MEC at BS1 can forward the task to the MEC at BS2, aligning with the user's current location. This ensures any MEC within the user's trajectory remains poised to execute the offloaded task, optimizing both energy consumption and computational efficiency.

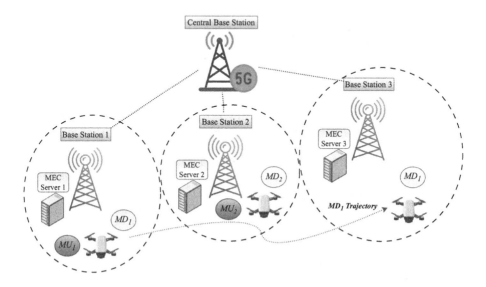

Fig. 1. Mobile Edge Computing Network.

The problem can be articulated as a mathematical optimization challenge with the objective of minimizing the total energy consumption for all mobile devices represented by the set N. The aim is to determine the optimal MEC server from a set of accessible servers, denoted for each trajectory of a device as S_i, that meets each stipulated task deadline. A pivotal hurdle lies in detecting available MEC servers when a user relocates and in orchestrating task computation at a designated server.

Let us denote $N = \{1, 2, \ldots, i, \ldots, N\}$ as the mobile devices traversing the area overseen by MEN. Every user possesses a task T_i, characterized as a triplet $(s_i, c_i, t_{\max})$, where s_i represents the size of the computational task, c_i is the essential computation resource measured in cycles, and $t_{\max}$ denotes the task's deadline. Furthermore, there are M base stations in total, with each having a signal range r_j and the corresponding MEC boasting a computation capacity of a_j.

3.2   Proposed Decentralized Energy-Efficient Algorithm

Given the complexity of the problem formulated in the previous sections, a novel decentralized algorithm is proposed to solve the problem in a scalable manner while preserving energy efficiency. This algorithm, referred to as the Decentralized Energy-efficient Offloading and Resource Allocation (EffiMEC), is designed to handle drone mobility and dynamically offload tasks to different edge servers following the trajectory of mobile drones. The EffiMEC approach is inspired by swarm intelligence, particularly ant colony optimization, with adaptations to suit the MEC context.

3.3   Algorithm Description

Each Mobile Device (MD) in the network runs an instance of the EffiMEC algorithm, enabling a fully decentralized system. The algorithm works as follows:

1. Each MD i initiates the algorithm by considering its current location and available MEC servers within its range. This set of servers is denoted by S_i^0.
2. The MD calculates the energy cost $E_{i,j}$ and execution time $t_{i,j}$ for each available MEC server j in S_i^0. These values are used to evaluate the suitability of each server.
3. For each server j in S_i^0, MD calculates the quality of the server, $Q_{i,j}$, as follows:

$$Q_{i,j} = \frac{1}{E_{i,j}} - \lambda \cdot t_{i,j} \tag{1}$$

   where λ is a tunable parameter representing the trade-off between energy conservation and time efficiency. A higher λ gives more importance to time efficiency, while a lower λ gives more importance to energy conservation.
4. The MD then probabilistically selects the next MEC server to offload the task based on the quality of the servers. The probability $P_{i,j}$ of selecting server j is calculated as follows:

$$P_{i,j} = \frac{Q_{i,j}}{\sum_{k \in S_i^0} Q_{i,k}} \tag{2}$$

5. After offloading the task to the selected MEC server, the MD moves to the next location, and the set of available MEC servers S_i^t gets updated. The above steps are repeated until the task is fully executed or the task deadline is reached.

3.4   Proposed Heuristic: Efficiency Maximizing Algorithm

In Algorithm 1, a series of symbols are utilized to define, calculate, and manipulate various parameters related to the task allocation problem, drones, servers, and other computational elements. A comprehensive list of these symbols and their corresponding definitions is presented in Table 2. These symbols represent various entities and metrics such as the drones, servers, task-related parameters, time intervals, and efficiencies, which are critical for the functioning and explanation of the EffiMEC algorithm. The specific use and context of each symbol are based upon the operations and calculations performed within the algorithm, and they collectively serve to establish a mathematical and logical framework to elucidate the heuristic's inner workings and methodologies. Understanding these symbols and their respective roles within the algorithm is vital for comprehending the mechanics, analyses, and results of the proposed heuristic approach.

Table 2. Symbol Definitions for EffiMEC Algorithm

Symbol	Definition
$P1$	The task allocation problem
i	Drone identifier
t	Time step or interval
mt_i	Final time step for drone i
N	Set of mobile drones
M	Set of base stations
S_i^t	Available MEC servers for drone i at time t
T_i	Task assigned to drone i
td_i	Deadline for task T_i
t_j^e	Time required for task execution on server j
$t_{i,j}^u$	Time to upload task from drone i to server j
$t_{i,j}^e$	Execution time of task on server j from drone i
eff_j	Efficiency of server j
$c_{i,j}$	Computational capacity of server j for drone i
$e_{i,j}$	Energy consumed for task execution on server j from drone i
$t_{j0...t-1}^{tr}$	Transmission time from server j at previous time steps
$t_{jt-1,j}^{tr}$	Transmission time from server j at time $t-1$ to j at time t
$e_{j0...t-1}^{tr}$	Transmission energy from server j at previous time steps
$e_{jt-1,j}^{tr}$	Transmission energy from server j at time $t-1$ to j at time t
y_i	Assigned server for drone i

The task allocation problem $P1$ is a combinatorial optimization problem, classified as NP-hard. To address this issue, we propose an efficiency-maximizing heuristic called "EffiMEC". Similar to the OptiMEC algorithm, each drone i offloads a task T_i with details about the task size, required computational resources, and deadline.

For each drone $i \in N$ and at each time interval $t \in [0, mt_i]$, the CBS identifies available MEC servers, denoted as S_i^t. The objective is to find an optimal server from S_i^t for computation and a suitable server for transmission of the task to another server in the next time step region. The time required for uploading, transmission, and computation is calculated and compared against the task deadline at each time step. The efficiency of each available server in S_i^t is computed by considering the computational capacity and the energy consumed during transmission and execution up to time step $t-1$.

Algorithm 1. EffiMEC Algorithm

Input: mobile drones N, base stations M

Output: $y_i, \forall i \in M$

1: **for each** drone $i \in N$ **do**
2:     $S_i^t \leftarrow$ get available MEC servers at final time step (mt_i)
3:     **for each** server $j \in S_i^t$ **do**
4:       **if** $t == 0$ **then**
5:         $t_j^e = t_{i,j}^u + t_{i,j}^e$
6:         **if** $t_j^e \leq td_i$ **then**
7:           $eff_j = (c_{i,j} - e_{i,j})/c_{i,j}$
8:         **else**
9:           $eff_j \leftarrow 0$
10:        **end if**
11:       **else**
12:         $t_j^e = t^{tr}j0 \ldots t-1 + t^{tr}jt-1,j + t_{i,j}^e$
13:         **if** $t_j^e \leq td_i$ **then**
14:           $eff_j = (c_{i,j} - e^{tr}j0 \ldots t-1 - e^{tr}jt-1,j - e_{i,j})/c_{i,j}$
15:         **else**
16:           $eff_j \leftarrow 0$
17:         **end if**
18:       **end if**
19:     **end for**
20:     $j_*^t = argmax_j(eff_j)$
21: **end for**
22: **return** $y_i, \forall i \in M$

This procedure is reiterated for all time intervals. The server with the highest efficiency is assigned to the task T_i for execution. The efficiency of a server at time step t can be calculated by subtracting the energy consumed for transmission up to time step $t-1$ and the energy required to offload the task from the server's location to the next time step's locality from the server's computational capacity. The algorithm finally outputs $y_i \ \forall i \in N$, the server assignment that maximizes efficiency while satisfying the delay constraints.

In addition, we propose a resource-allocation algorithm. This heuristic ensures the efficient use of available resources by balancing the computation load among servers. This algorithm is provided in Algorithm 3.

3.5 Complexity Analysis of the EffiMEC Algorithm

The time complexity of the EffiMEC algorithm arises from its nested loop structure. The outer loop traverses all N mobile drones, while the inner loop iterates over M MEC servers available to each drone. As such, the worst-case scenario presents a time complexity of O(NM). The operations within these loops, including computations, condition checking, and assignments, possess a constant time complexity of O(1). Therefore, it does not affect the overall time complexity. It is important to note, that the complexity could increase if the invoked functions, such as getting available MEC servers at the final time step have higher time complexities. Regarding space complexity, the EffiMEC algorithm appears to use a constant amount of space ($O(1)$), not necessitating data structures that scale with the size of the input. This analysis considers the worst-case scenario. Depending on server distribution and specific implementation, the actual performance may vary.

3.6   Proposed Scheduling Framework

Our problem $P1$ has been identified as a constraint satisfaction problem and is of NP-complete nature. To solve it, we put forward a scheduling heuristic. The heuristic works as follows: Every drone i offloads the task T_i along with necessary information such as the size of the computational task, required computation resources (expressed in cycles), and task deadline. The Central Base Station (CBS) allocates each task to a Multi-access Edge Computing (MEC) server that fulfils the task deadline and ensures minimum energy consumption. We call this mechanism the Energy-efficient Optimal Multi-Access Edge Computing (E-OptiMEC) algorithm, and its procedure is detailed in Algorithm 2.

At each time step $t \in [0, mt_i]$ for every drone $i \in N$, the heuristic identifies the available MEC servers, denoted as S_i^t. Among the available servers, the goal is to identify two servers - one for task execution, and one for task transmission, to offload the task to a server in the subsequent time step's location. Given that the task assignment must adhere to the delay constraint, the time required for uploading, transmission, and execution is calculated and checked against the delay constraint at each time step. The algorithm also computes the energy consumed due to transmission and execution for each available server.

Algorithm 2. E-OptiMEC Algorithm

Input: mobile drones N, base stations M

Output: $x_i, \forall i \in M$

1: **for each**   drone $i \in N$ **do**
2:     $S_i^t \leftarrow$ identify available MEC servers at the final time step (mt_i)
3:     **for each**   server $j \in S_i^t$ **do**
4:         Calculate time and energy for task execution and transmission
5:         Identify suitable servers for task execution and transmission based on least energy consumption and deadline satisfaction
6:     **end for**
7:     Select the server with the minimum total energy consumption
8: **end for**
9: **return** $x_i, \forall i \in M$

This process is replicated across all temporal instances, whereby the server demonstrating the lowest energy expenditure is elected for executing task T_i. The transmission energy at a given timestamp t can be derived by combining the cumulative transmission energy until timestamp $t-1$ and the energy mandated to transfer the task from the incumbent server's location to the drone's position at the ensuing timestamp $t+1$. In the final analysis, the algorithm yields $x_i \ \forall i \in N$, specifying the server that optimizes energy utilization while adhering to the latency stipulations of task T_i.

3.7 Complexity Analysis of the E-OptiMEC Algorithm

The time complexity of the E-OptiMEC algorithm derives primarily from its nested loop construction. The outer loop iterates over each of the N mobile drones, while the inner loop traverses M MEC servers accessible to a given drone. Consequently, the worst-case time complexity is O(NM). Within these loops, operations such as calculations, server identification based on energy consumption and deadline satisfaction, and server selection all carry a constant time complexity, O(1). Thus, they do not impact the overall time complexity.

However, the total time complexity could be greater if the internal functions, like identifying available MEC servers at the final time step, have higher time complexities. As for the space complexity, the E-OptiMEC algorithm uses a constant amount of space, O(1), since it does not require data structures scaling with the size of the input. This analysis represents a worst-case scenario. The actual performance may be more efficient, contingent upon the specific server distribution and implementation details.

Moreover, we offer an example of a load-balancing heuristic algorithm designed to balance each mobile drone's energy consumption across available servers. This algorithm is depicted in Algorithm 3.

Algorithm 3. Power-Efficient Workload Distribution Using E-OptiMEC

Input: UAVs N, base stations M, energy cap e_t
Output: $x_i, \forall i \in N$
1: **for each** UAV $i \in N$ **do**
2:    **for each** timestep $t \in [0, mt_i]$ **do**
3:       S_i^t locates reachable MEC servers at timestep t
4:       Evaluate energy usage for each UAV i
5:       Pinpoint server with smallest energy drain (j_t)
6:       Amend energy balance record for UAV i
7:       **if** UAV i energy balance $< e_t$ **then**
8:          defer task or diminish task sophistication
9:       **else**
10:          consign the task to server j_t
11:       **end if**
12:       Renew the transmission energy $(e_t r)$ and transmission interval $(t_t r)$
13:    **end for**
14: **end for**
15: **return** $x_i, \forall i \in N$

Algorithm 3 makes use of the energy consumption information of each mobile drone among the available servers. It selects the server with the lowest energy consumption for task assignment. If the energy balance for mobile drones falls below the threshold e_t, the algorithm includes a step to postpone tasks or reduce task complexity. Moreover, the algorithm updates each drone's energy balance after each workload distribution, facilitating more precise load-balancing decisions.

3.8 Complexity Analysis of the Energy-Efficient Load Balancing Based on E-OptiMEC Algorithm

The Energy-Efficient Load Balancing Based on E-OptiMEC algorithm introduces an additional layer of complexity through its use of two nested loops. The outer loop iterates over the N mobile drones, while the inner loop goes through each timestep t within the range $[0, mt_i]$ for each drone i.

Without specific knowledge of the variable mt_i, the worst-case scenario would suggest it's a value of T where T is the maximum number of timesteps. Therefore, in the worst case, the inner loop would run T times for each drone. This results in a worst-case time complexity of $O(NT)$ for each drone, and with M base stations, it becomes $O(NMT)$, given that M base stations are checked in each timestep for each drone. The operations within these loops have a constant time complexity of $O(1)$. However, as before, the overall time complexity may be higher if the internal functions like determine available MEC servers at timestep t have time complexities exceeding $O(1)$.

As for the space complexity, the algorithm appears to use a constant amount of space $(O(1))$, as it doesn't employ data structures that grow with the input size. Note that this analysis is for the worst-case scenario. The actual performance may be more efficient depending on specific server distribution, the distribution of timesteps per drone, and implementation details.

The prior discourse outlined a load-balancing mechanism among mobile drones in a network, the advantages of which can be enumerated as follows:

1. **Energy efficiency:** The proposed method significantly enhances energy efficiency within a mobile edge computing network. This is achieved by offloading computational tasks to proximate servers, which reduces the energy consumption of mobile devices. Therefore, by regulating the energy expenditure among mobile drones, the cumulative energy consumption of the system can be reduced, fostering a more energy-efficient network.
2. **Equitable workload distribution:** The suggested algorithm ensures a fair distribution of workload among the available servers. This equitable distribution forestalls the overloading of certain servers while others remain underutilized, leading to enhanced resource utilization and improved energy efficiency.

To elucidate the proposed load-balancing algorithm, let's contemplate a hypothetical scenario. Drone 1 offloads tasks to MEC servers BS_1 and BS_2 at timestep 0, as displayed in Table 3. Here, BS_2 is selected for task execution due to its lesser energy consumption post uploading and execution. Concurrently, BS_1 is employed to offload the task to MEC servers in the subsequent timestep due to its lower energy consumption for transmission (refer to Table 4).

Table 3. E-OptiMEC at timestep 1

Execution	Transmission
$drone1 \rightarrow BS_1$	$BS_1 \rightarrow drone1$
$t_1^u + t_1^{ex} = 0.6 \, (<1)$	$t_1^u + t_1^{tr} = 0.3$
$e_1^u + e_1^{ex} = 0.9$	$e_1^u + e_1^{tr} = 0.6$
$drone1 \rightarrow BS_2$	$BS_2 \rightarrow drone1$
$t_1^u + t_1^{ex} = 0.7 \, (<1)$	$t_1^u + t_1^{tr} = 0.4$
$e_1^u + e_1^{ex} = 0.8$	$e_1^u + e_1^{tr} = 0.7$

Table 4. E-OptiMEC at timestep 2

Execution	Transmission
$drone1 \rightarrow BS_1 \rightarrow BS_3$	$BS_3 \rightarrow drone1$
$t_1^u + t_1^{tr} + t_1^{ex} = 0.9 \, (<1)$	$t_1^u + t_1^{tr} + t_1^{tr} = 0.5$
$e_1^u + e_1^{tr} + e_1^{ex} = 0.7$	$e_1^u + e_1^{tr} + e_1^{tr} = 0.9$
$drone1 \rightarrow BS_1 \rightarrow BS_4$	$BS_4 \rightarrow drone1$
$t_1^u + t_1^{tr} + t_1^{ex} = 0.7 \, (<1)$	$t_1^u + t_1^{tr} + t_1^{tr} = 0.6$
$e_1^u + e_1^{tr} + e_1^{ex} = 0.8$	$e_1^u + e_1^{tr} + e_1^{tr} = 0.8$

In the subsequent timestep, the MEC servers at disposal are BS_3 and BS_4. BS_3 is elected for execution as it consumes lesser energy post uploading and execution. On the other hand, BS_4 is chosen to offload the task to the accessible MEC servers owing to its lower transmission energy requirement. At the final timestep, the available MEC servers are BS_5 and BS_6. BS_5 is ultimately selected for execution due to its lower energy consumption post uploading and execution (Table 5).

Table 5. E-OptiMEC Execution Phase

Execution Phase
$drone1 \rightarrow BS_1 \rightarrow BS_4 \rightarrow BS_5$
$t_1^u + t_1^{tr} + t_1^{tr} + t_1^{ex} = 0.7 \, (<1)$
$e_1^u + e_1^{tr} + e_1^{tr} + e_1^{ex} = 1.2$
$drone1 \rightarrow BS_1 \rightarrow BS_4 \rightarrow BS_6$
$t_1^u + t_1^{tr} + t_1^{tr} + t_1^{ex} = 0.6 \, (<1)$
$e_1^u + e_1^{tr} + e_1^{tr} + e_1^{ex} = 1.3$

Subsequently, as this is the final timestep, there are no further transmissions from BS_5 or BS_6. The CBS will then delegate the task to either BS_2, BS_3, or BS_5, contingent on the server that consumes the least execution energy.

The simulation parameters are as follows: the coverage radius of the base station ranges from 70 to 100 m; the CPU capacity of the MEC is within the range of 7 to 20 GHz; the computation power varies between 3 to 5 W; the transmission power lies within 0.1 to 1 W; the channel bandwidth is set at 1 MHz; the mobility speed of the drone is between 1 to 3 Km/h; the task requirement as per CPU capacity ranges from 1 to 10 GHz; the input data size is between 1 to 3 MB; and the task deadline constraint is within 0.1 to 1 s.

For empirical analysis, the proposed algorithm is evaluated in comparison to the random waypoint model and mobile execution (which refers to executing a task on a mobile device instead of a remote server). This comparative analysis provides a robust performance assessment, underscoring the merits of the proposed algorithm.

4   Experimental Results

In this section, we evaluate the efficacy of our suggested algorithms in accomplishing minimal-energy task allocation, taking into account the mobility of devices. Moreover, we carry out trials with diverse drone devices, spanning a range of 1 to 10 units. In terms of mobility, we employ data sourced from 57 base stations situated in the central region of London, UK. Moreover, we assess the performance of our proposed algorithms through rigorous experimentation. The primary objectives of these evaluations are twofold as shown in Table 6.

Table 6. Evaluation Metrics Description.

Metric	Description
Task Completion Efficacy	Evaluates task completion rates in relation to task deadlines for different drone counts
Energy Consumption Efficiency	Assesses energy usage concerning drone count and task input size. Lower values indicate efficient, sustainable operations

As depicted in Fig. 2, it is observed that the Task completion percentage surpasses that of the other three methods when varying Task deadline constraints are applied. The load balancing technique consistently outperforms the other three methods, with EffiMec following closely as the second most effective solution. OptiMEC displays a significant improvement, being 12.56% higher than Random-Allocation and a substantial 29.10% higher than Local-Execution on average. Additionally, a noteworthy observation is the proportional relationship

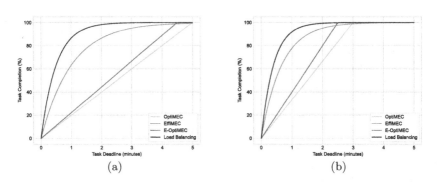

Fig. 2. Percentage of Task Completion in correlation to Task Deadline for (a) a single drone and (b) ten drones.

between the Deadline constraint and the Task completion percentage; as the Deadline constraint is increased, the Task completion percentage likewise sees an increase.

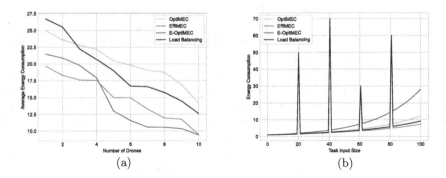

Fig. 3. (a) Average Energy Utilization in correlation with Drone Count and (b) Correlation of Task Input Dimension with Energy Expenditure.

Figure 3 illustrates the fluctuations in energy consumption with varying task input sizes. It becomes abundantly clear that as the task input size escalates, there is a commensurate increase in energy consumption, attributable to the amplified transmission energy required for task distribution. OptiMEC's energy consumption is more efficient by 10.42% compared to the Random-Allocation method. However, EffiMEC provides an even more efficient solution, boasting the lowest average energy usage, while E-OptiMEC exhibits similar performance. Lastly, within the dimension of Task input size, we notice some spikes coinciding with task arrivals, but the E-OptiMEC technique exhibits superior resilience to these energy fluctuations.

5   Conclusions and Future Work

In this work, two novel heuristics are proposed to solve an NP-hard task allocation problem in a Mobile Edge Computing (MEC) context. The first one, EffiMEC, is an efficiency-maximizing algorithm designed to maximize the computational efficiency of servers in the MEC network, while the second one, E-OptiMEC, is an energy-optimizing heuristic aimed at minimizing energy consumption during task execution and transmission. The proposed heuristics operate within a constraint satisfaction framework, wherein tasks from mobile drones are allocated to suitable MEC servers based on energy consumption and computational efficiency while satisfying task deadlines.

EffiMEC algorithm, whose worst-case time complexity is O(NM), operates by selecting, for each drone at each time interval, the server with the highest efficiency. Efficiency here is determined by computational capacity minus energy consumed for transmission up to the previous time step and the energy required for offloading the task to the next time step. The output of the algorithm is the server that maximizes efficiency while satisfying the delay constraints.

On the other hand, the E-OptiMEC heuristic operates by allocating each task to a MEC server that fulfils the task deadline and ensures minimum energy consumption. At each time step, for each drone, the heuristic identifies available MEC servers and chooses the one with minimum total energy consumption for task execution. The output of this algorithm is the server assignment that minimizes energy consumption while meeting delay constraints. These two heuristics, based on their designs, could provide more efficient and energy-saving solutions for task allocation problems in MEC networks. However, they are heuristic solutions, and there's no guarantee they'll always achieve the optimal solution. Further, the actual performance of these algorithms may vary depending on server distribution and specific implementation.

As future work, it could be beneficial to conduct comprehensive performance analysis and comparisons of these heuristics in different scenarios or under varying constraints. For instance, scenarios where energy availability or computational capacity is extremely limited, or where task deadlines are particularly stringent. Moreover, while these heuristics are promising, it might be interesting to explore potential enhancements to these algorithms, such as incorporating machine learning techniques for dynamic adaptation, considering other performance metrics like task failure rate, or addressing additional real-world considerations like network congestion and server failure. Finally, the scalability of these heuristics could be evaluated. Given that their complexity scales linearly with the number of drones and servers, understanding how these heuristics perform under heavy network loads could provide valuable insights into their practical applicability in large-scale MEC deployments.

Acknowledgements. This research has been co-financed by the European Regional Development Fund of the European Union and Greek national funds through the Operational Program Competitiveness, Entrepreneurship and Innovation, under the call RESEARCH-CREATE-INNOVATE (project code: T2EΔK-00127).

References

1. Angel, N.A., Ravindran, D., Vincent, P.D.R., Srinivasan, K., Hu, Y.C.: Recent advances in evolving computing paradigms: cloud, edge, and fog technologies. Sensors **22**(1), 196 (2021)
2. Calheiros, R.N., Ranjan, R., Beloglazov, A., De Rose, C.A., Buyya, R.: CloudSim: a toolkit for modeling and simulation of cloud computing environments and evaluation of resource provisioning algorithms. Softw. Pract. Exp. **41**(1), 23–50 (2011)
3. Chauhan, N., Kaur, N., Saini, K.S.: Energy efficient resource allocation in cloud data center: a comparative analysis. In: 2022 International Conference on Computational Modelling, Simulation and Optimization (ICCMSO), pp. 201–206 (2022). https://doi.org/10.1109/ICCMSO58359.2022.00049
4. Chekired, D.A., Khoukhi, L., Mouftah, H.T.: Decentralized Cloud-SDN architecture in smart grid: a dynamic pricing model. IEEE Trans. Industr. Inf. **14**(3), 1220–1231 (2018). https://doi.org/10.1109/TII.2017.2742147

5. Chen, S., Chen, J., Miao, Y., Wang, Q., Zhao, C.: Deep reinforcement learning-based cloud-edge collaborative mobile computation offloading in industrial networks. IEEE Trans. Signal Inf. Process. Netw. **8**, 364–375 (2022). https://doi.org/10.1109/TSIPN.2022.3171336

6. Fernandez Blanco, D., Le Mouel, F., Lin, T., Ponge, J.: An energy-efficient FaaS edge computing platform over IoT nodes: focus on consensus algorithm. In: Proceedings of the 38th ACM/SIGAPP Symposium on Applied Computing, pp. 661–670 (2023)

7. Fu, W., Wan, Y., Qin, J., Kang, Y., Li, L.: Privacy-preserving optimal energy management for smart grid with cloud-edge computing. IEEE Trans. Industr. Inf. **18**(6), 4029–4038 (2022). https://doi.org/10.1109/TII.2021.3114513

8. Han, T., Muhammad, K., Hussain, T., Lloret, J., Baik, S.W.: An efficient deep learning framework for intelligent energy management in IoT networks. IEEE Internet Things J. **8**(5), 3170–3179 (2020)

9. Jayanetti, A., Halgamuge, S., Buyya, R.: Deep reinforcement learning for energy and time optimized scheduling of precedence-constrained tasks in edge-cloud computing environments. Futur. Gener. Comput. Syst. **137**, 14–30 (2022)

10. Karras, A., Karras, C., Giannaros, A., Tsolis, D., Sioutas, S.: Mobility-aware workload distribution and task allocation for mobile edge computing networks. In: Daimi, K., Al Sadoon, A. (eds.) ACR 2023. LNNS, vol. 700, pp. 395–407. Springer, Cham (2023). https://doi.org/10.1007/978-3-031-33743-7_32

11. Khan, U.A., Khalid, W., Saifullah, S.: Energy efficient resource allocation and computation offloading strategy in a UAV-enabled secure edge-cloud computing system. In: 2020 IEEE International Conference on Smart Internet of Things (SmartIoT), pp. 58–63 (2020). https://doi.org/10.1109/SmartIoT49966.2020.00018

12. Li, Y.: Resource allocation in a Cloud partially powered by renewable energy sources. Ph.D. thesis, Ecole nationale supérieure Mines-Télécom Atlantique (2017)

13. Lim, W.Y.B., et al.: Decentralized edge intelligence: a dynamic resource allocation framework for hierarchical federated learning. IEEE Trans. Parallel Distrib. Syst. **33**(3), 536–550 (2022). https://doi.org/10.1109/TPDS.2021.3096076

14. Liu, P., Chaudhry, S.R., Huang, T., Wang, X., Collier, M.: Multi-factorial energy aware resource management in edge networks. IEEE Trans. Green Commun. Netw. **3**(1), 45–56 (2019). https://doi.org/10.1109/TGCN.2018.2874397

15. Marozzo, F., Orsino, A., Talia, D., Trunfio, P.: Edge computing solutions for distributed machine learning. In: 2022 IEEE International Conference on Dependable, Autonomic and Secure Computing, International Conference on Pervasive Intelligence and Computing, International Conference on Cloud and Big Data Computing, International Conference on Cyber Science and Technology Congress (DASC/PiCom/CBDCom/CyberSciTech), pp. 1–8. IEEE (2022)

16. Pantazoglou, M., Tzortzakis, G., Delis, A.: Decentralized and energy-efficient workload management in enterprise clouds. IEEE Trans. Cloud Comput. **4**(2), 196–209 (2016). https://doi.org/10.1109/TCC.2015.2464817

17. Rafique, H., Shah, M.A., Islam, S.U., Maqsood, T., Khan, S., Maple, C.: A novel bio-inspired hybrid algorithm (NBIHA) for efficient resource management in fog computing. IEEE Access **7**, 115760–115773 (2019). https://doi.org/10.1109/ACCESS.2019.2924958

18. Rey-Jouanchicot, J., Del Castillo, J.Á.L., Zuckerman, S., Belmega, E.V.: Energy-efficient online resource provisioning for cloud-edge platforms via multi-armed bandits. In: 2022 International Symposium on Computer Architecture and High Performance Computing Workshops (SBAC-PADW), pp. 45–50. IEEE (2022)

19. da Silva, M.D.M., Gamatié , A., Sassatelli, G., Poss, M., Robert, M.: Optimization of data and energy migrations in mini data centers for carbon-neutral computing. IEEE Trans. Sustain. Comput. **8**(1), 68–81 (2023). https://doi.org/10.1109/TSUSC.2022.3197090
20. Tian, Z., Li, H., Maeda, R.K.V., Feng, J., Xu, J.: Decentralized collaborative power management through multi-device knowledge sharing. In: 2018 IEEE 36th International Conference on Computer Design (ICCD), pp. 409–412. IEEE (2018)
21. Wang, S., Xin, N., Luo, Z., Lin, T.: An efficient computation offloading strategy based on cloud-edge collaboration in vehicular edge computing. In: 2022 International Conference on Computing, Communication, Perception and Quantum Technology (CCPQT), pp. 193–197 (2022). https://doi.org/10.1109/CCPQT56151.2022.00041
22. Xiong, Z., Kang, J., Niyato, D., Wang, P., Poor, H.V.: Cloud/edge computing service management in blockchain networks: multi-leader multi-follower game-based ADMM for pricing. IEEE Trans. Serv. Comput. **13**(2), 356–367 (2019)
23. Zahoor, S., Javaid, N., Khan, A., Ruqia, B., Muhammad, F.J., Zahid, M.: A cloud-fog-based smart grid model for efficient resource utilization. In: 2018 14th International Wireless Communications and Mobile Computing Conference (IWCMC), pp. 1154–1160 (2018). https://doi.org/10.1109/IWCMC.2018.8450506
24. Zahoor, S., Javaid, S., Javaid, N., Ashraf, M., Ishmanov, F., Afzal, M.K.: Cloud-fog-based smart grid model for efficient resource management. Sustainability **10**(6), 2079 (2018)
25. Zhang, W., Zhang, Z., Zeadally, S., Chao, H.C., Leung, V.C.M.: Energy-efficient workload allocation and computation resource configuration in distributed cloud/edge computing systems with stochastic workloads. IEEE J. Sel. Areas Commun. **38**(6), 1118–1132 (2020). https://doi.org/10.1109/JSAC.2020.2986614

Author Index

Printed in the United States
by Baker & Taylor Publisher Services